DISCOVERING MY EMPATHETIC HEART

MELANIE BAKER RMN

For the wonderful patients and staff I worked with throughout my nursing career.
Thank you for being part of my life.

INTRODUCTION

The COVID-19 world pandemic announcement from the UK government stated that you should isolate yourself at home until further notice if you have any underlying health conditions. Living in Portugal as a UK resident, I had already begun to do so before the UK, as Portugal described itself as being 'in a state of Calamity'. This description made me laugh, as the family always thought of me as 'Calamity Jane'. If there is ever the opportunity for a stumble or a trip or an illness to get, you can bet your bottom dollar I would be the person to succumb to it. Sadly, I have four of the most significant health conditions on the list: Diabetes, low immune system, asthma, and a rare blood condition. The only thing going for me was that I am a female and statistically less likely to die from it. "Just great!" I thought, "the first time in history that women have had the upper hand!" Therefore, with a sense of national duty and self-preservation, I headed to the sofa with a bottle of wine and a bar of chocolate. How hard could it be to sit with my feet up, watching movies and my favourite TV shows for a few months, all to adhere to the national guidelines? Bring it on! Bliss!

After four weeks of self-isolation up to the 4th of April 2020,

I was going stir crazy. I had washed clothes, cleaned the house, ironed, tended to the garden, redecorated and rearranged furniture; I baked, cooked, blanched and pickled food. When completed, I watched box sets, films, and TV reruns. I played Candy Crush and Scrabble; chatted for hours on Facebook and Messenger. I video-called my son, grandson and other family and friends. I even spoke to my 98-year-old mum on her new tablet via video call. Now that is a sentence, I never thought I would say! Modern technology and my mother do not go together. It certainly filled the time though. She kept forgetting to turn on her hearing aid and insisted on keeping the tablet in the other room. "That is where it charges," she'd say. I would also have to teach her repeatedly to "Tap the green button!" to answer it.

Like millions of others worldwide, I googled every piece of information about COVID-19 and shared the hell out of it to family, friends or anyone who would listen really. One day, while sorting cupboards and drawers out for the umpteenth time in a month, I found myself putting all the rubbish I had just taken out, back into the drawers; this was an example of my 'Just in case I might need it' mentality. I burst into tears, feeling so frustrated as I realised that I was doing things for doing sake to keep my mind off Covid-19. It wasn't just the boredom that was getting to me; it was also the fear of catching the deadly virus. I knew if I did, I wouldn't stand a chance. The fear was slowly taking over my every waking and sleeping thought. I was anxious beyond anxious. I was having nightmares of losing all my hair and teeth. (According to dream interpretation this signifies a feeling of helplessness and that you are afraid of a situation in your life - I couldn't have been anymore textbook if I tried!)

One minute I was laughing and over-talkative to my husband, or over the fence to my neighbour's, and then next I would have a big black cloud over me, causing me to retreat to my bed and cry again. My blood sugar levels were sky-high from the comforting little treats of chocolate, ice cream, cakes, and scones, but I had to keep treating myself for sanity's sake. I began depending upon a wee little drop of Brandy at night or even in the day to take the edge off. (Oh, okay, I lied. It was an extra-large Brandy to take the anxiety away). I completed the trip to the bottle bank during the hours of darkness wearing a mask, not just my COVID-19 one! Anything would do so long as the community didn't recognise me as the local alcoholic.

The Shirley Valentine within me started having conversations in my head to boost my sanity. "Come on, Mel; you're a trained mental health nurse and cognitive behavioural therapist. You were the Director of your own home care company. You've managed and trained hundreds of staff and provided care for thousands of clients in the community. With well over 50 years of life experience, you have dealt with a lot of stress, and your emotions have been to hell and back many times. You have always got through it! Pull yourself together. No one is asking you to go to war! You are sat on your arse, basking in the Portuguese sun. Come on, girl; you've got this! What would Mel say to someone else behaving like this? You'd tell them to think of something they would love to do; to make this time in isolation count!"

One evening, as I sat there lost within my mind, sipping on my favourite Portuguese red wine, the thought of how much I missed my grandson, Jacob, sparked a memory of a conversation I'd had with him on my last visit to the UK in February.

Jacob loved getting in bed with me so we could have Nanny and Jacob time, where I would tickle his back and massage his feet, which he had loved since he was a baby. We would chat about his day and generally put the world to rights. I would read him some stories, or he would ask me questions. He would often ask me to tell him about when I worked as a Nurse as he shuffled himself onto his pillow to listen. He loved stories, and I had hundreds of stories about nursing from my thirty-one years of being a psychiatric nurse. His reactions were priceless as I recounted my most treasured nursing memories. One minute he was laughing, then the next teary-eyed and sad. He was genuinely interested in the real-life events of my nursing career and my life before I became a nanny. He asked lots of questions and seemed fascinated by my answers. After an hour in bed telling stories, and devouring a tub of popcorn, he sat up and said, "You should write a book, Nanny!" So here I am, doing exactly that.

MY CHILDHOOD YEARS

*A*t an incredibly young age of about three, my first recollection was when I got a nurse's uniform from Santa. I squealed with delight as I opened my present and discovered it had a hat, uniform dress, and a white case with a red cross on the middle of the lid. The case contained a watch, thermometer, syringe, and stethoscope. I couldn't wait to get my Christmas nighty off and put on my uniform. I looked proudly in the hall mirror at the reflection of a nurse. I ran upstairs to my bedroom to collect my dolls and teddies and every shoebox I could find. Mum gave me some old bandages and medicine spoons too. I placed the shoeboxes on each stair, which became the hospital beds for my toys. At the bottom of the stairs was an old stool. I turned it upside down and sat in the middle of it, my instant makeshift ambulance. I threw my dolls and teddies all over the floor then shuffled the stool backwards and forwards, making a siren noise, and proceeded to rescue every one of my injured toys. Each doll or Teddy received an examination before I put them into their shoebox beds. I listened to their hearts, took their temperatures, gave injections into their tummies. I bandaged broken limbs and heads, while all the time, cuddling and reassuring them that they would be okay as I was there to make them feel better. Unusual behaviour for a child so young it seems, as I had never been in a hospital, apart from when I was born prematurely and had to stay in the hospital for a few months. The only nurse I knew was at the doctor's surgery. It just seemed natural for me to be a nurse.

I lived in a three-bedroomed council house in a small mining village called Darfield in South Yorkshire with my mum, dad and two sisters. I was the youngest of three daughters: the mistake. Fortunately, I didn't know what that meant until later in life. Sondra was sixteen years my senior and was starting to have boyfriends and had a dance school; Tina, at ten years old had friends her age on the street with whom to play. Being a preschool infant meant they had little interest in playing with me, but they always loved and protected me. As a toddler, I was like Houdini. I escaped the house most days and headed into the cornfield at the bottom of the garden. Mum would have the whole street looking out of their windows to see if the corn moved as I ran through it.

No matter how many smacks I got, I still did it. It was only me playing in the garden or house. My imagination and I became a great team; it's no surprise that I had an imaginary friend called Peep. My family said he was fictional, but I can still remember him being a little boy aged the same as me. He was smaller than me with blonde hair and blue eyes; dressed in blue shorts, a white shirt and big brown boots with hooks and laces. He told me he was lonely and lost and couldn't find his way home to his mummy and daddy. We chatted and played all the time and, in the absence of anyone else to talk to, I told him my secrets and fears.

We would cuddle up together at night, secure in each other's arms. He was my best friend; in fact, he was my only friend. I took him with me everywhere, much to my parents' dismay. I remember going out in the car one day, and I couldn't find Peep to take with me. I shouted and shouted for him, but I could not find him anywhere. Mum and Dad made me get in the car without him, and I cried and screamed so loud during our fifteen-minute journey that my dad stopped the car and shouted, "Bloody hell, I can't stand this noise anymore!", and turned the car back around to go and find Peep. I entered the front door, and there he was, sitting on our sofa crying; waiting for me to collect him. I cuddled him so tight and skipped happily back to the car where we both fell fast asleep. Of course, no member of my family saw him, but he was real to me. We were together for a few happy years before one day waking to find he had disappeared. I couldn't find him anywhere. It left me confused and broken-hearted that he had just left me and not said goodbye. I was so sad and lonely. I hoped every day that he would come back, but sadly not. A few weeks later, I started infant school, and the memory of Peep slowly faded away.

From day one of infant school, I was called the soft fat lass. I wore hand-me-down clothing or clothes made by my mum because we didn't have very much money. As a result, they bullied me for being fat and wearing clothes different from everyone else. They included me with the odd kids, like the dirty kid that smelt of old socks, the ginger-haired kid nick-named 'Carrot' and the boy with jam-jar-bottomed glasses called 'The Milky Bar Kid'. I hated the bullying. They would call me fatty and push or hit me. Playtime was always a trauma, and I would try to stay as close as possible to the teacher or dinner lady, but the bullies managed to find a way to bully me at some point during the day. As much as I hated the bullies, it was also my first real exposure to my desire to care for others. On the occasions when it was another kid's turn to be bullied, I would make sure that I was in the background waiting until the bullies had finished their bullying and be the first to help and offer comfort. I felt their fear and pain in my heart, and yet I enjoyed the feeling I got when helping others, even if it meant I would get bullied again later for doing so. I realise now it was the feeling of empathy.

My sister, Sondra, owned her dance school in the next village, which I loved attending to learn ballet, tap and stage. I had been dancing since the age of two and passed my exams with highly commended or honours. I would perform at concerts and competed at local festivals in Yorkshire and Lancashire a few times a year. I always won a medal or trophy for my dance routines. At first, it was fun, and it became my escapism from bullying. That soon changed once my mum got involved with making me practice for the competitions.

Every day, as soon as I walked in from school, Mum told me to change into my dance shoes and practice up to six dances, one after the other. I just wanted to watch a bit of TV or play with my toys as most kids did, but I couldn't play or even have my tea until I had practised. I couldn't just run through the routines. I had to perform them as if I were on the stage, and my life depended on it. If I didn't execute them to the best of my ability, Mum would hit me with a ballet or tap shoe, and I would have to dance them all over again. This punishment took place in the front room, where the windows faced out onto the street where other children from my school would hide behind the front bushes and laugh. I began to hate dancing; mostly when a competition was near. Mum would threaten me that if I didn't win, it would reflect poorly upon her and I would get a good hiding. As a small child, this filled me with fear and anxiety, which I can still feel to this day.

Whenever I would walk on to the stage, I would be so afraid, knowing that Mum would be in the audience somewhere, scrutinising every movement of my performance. The anxiety would build within me until the music began, where I would perform to the best of my ability. Most of the time, I would win bronze, silver, or gold medals. However, Mum would always be angry or extremely disappointed with me if I didn't get a gold medal. It is sad to think how the adjudicators' decision could result in a child being hit with a tap shoe, causing a welt on the skin, and the lesser award discarded in a case like rubbish in the bin. My sister, Sondra, married and moved away, and my other sister, Tina, took over the dance school where I continued to perform and compete for her. I had no choice in the matter. Mum insisted I was going to be a dancer and had to follow the family tradition.

At the age of fourteen, my rebellious teenage side must have gotten the better of me when I asked Mum to let me practice by myself and go to the next festival without her. Reluctantly she agreed, but parted with the words, "You will win nothing because you need me to push you."

In the run-up to the next festival, I practised at the times I wanted and how I wanted. My favourite dance to perform was a character dance choreographed by Tina called 'The Broken-Hearted Clown'. She had based it on Pierrot, a stock character whose origins are in the late seventeenth-century Italian troupe of players performing in Paris and known as the Comédie-Italienne. My story, told through dance, was that of a dying clown performing at his last circus show.

The competition was in Leeds, in an old theatre with red swish stage curtains and ornate gold ceilings. It made me feel special to walk out onto the stage; it filled my heart with pride and confidence to give my best performance. I danced my heart out for every routine and thoroughly enjoyed myself without the fear of Mum watching over me. Out of six dance categories, I attained six gold medals and got the trophy for the competition's best dancer. I got ninety-nine points out of a hundred. The adjudicator requested that I perform for her again at the end of the festival; this was mostly unheard of at the time. I was so proud of myself, especially when I got a standing ovation at the end of my performance. It was the first time in my life that I felt I was good enough. I couldn't wait to get home and tell my mum. I thought she would be so happy and proud of me.

After being dropped off by the dance bus, I ran excitedly into the house and couldn't wait to show her my six gold medals and trophy for being the best dancer of the competition. I told Mum about performing for the adjudicator at the end of the presentations, and how I got a standing ovation. Mum just scowled at me and got up from her chair. You might think this was to hug me and say, 'well done', but instead, she grabbed me by the hair and slapped me. She accused me of stealing the medals from the festival to make myself look good and make her look a fool. I managed to wriggle free of her grip and ran upstairs to lock myself in the bathroom. She ran after me shouting, "Come down here, you little thief!" I was terrified, but thankfully, the bolt kept her away from giving me a good hiding.

I sat on the loo, crying, as she continued to bang on the bathroom door. All that excitement and feeling of self-worth disappeared in an instant. Thankfully, my dad came home from the pub not long afterwards, and I knew it would be safe to leave the bathroom. Mum would never hit me in front of anyone else. I opened the bathroom door, and as I ran past, Mum gave me a backhanded flick to my head. I ran straight to my dad and told him what I had won and about dancing for the adjudicator. He was so proud of me and hugged and kissed me, then spun me around in a circle. He had promised to give me ten pence for every gold medal I won, but when he put his hands in his pocket, he gave me not sixty pence but a crisp pound note and said, "That's for you, bonny lass, you deserve it."

The phone rang, and it was my sister, Tina, to see if I was okay. She had an inkling that Mum might not be happy with me achieving these medals without her tuition. Tina spoke to her and confirmed it was all true, and that the whole dance school was proud of how beautifully I had danced. Mum just listened and nodded along and said "Okay," before ending the call and going up to bed. No apology and no 'well done' forthcoming. We never spoke about it again.

The following week the local newspaper published an article saying, 'MELANIE THE GOLDEN GIRL'. It was Mum's way of showing her pride in me, but it just gave the bullies something else with which to bully me. Mum rarely offered to go to a dance festival with me again, thank God, but I guess without her tuition in the early days I wouldn't have been as good at dancing, or as determined in life.

The following month, Tina was reading through one of the professional dance magazines when something caught her eye. Always interested to see who had been offered auditions for the well-known dance school scholarships, she nearly fell off her seat when she saw my name under the Sadler's Wells list of auditions. I didn't know that the Leeds festival's adjudicator had referred me to Sadler's Wells ballet school for an audition to become a professional ballerina. Once Tina had phoned and let us know, she contacted Sadler's Wells to find that they had sent a letter and that I had missed the audition. Tina pleaded with them, explaining that it must have gotten lost in the post and that had I received it I most certainly would have attended. Fortunately, they asked me to go to London the following month for the next round of auditions. I couldn't believe it!

In July, Mum and Dad took me to London for my audition. I changed into my black leotard, pink tights and headband and put on my new silk ballet shoes. I felt extremely nervous, not knowing what they expected from me, but the nerves disappeared after chatting with the other girls. I felt safe being a part of a group of dancers who were the same as me; I knew I wouldn't be bullied for being different, even if |I was a little chubbier than most of them.

The dance Principle was very tall. She wore black Dame Edna Everidge style glasses, which she peered over whenever she spoke with someone. She carried an ornate gold-handled cane in her left hand and banged it on the floor to get our attention, which prompted the other girls and me to jump straight into first position with our feet. She asked us to follow her to the dance studio, lined with floor to ceiling mirrors and wooden ballet barres. You could tell she had been a ballerina in her time as she didn't just walk, in front of us, she glided across the floor with grace and poise.

We did barre exercises to classical music first, played by a male pianist in the corner. The Principle walked up and down checking each of our foot positions as she went by. She rearranged feet with a cane tap and lifted arms higher to achieve a better transition from the fourth to fifth position. Following the exercises, we had to learn a small, choreographed routine that we performed as a group. Simultaneously, the instructor walked round and round the studio, watching us from different angles. At the end of the sequence, she saw us individually in another studio, where we performed a dance routine of our own to a piece of music of our choice. I chose one of the standard ballet routines that I would regularly perform at festivals, but halfway through I completely forgot the steps and had to make it up on the spot until the end of the piece. As this was in front of a panel of four different dance Principles that were watching and writing notes, I was concerned. Fortunately, they didn't seem to notice my improvisation. I went home, buzzing with excitement at this experience. Yet deep down, I knew I didn't want to be a professional ballerina; I was just a young girl who loved to dance.

Two weeks later, a letter arrived with an embossed stamp saying 'Sadler's Wells'. I opened it to find I had been successful, and they were offering me a scholarship to start in September in London. My chest filled with pride having achieved this, but an inner conflict soon replaced it. I told Mum I didn't want to go because even though I loved to dance, I didn't want to be a ballerina; I wanted to be a nurse. She was so cross with me and shouted and walloped my backside. I guess she was frustrated and thought me ungrateful for such an excellent opportunity. But I didn't want it, and that was that! Thankfully, Tina intervened, and I didn't get forced into it.

I continued dancing until I was eighteen years of age, with my last dance finale at Tina's annual Christmas concert. It was a sort of goodbye-dancing/hello-nursing send-off. We wore pale blue, floaty, silk dresses. They were long silk nighties from M&S, and we had pale blue flower buds in our hair. We danced to *Don't give up on us baby* by David Soul. It was regrettable to take my final curtsy but a memory I cherish. Whenever I hear the song today, I dance around the lounge, remembering the steps and memories of dancing with my sister, Tina, who died in 2011.

SEWING THE SEED THROUGH VOLUNTEERING

When I was nine years old, I joined the Junior British Red Cross to learn first aid and nursing. I just loved going every Monday evening after school to be trained and to meet other like-minded kids who enjoyed it as much as me. I made great friends and was never bullied, which was a blessing. At the age of nearly eleven, the Red Cross chose me to help on their disabled children's holiday. I was mature for my age, but I didn't know what to expect as this was the first time I had met people with disabilities. I needn't have worried, and I fitted right in.

The young girl assigned to me to care for was a twelve-year-old girl with Downs Syndrome, called Susan. She was taller, more muscular and heftier than me. She was sweet and allowed me to help her, loved holding my hand and chatted a lot - and I mean a lot! I don't think she stopped to draw breath from morning until night. When she got excited, boy, did I know it. She would scream very loudly and fling her arms around me and pick me up to spin me around, then threw me onto the floor. She would then dive on top of me, giving me hugs and sloppy kisses. I was covered in bruises by the end of the holiday, but I thoroughly enjoyed this wonderful, privileged experience. I knew there and then that I wanted to be a nurse in the future.

This first disabled kids' holiday was where I first met my future husband, Steve. He was two years older than me, and we hit it off straight away. We enjoyed each other's company, sharing the same sense of humour and dedication to let these kids have the holiday of a lifetime. Steve had matching bruises to me, as the little boy he was looking after had a false leg, and when he couldn't get his own way or got frustrated, he would take his leg off and proceed to hit Steve with it. He was certainly a handful, and Steve handled him beautifully with kindness and love.

Every year this holiday took place, I would meet up with old and new friends from the Red Cross, including my Steve, new children with different disabilities, or socially deprived backgrounds. I learnt so much from this yearly experience. Some of the deaf children taught me sign language. The staff showed me how to manoeuvre a wheelchair up and down pavements and stairs. Also, how to empty and change catheter bags. I also had physiotherapy lessons to learn how to stop muscular spasms for children with spina bifida or cerebral palsy. Most of all, I learnt the importance of fun and laughter as medicine. Of which these kids had seen extraordinarily little in the past.

Robert was one of the children that they referred to the Red Cross for most years. He had cerebral palsy and came from a very disadvantaged social background. Robert had dark hair, wore thick-rimmed glasses, and had great difficulty walking. Especially long distances. His smile and infectious laughter would brighten the room, and he stole my heart from the first second I met him. His home life was sorrowful; he was mostly left by himself, alone in his room and ignored. When Robert was with us, he would always be the first to volunteer for playing games, even if it were beyond his capabilities. We played rounders and football on the beach. We paddled in the sea and built sandcastles. Despite him using walking aids and a wheel-chair for long-distance, he always volunteered to be the first batsman at rounders. He put his heart and soul into hitting the ball, even though nine times out of ten he missed it, and ran with his limbs flailing around like a windmill, squealing with delight towards first base as we all cheered him on. His main passion was singing his favourite song, *Chirpy Chirpy Cheep Cheep*, which was number one in the music charts of 1971. He would dance and sing at the top of his voice with a smile that radiated from ear to ear. We encouraged him to try everything in life, despite his disability, and never let it get in his way. Each time he came on holiday, he improved himself. His walking became more robust. His speech got more intelligible, and his attitude to life became full of positivity and optimism. I loved him and his spirit.

Years later, Steve and I continued to run the kids' holiday for the Red Cross. Robert lived only a few miles from us, and on his birthday and Christmas, we would buy him a few presents and visit him at home. One Christmas morning, we arrived to give him a few small gifts to find his mum drunk on the sofa. We could see no Christmas decorations or presents anywhere, and Robert was all alone in his room. He heard our voices and ran so fast he nearly fell down the stairs to get to us, leaping into my arms and cuddling me so tight. His mum opened her eyes and said, "You can have him for the day if you want," and fell back to sleep.

The poor little guy: I was so sad for him. No kid should have to be alone, especially on Christmas day. I left his mum a note and our contact number, explaining that he was with us. We took a very excitable Robert to our house for the whole day. He tucked into an enormous Christmas dinner and pulled Christmas crackers, which he had never seen before. He ate lots of sweets and chocolate pennies, played games, sang Christmas songs, and, of course, *Chirpy Chirpy Cheep Cheep*. His beautiful smile and giggles continued all day and filled our home with love and happiness until at 6 pm when we said, "Sorry love, it's time to go home."

Bless him, he clung on to me so tight and cried his eyes out. He pleaded to stay, saying "Mummy won't mind." I couldn't help but cry with him. It was the quietest, saddest journey back to his home. He clung onto the car seats, and I hated being the person making him get out of the car, as he continued pleading with me to stay. His mum was still asleep on the settee, but she raised her head to say thanks. Poor Robert said goodbye through his sobbing and slowly walked up the stairs to his room, carrying his carrier bag full of sweets, Lego, a colouring book, pencils, and fuzzy felt. At the top of the stairs, he just turned to look back at us with tears rolling down his face and said, "Thank you, it was my best day ever."

I remember crying all the way home—such a great lad with such a generous spirit. There weren't whistleblowing policies for reporting to social services in the early seventies; otherwise, I would have contacted them. Looking back in hindsight, he and his family needed support and guidance.

Many years later, Steve and I were in a shopping centre, and we heard a voice shout our names. It was Robert. He was now seventeen years old, and he ran and hugged me and shook Steve's hand. He said he wanted to thank us both for giving him support and encouragement to progress in life and said very proudly that he now had a job. He planned to get his driving test the following week and that the council were giving him a flat the next month. I was so happy when he introduced us to his girlfriend Jenny, who I recognised from one of the holidays with us. He explained that they had been together ever since. We were so pleased to see him and so enormously proud of him knowing that we had played a small part in getting him to where he was today; Happy, confident, and healthy.

As a teenager, I worked voluntarily for the Red Cross in the hospital on alternate Sundays. I would visit the hospital matron's office and be allocated to a ward. I served tea and biscuits and collected chocolate, toiletries, magazines, or newspapers from the hospital shop for the patients who couldn't get out of bed. But mainly, I was asked to sit and chat with the patients. I loved finding out what treatment they were having. Or what brought them to the hospital. I learnt such a lot about the signs and symptoms of different illnesses. I even became an expert in how to fold hospital corners when making beds.

I remember a young lad, aged about thirteen, being admitted from theatre to the ward. He and his friends played on the railway track, as most boys stupidly did back then, but unfortunately, a train hit him while playing chicken. He got his foot caught under the track, and the train severed his leg as it passed. He had just got back from the theatre, and the nurses asked me to sit with him until he woke up. A cage covered the bottom half of his body, and a sheet lay over that. He had a drip in each arm; one of blood and the other of saline. When he woke, he was very groggy and confused and felt sick from the anaesthetic. Abruptly, he began to scream and shouted, "Where's my leg? What's happened to my leg?"

His screams were horrific. I tried my best to comfort him until the doctor came to talk to him, but at fifteen years of age, I had no training for this kind of situation. I felt so deeply in my heart that I had failed him. The ward sister and doctor asked me to leave his bed and pulled the curtain around. After a few minutes, they managed to calm him as they explained what had happened and sedated him to help his physical and mental pain. At that point, I realised I wanted to learn more about a person's mental health and well-being, not just their physical well-being. I realised that they go hand in hand and are forever intertwined; this is now known as the bio-psycho-social approach within nursing care. I continued to work voluntarily for the Red Cross at organised events administering first aid, working on hospital wards, and nursing homes; gaining as much experience as possible, for a future nursing career.

At seventeen years of age, I remember reading a magazine during my break in the hospital canteen. It had an article about a man who suffered from severe depression and had suicidal thoughts. It explained all about the care and treatment he received from a psychiatric nurse who helped him get through his illness. At the end of the article, it said, *'Could you be the next nurse to help someone with depression? If so, please contact the NHS to train as a psychiatric nurse.'* It felt like the article was written just for me, a calling; this is what I wanted to do. All my life had been leading to this moment. It all suddenly made sense.

MY CHOICE, MY CAREER

The following week, I visited my careers officer at school, armed with the magazine and information that I had received from the NHS, to discuss my new career choice. He wasn't impressed at my change of mind to go from general nursing to psychiatric nursing. He sat back in his swivel chair and put his glasses on top of his head and tutted. "No, no, no," he said. "You would be better off being a general nurse."

"Why?" I asked.

"Well, you don't want to look after nutters and murderers, do you? It will be extremely dangerous! It's more of a man's job, not a woman's job! You won't be strong enough as they can be overly aggressive, and it's not a proper nursing job anyway."

I couldn't believe what I was hearing. I just looked at the careers officer in disbelief and showed him the magazine, saying, "This is MY kind of nursing, and it's my choice!" He carried on stating it wasn't for me, so I dug my heels in and said, "Stop spouting rubbish at me, I'm going to apply with or without your help." I grabbed the magazine out of his hands and flounced out of the room in typical teenage fashion. He didn't realise that people with mental health illnesses could have physical issues, just like the rest of the population. I knew I would learn all about general nursing too. I thought, what a stupid, ignorant, condescending little man he was.

In July 1976, at the age of seventeen, I was sat in the waiting room of Middlewood Hospital Training Centre, waiting to be called for my 1 pm psychiatric student nurse interview. I was very anxious, but mainly, I felt excited to be taking the next step towards my dream career. At least ten more people were waiting for interviews too; all fidgeting, pacing up and down like me. A girl came over and sat next to me. She introduced herself as Karen. We chatted for a while to take our minds off the pending interview and discovered if we were successful, we would be in the same class starting in September.

I had never been to an interview before, and my heart was pounding, my legs were shaking. I looked at the clock, and it was 12.55 pm; just five minutes to go. I closed my eyes and took a few deep breaths and tried to remember the interview techniques I had learnt from the career officer's class: Look relaxed, but confident, sit up straight in the chair and look into the interviewer's eyes, smile, don't fidget, don't rush your answers, and don't forget to breathe. How the hell would I remember it all, never mind put it into practice? I heard a man call my name and thought, *Oh shit, here goes*! I put on my biggest smile and tried to look confident as I followed him into the interview room.

THE MIDDLE-AGED MAN that was about to interview me had slicked black hair and wore a black suit, white shirt, and a loud red kipper tie. He looked over the rim of his glasses, giving me a friendly smile that instantly put me at ease, and pointed to a chair opposite him, telling me to take a seat. He re-read my application form, nodding his head, and smiling as he read, before sitting back in his chair to ask me my first question. "Tell me, do you think that at the tender age of seventeen you're too young to do this type of nursing?"

"Of course not," I replied. I then explained my Red Cross experiences, the disabled children's holidays, and my voluntary hospital work. I also explained that I had just returned from Sweden after representing the British Red Cross at a camp looking after disabled children from all over the world.

He asked me, "What qualities do you have to become a good psychiatric nurse?"

I told him, "Well, I love to look after people, and my experience of looking after a variety of disabled children with both mental and physical needs has helped me to understand the importance of caring for both aspects of a person. I have good listening skills. I'm kind and sympathetic and have a genuine interest in people, but some will probably just say that's because I'm a nosey parker!" He laughed at the last part of my answer and proceeded to tell me all about the training. I left the interview feeling confident I had done my best and was relieved the interview wasn't as hard as I thought it might be. I looked in the waiting room and saw Karen and gave her the thumbs up and said, "Good luck. I hope to see you in September." I would have to wait six weeks before I would find out if I had been successful or not.

A letter arrived on the doormat at the end of August, and I was terrified to open it. I would have been devastated if they declined my application, and I didn't want the careers officer to say, 'I told you so.' I opened the letter and screeched with delight, as the first thing I saw was the start date halfway down the page in bold black letters. The feeling of pride bubbled up within me as the tears rolled down my cheeks. I don't know how I managed, but through my mascara-stained eyes, I read through the rest of the letter, congratulating me, and offering me the position to train as a psychiatric nurse for three years. At the end of it, it asked me to confirm the acceptance of my training and to make a request for a room at the nurse's residence if I required accommodation during my training, as there were limited spaces available. I hadn't even thought about getting to and from work or even where I would live. I just knew I wanted to be a nurse, and that was as far as my seventeen-year-old brain had thought. How naive was I? I lived twenty miles and three bus rides away from the hospital so travelling from my home every day was impractical. I rang immediately and accepted my position as a student nurse and confirmed I would like a place in the nurse's residence to live. I suddenly felt incredibly grown-up, after all, I was starting a new chapter in my life, and I was in control of my destiny.

NAIVETY AND DEAD BODIES

On 26th September 1976, which was my 18th birthday, I left home to start my new life and career in the big wide world. I had a box full of goodies, food, toiletries, two mugs, knives, forks, spoons, plates, dishes, and a suitcase full of naivety. Moving from a small Yorkshire village to the Sheffield city centre's bright lights was exciting, yet I didn't know what city life, nursing life, or adult life indeed was. My wings were unclipped, and I was leaping blindly from the highest nest. I was feeling every bit the grown-up, armed with my very own 12-inch black and white telly, a record player, a few records; new clothes, make-up and a bottle of Charlie perfume completed the transition from a young girl to womanhood. Long shifts at the Longbow pub as a barmaid helped me buy black nursing shoes, ready to be paired with a new nursing uniform. My pride and joy was a new silver nurses pendant watch that had been presented to me by my local Red Cross friends to wish me luck in my future career as a nurse.

Mum and Dad drove me from my home in Darfield to Middlewood hospital, Sheffield, in their small mustard coloured Austin Marina car, packed to the hilt with all my worldly possessions. As we entered the turning into Middlewood hospital, their faces were a picture with mouths agape as we drove slowly through the big gates and vast grounds, surrounded by the intimidating days of gone by Victorian asylum buildings. Massive oak trees and willow were blowing in the wind, with black ravens and crows flying low in front of the car, as if checking us out. It was like a scene out of an Alfred Hitchcock movie.

When we arrived at the nurse's residence building, I saw a hunched over man with two cigarettes behind his ears, shuffling towards me and muttering to himself in between frantic puffs of a lit cigarette. He came right up to me, leaning into my face, with the stench of stale cigarettes invading my senses. "Got a cigarette, nurse?" he asked gruffly. I told him I didn't smoke, to which he glared at me and swore under his breath as he shuffled away down the drive. I would learn the significance of always having cigarettes in my pocket later in my training.

With a sense of urgency to get inside, Mum and Dad hastily grabbed my belongings and carried them through the large glass doors of the nurse's residence building. While I felt entirely unfazed by this first encounter with a patient, Mum and Dad were undeniably anxious for my safety. I signed in with Annie, the Warden, who gave me her contact details in case of an emergency. She told me all about the residence rules and essential safety information, such as not having visitors after midnight and where the fire escapes were. I signed for two keys for room number two, located on the ground floor. I made my way towards my room with Mum and Dad in tow, ladened with bags and boxes. I had the hard job of carrying the key!

I opened the door to find a single bed, a wardrobe, a small desk, and a chair. Still not entirely reassured of my welfare from Annie's greeting, Dad proceeded to check if the single window in my room was secure and that it locked firmly. He didn't seem happy to be leaving me in such a daunting place, but I assured him I was okay and not to worry; secretly just wanting them to hurry and go so that I could begin my newfound independence. Mum and Dad kissed and cuddled me and said their goodbyes. Mum told me to phone them if I got scared, even if it was in the middle of the night. It was unusual for her to let her guard down and show her genuine emotions, but she became tearful as she realised that her little girl was all grown up and leaving the nest. They got in the car and drove away, waving frantically out of the windows until out of sight. Mum later told me that Dad had cried most of the journey home after leaving his little girl in a mental hospital.

Without any further thought, I turned straight to unpacking my belongings and most importantly, looking where I should plug in my telly. A knock at the door made me jump and in came two other newbies, Alison, and Sarah, asking if I wanted to join them for a coffee in the kitchen. Having been bullied throughout school, this felt entirely alien to me; to feel included and have new people want to make friends genuinely. I found my mug and a packet of Ginger Nut biscuits and left the rest of my unpacking until later. I wasn't going to miss the opportunity to make new friends. I joined them in the kitchen where we chatted and laughed the afternoon away. We discovered that we were all going to be in the same class of September 1976. Later, I found the communal telephone (No mobiles in those days) at the end of the corridor and rang Steve, who was now my new boyfriend of three weeks. I asked him to join my new friends and me for a drink in the hospital social club; after all, it was my eighteenth birthday, and I deserved my first legal drink to celebrate this doubly special day.

~

THREE WEEKS before I started my training, Steve asked me out on a date to a friend's party. I had always fancied him and had even had a few sneaky snogs with him over the years during the disabled kids' holidays. Unfortunately, our first kiss was a disaster.

While having the longest snog on the staircase of an old hotel in Morcombe, there was a noise from above our heads and the ceiling fell in on top of us, covering us in white plaster. Not the best of omens. I have heard the saying "Did the earth move for you, darling?" However, never have I heard, "Did the ceiling fall for you, darling?"

Steve picked me up in his dad's car; a red Ford Cortina, registration XWE 113M. How I still remember that registration, I don't know. I struggle to remember what I was doing yesterday, never mind forty-four years ago. He asked what drinks I wanted from the "off-y" (Yorkshire for the off-license store). As it was our first date, I wanted to appear sophisticated, and so instead of saying wine or cider, which I usually drank, I asked for Pernod spirit and blackcurrant cordial.

He didn't look impressed on returning to the car as the Pernod's cost didn't leave much change from his five-pound note. We arrived at the party and Steve poured me a large glass of Pernod and blackcurrant and added an ice cube. Gosh! It was bloody gorgeous, like Blackpool aniseed rock in liquid form. I chatted, kissed and danced with Steve while drinking my drink like it was blackcurrant squash, until suddenly, I didn't feel very well, and the room began to spin. I hadn't realised that Pernod had a 40% alcohol content and I had been necking it like it was going out of fashion; not that I knew back then that alcohol had different strengths! I was new at this drinking malarky. Steve took me outside for some fresh air to help me feel better, but as soon as it hit me, I felt sick and proceeded to vomit all over the floor and on Steve's shoes.

I was in a right old alcoholic state; embarrassingly vomiting and farting simultaneously with projectile force. "Come on, Melanie, I think I need to get you home," Steve said and bundled me into the car. I continued to feel sick as my head spun as if I were on a fairground ride; this was one of the longest journeys of my life. Steve had to stop every five minutes for me to get out of the car to be sick. I begged him for a drink after the umpteenth time of vomiting, and luckily, he found a bottle of water in the boot of the car. I drank it all down in one because I was so thirsty, and my mouth tasted vile. The water didn't seem to help much, and I continued vomiting as we travelled to my house. Even when there was nothing more to come up, I continued to wretch and fart; this would be embarrassing at any time, never mind on a first date! Steve got me out of the car and held me up. By this time, I could hardly stand or focus. He knocked on my parent's front door and handed me over to my sister Tina, stating, "I think she's had too much to drink," before scarpering as quickly as he could into his car and drove off. What a coward!

I was in bed for a further five days with bad headaches, dizziness, and vomiting. I felt so ill I thought at one point I would die. On the sixth day, I started to feel a bit better, and I even managed to keep a slice of toast down. I hadn't phoned Steve all week because I was so embarrassed, but that evening Steve called to see how I was. I was surprised as I thought I had blown my chances with him. What a vision of loveliness I must have looked that night as he handed me over to my sister at the end of our date. Over the phone, he said, "I have something to tell you, and you might not like it."

Here we go, I thought, *I'm getting dumped*.

"I think I need to apologise to you," he said.

Really? I thought. It should be me apologising to him, after all, it was me that got into a drunken state and vomited on his shoes.

"I'm afraid I don't know how to tell you this, but the water I gave you to drink in the car was in fact water laced with antifreeze that my dad had put in the boot. I thought it was just water. I'm so sorry. I didn't know."

My God! Poisoned from not only alcohol but bloody antifreeze; no wonder I was so ill.

Steve had tried to kill me on our first date. He tried to make light of it and said, "Well, at least you will be a good little starter on a cold morning." He even had the cheek to ask me out on a second date.

Of course, I played it cool at first and let him grovel a bit, before saying that I would. After all, I did rather fancy his 6ft 4-inch-tall frame, long strawberry wavy blonde hair, piercing blue eyes, and sexy smile. Finally, after much grovelling and flattery, I agreed to a second date. Secretly I was falling for him, but I wasn't going to make it easy for him, besides, he might have been a murderer in the making.

THE FIRST SIX weeks of nurse training was in a purpose-built training unit in Middlewood hospital. Here we would learn the basics of nursing care. The tutors introduced themselves and gave us the itinerary for those weeks ahead. I couldn't wait to get started. My first lecture was 'Terminology in Nursing' where we learned about the meaning of words and phrases, we would use in our nursing careers. I found it fascinating, seeing as the most complicated expression I knew was 'Ee, by gum.' We learnt what terms 'signs and symptoms', 'institutionalisation', 'confusion', 'agitation', 'delusions', and 'hallucinations' meant.

The list went on and on, and I realised that I didn't know as much as I thought I did. For example, I thought delusions and hallucinations were the same, but they are different entirely. A 'delusion' is a distortion that affects the thought process, and a hallucination is a distortion that affects the senses. As we continued through the lecture, one particular word, and explanation made a profound emotional connection with me: 'EMPATHY'. The definition of empathy is the ability to understand another person's thoughts, feelings, or emotions. We discussed how to be empathetic as nurses by understanding others' needs and treating people how we would want to be treated ourselves in this situation. I had never even heard of the word 'empathy'. A particular word had never impacted me before, but this word 'empathy' totally resonated with me. It made complete sense of how to care for a person, and I decided there and then that I wanted to be that kind of nurse and person. Empathy and I would go forward from this day hand in hand. Little did I know how true this would be in later life.

As we continued through the following weeks, we learned and practised various practical nursing skills on each other. We learned how to take blood pressure, temperature, pulse, and respiration. We measured, gave, and recorded medication; performed aseptic technique when changing dressings; made beds with crisp linen and neat hospital corners, built our knowledge in various mental health illnesses, and food categories. We even practised our injection technique into poor old Jaffa the Orange repeatedly until he'd been well and truly juiced. My brain was just as full.

During the last week of initial training, we were taken around the hospital to different departments and were introduced to the various staff to know where to go once we started working on the ward. As a student nurse, you were the gopher of the wards. You collected drugs from the pharmacy; fetched a wheelchair from the stores or even took dead bodies from the ward to the Mortuary with a porter.

On our visit to the Mortuary, situated in an outer building of the grounds, I had my first experience of seeing a dead body. The idea of it gave me the jitters! Looking back now, it seems an awful lot to expect of someone at the sweet age of eighteen. As we entered the Mortuary room, there was a very distinctive smell which I had never smelt before, and it got right up my nose. I had to put my hand over my mouth and nose, as I didn't like it. It was a combination of stale, stagnant air, pungent chemicals and, what I now know to be the unmistakable smell of death, that made me want to wretch. The room was clinical with white tiled walls and surgical metal trolleys and equipment at the outer edges. At the centre of the room was a space awaiting the next deceased patient to arrive. We were taken through the back of the room through a heavy metal door into a tiny, chilled room where two dead bodies, bound in white sheets and labels attached, laid on silver trolleys. A group of us students and the mortician crammed in with the bodies.

The mortician explained all about what his job entailed and how he prepared the deceased for the undertakers. This explanation was all lost on me as I felt the walls closing in; my ears began to buzz as my face flushed up with heat, despite the room's cooler temperature. I stood at the back of the room, pressed up tight against the closing wall, as far away from the bodies as possible.

Honestly, I wouldn't say I liked this situation, and it made me question how I would ever deal with a dead patient in the future. I just wanted to get out of the room as soon as possible, but everyone else kept asking questions, prolonging this nightmare of a visit. When the mortician had finally finished his presentation, the group slowly made their way out of the tiny room. As I approached the door to leave, two of the lads from our group, called Bernie and Brian, thought it would be funny to push me backwards towards the bodies before running out and shutting the mortuary door, leaving me still inside.

I was terrified! The room instantly plunged into darkness, and I couldn't find the light switch or the door handle to get out. I remember screaming frantically for someone to let me out, but either nobody could hear me or chose not to. I started to panic; gasping for breath as my imagination ran riot that the bodies would reach out and grab me. I continued to scream hysterically for what seemed like forever until eventually, the door opened, and the two lads stood there laughing at me.

I flew past them, pushing them aside, and ran back to the nurse's residence. I flung myself onto my bed, crying, and shaking, still unable to catch my breath. Alison, who had seen me run into the building in a state, came to see if I was okay and tried her best to calm me down. *That was it,* I thought, *I was giving up nursing, and I was going home right now; today.* As a kid, they'd bullied me, and I certainly wasn't going to be bullied or intimidated as an adult. I jumped off my bed and started packing my things up into boxes as I continued to sob. Alison tried her best to reassure me that I should carry on and not let two immature arseholes stop me from becoming a nurse.

As if by magic, Bernie and Brian arrived at my door to apologise for their stupidity. At first, they still seemed to find it funny, but when they saw the state of me, they realised they had gone too far and that it had scared and upset me. They explained that they hadn't meant to scare me so much and that they just did it as a joke. They said they had seen how freaked out I looked when I was in the chilled room and thought it would be funny to shut me in and that I would just let myself out and shout at them. After ten minutes (which seemed like an hour to me) they realised that I hadn't followed them and came back to let me out. When they found out that the lights had gone out once the door shut, and there was no handle on the inside either, they were horrified.

I was still crying and still terribly angry at them, but eventually, I calmed down and accepted their apologies and accepted it was a prank that had gone wrong. They both promised never to be so stupid again and begged me not to leave nursing. They were worried they would be thrown off the course if the school of nursing found out. We shook hands, and they left for lunch with their tails between their legs. I didn't join them; strangely enough, I had lost my appetite. I didn't go back to lectures that afternoon either and fell asleep, exhausted from the trauma of the day.

The following day, I woke up feeling optimistic about what lay ahead. I put the previous day's events behind me, and I made my way over to the sewing room, where hospital staff had their uniforms fitted. The seamstress measured me for six starched blue and white small, checked uniforms complete with two white belts to identify as a first-year student nurse. My body shape created some difficulty for the seamstress who struggled to find the right size uniform for, what she called, my 'dumplings'. Having 38 F sized breasts in a nursing uniform meant that I either looked like Barbara Windsor in *Carry on Nurse*, or Hattie Jacques in *Carry on Matron*. The uniform was either too tight on my boobs, just waiting for the poppers to give way when I bent over, or too big, drowning any thought of curves and figure. In the meantime, while she made alterations, we decided that I would take two of the Hattie Jacques and fasten my white belt a bit tighter.

They gave us a skeleton key to fit all the hospital doors on-site, which they locked throughout the hospital to prevent vulnerable and confused patients from leaving the wards. As my first placement, they allocated me to Ward 15, a long-stay female geriatric ward. At last, I was going to start my nursing career. I couldn't wait until Monday morning.

LET THE NURSING BEGIN WITH POO AND CHOCOLATE

$\mathcal{M}$y first shift started at 6 am. At 5 am I was up, showered and dressed, wearing my pristinely ironed uniform staring at the four walls of my room. With a combination of excitement and apprehension, I set off walking through the grounds of the hospital. It was still dark, and I don't think I had ever walked so fast in my life. The wind was howling, and the birds were just about waking enough to give a few squawks and whistles to make me jump as I went by.

The main building had stone steps leading up to a big main entrance door, which was incredibly heavy to push open. I turned left and followed the signs for Ward 15; down a long corridor and up the red steps to the door. I took a deep breath and then became confused as I didn't know if I should use my skeleton key or ring the bell, but fortunately for me, another member of staff came up behind me to let us both in. The ward felt open and spacious with high ceilings and cream walls that held tiny night lights; giving just enough light to see and walk. I felt so glamorous and essential to be a nurse in my uniform, walking through the grandeur of this Victorian hospital ward. That was until the pungent smell of urine hit my nose. I would soon be taken back down a peg or two and learn that there was extraordinarily little glamour in nursing.

I followed the nurse into the staff office and introduced myself, met with mixed reactions of "Hello, pleased to meet you," and "Oh, good we could do with an extra pair of hands today."

Then a middle-aged woman piped up from the back of the office, "Oh God! Not another student nurse," while rolling her eyes. They taught us how to identify the various nursing positions based upon the colour of their uniform. This battle-axe-looking nurse was wearing an Olive-green uniform, which meant she was a State Enrolled Nurse or SEN.

I said, "Hello, nice to meet you."

She only turned and pointed out the door and said, "Make yourself useful and go to the kitchen and make a pot of tea and one of coffee. Bring a large jug of milk, sugar cubes and six mugs." I tried not to look flustered and did so, wanting to make an excellent first impression.

I took a guess and walked down one of the corridors of the ward. Luckily for me, I found the kitchen just a few doors away from the office and got to it. Not knowing where they kept things, I opened and closed each kitchen cupboard until I found everything, I needed to complete my first assigned task; this would take some time as I was trying to locate everything in all the unlabelled cupboards. The next thing I knew, the same battle-axe came storming into the kitchen in her shoes that made a clip-clop sound as she walked and said, "Nurse! How stupid do you have to be not to make up a morning tray for the staff? It will be afternoon by the time we get our drinks, if you carry on at this snail pace." She snatched the tray out of my hands and stomped down the corridor, with me scuttling behind her like a naughty schoolgirl.

In the staff office, we had a 'handover' from night staff to morning staff. A handover is where the previous shift's staff relay any problems or changes in patients' conditions. Not knowing what to do, I just sat there drinking my coffee and listening, feeling every bit the lemon because I didn't know the patients or what to do next. They informed us that sadly a lady, called Harriet, had just died an hour before I had arrived on the ward. They told us that they had left her for us to deal with. I thought, *What the hell does that mean?* But I was soon going to find out.

The battle-axe, called Joan, stood up and said, "The student and I will see to Harriet." I was just taking my last gulp of coffee and nearly choked at her statement. Did she mean I would help with a dead body within the first hour of my first shift, on my first ward? *Bloody hell!* I thought. I had only just recovered from the horrible experience in the mortuary the week before. I was so scared I could hear my heart thumping in my ears and pounding in my chest, but I put a brave face on and pretended I was okay. I call it my tits-and-teeth face — I stand tall, stick out my chest and smile!

I followed Joan to a small, cramped room full of medical equipment. She instructed me to collect a stainless-steel trolley, a large bowl of hot water, towels, a comb, a small tray with cotton wool balls, tweezers, tape, two bandages, a shroud, two sheets, a card tag, a large piece of paper, a pen, and a safety pin. Thankfully, I had a pen and pad in my pocket to write the list down, or I would never have remembered it all. Once again, it took me ages as I had to look in every cupboard and drawer to find everything that she had requested. She left me for about ten minutes and returned, then said, "Follow me, nurse," in a quick sing-song manner, leaving me to bring the ladened trolley.

I trekked along the corridor with the bowl of water sloshing about as I went. When I was halfway along, Joan screeched at me, "You're bloody useless, nurse! Just look at those sheets." I had placed the bowl of water on the top shelf of the trolley. At the same time, I'd put the towels and sheets on the bottom one.

Now, the towels and sheets were well and truly soaked through because I had filled the bowl of water too full. Off I went, back to the room, still sloshing away as I returned, with the ward cleaner mopping up behind me and giving me a motherly wink as if to say that it was all okay. I learnt my lesson and would always place the bowl on the bottom shelf and only half fill it from then on.

I returned to Joan. She stood, huffing, and tutting in the small six bedded bay, by a bed surrounded by curtains. I followed Joan through the curtains with the trolly and looked at the tiny body shape inside, covered with a sheet. I just stood looking, frozen to the spot and not knowing what to do next; this was a real dead person I was going to meet. All I did know was that the voice in my head was saying, "Run Mel, run!", but somehow, I managed to talk myself into staying.

Joan instructed me to take the sheet off the lady and said, "We're going to wash her, stuff her and dress her in a shroud." It was said so matter of fact as if I knew what the hell she was talking about, but I stood there like a rabbit caught in headlights.

I just said, "Okay," not wanting to appear a fool and stood at one side of the bed, with Joan at the other. I still couldn't bring myself to actually take the sheet off the body. Joan impatiently pulled the sheet off and put it into the laundry basket, revealing the skeletally thin and crumpled up body of dear Harriet. Thankfully, I didn't even get the time to let the fear within me take hold as Joan proceeded to roll Harriet towards me to hold her while she washed her back. I was pleasantly surprised to find Harriet was still warm and soft to touch, but even more surprised to see her eyes flash wide open and stare right at me, followed by a loud, large burp. I nearly shit myself and wanted to run for the hills again. Joan said, "Just hold her tight. She won't hurt you. Sometimes bodies do that — they belch and fart, and their eyes and mouths fall open."

"Okay," I said, as Harriet continued to stare up at me with vacant eyes. We washed and dried her gently, with Joan showing me how to keep a patient's dignity by placing towels over their private areas. This effort seemed in vain when Joan explained that the next stage was to put cotton wool into each orifice because there was no muscle control after death. I was horrified!

Bear in mind that we didn't have the usage of gloves and aprons for any personal care, including when a person had died. But we proceeded to put cotton wool into her back passage and vagina to prevent the leakage of poo and discharge and a pad placed between her legs to catch any urine. Once dressed in a starched white shroud, I brushed her hair and put her false teeth in her tiny mouth. They looked so big as if they belonged to a racing horse, and I had to pull her lips over to cover them.

By the time we finished, she had the appearance of a normal old lady sleeping peacefully in her bed. The hospital had contacted the family, and they were on their way to visit Harriet. I was so proud of myself that I had been able to overcome my fears and help Harriet look dignified for her final goodbyes with her family. I even got a "Well done" from the battle-axe who, in hindsight, actually made me face my fears and meant I just had to get on with whatever nursing threw at me. For someone so stern, she was surprisingly tender and caring for the patient, and I learnt a lot from her that day.

Before the family arrived, I saw that Harriet had a bunch of flowers on her bedside locker. I took a pink rose from the vase, placed it in her hands and laid them across her chest. The last memory for her family was complete. Joan smiled and acknowledged my effort to make Harriet look beautiful and at peace. When the family had said their goodbyes to Harriet, they came to meet with us to collect her belongings and thanked us for the care and compassion we had given her. I made them a hot drink, and they told me all about Harriet's life as we sat in the visitors' room. Although I had met Harriet in death, it was lovely to hear the stories of her life and the person she was to them; a loving wife, mother, and grandmother, who had dedicated her life to caring for her family.

Knowing Harriet in life reinforced my understanding of a nurse being compassionate in both life and death, and that Harriet was not merely a dead body but a person who had led a real life with real thoughts and feelings. As nurse Joan talked me through the final preparations for Harriet, I connected with her and was no longer afraid of a dead person. Joan taught me how to tie Harriet's jaw with a bandage to prevent it from falling open. We placed tape on her eyelids to keep them shut and tied her feet together using a bandage in a figure-eight application to stop them falling apart or off the trolly. Strangely, the most impersonal aspect of all the care we gave was to write a label with her name and tie it around her big toe. Once completed, we wrapped her in an outer sheet and safety-pinned her named piece of paper to the top sheet. We then arranged for Harriet to be taken by a porter to the Morgue. I took a great sigh of relief that no one requested me to escort Harriet to the mortuary with the porter. Instead, Joan sent me on my breakfast break. I sat eating my well-deserved bacon butty, feeling physically and mentally exhausted, and it was only 9.30 am.

As the weeks went by, I began to enjoy my time on this forty-two bedded ward. I was learning how to physically and mentally nurse the confused old ladies with dementia who were the permanent residents. Each patient was at a different stage of their illness; some were just pleasantly confused, and others were in bed in the foetus position, unable to communicate, walk, or eat independently.

I learned about pressure area care for bedridden patients to relieve their bodies' weight onto the mattress against their skin and bony joints. They needed to change position every two hours at a minimum. They needed to move from a side position, onto their backs, and over to the opposite side. Sadly, even with this attentive care, their skin could still break down, and big sores could appear in a matter of hours.

The worst I witnessed was a little old lady called Jenny; not weighing much more than five stone, she had been bedridden for months and was terminally ill with cancer and dementia. Her sore grew so big at the bottom of her spine that I could have put my fist in the hole. We had to clean the area and pack it with ribbon gauze every other day. It took two packs of ribbon gauze to fill the wound, followed by a large dressing to protect the area. It was sad to see someone in so much pain despite being given medication to help with it. Thank goodness I had learned old-time songs during my voluntary work at Darfield nursing home; I would gently sing to her to try and distract her mind from the pain of packing the hole at the bottom of her spine. Sometimes she would stop screaming and lift her head from her pillow and smile the most beautiful toothless grin I had ever seen, joining in to sing the odd word, or humming the tune with me. I didn't like having to change her dressing and cause her pain. To be the one inflicting pain upon a person did not sit well with me. It was the first time I realised that my role as a nurse was not just to help someone get better, but a careful balancing act of doing no harm, while easing discomfort. Without this dressing, we would have caused her more damage by allowing her wound to deteriorate and get sepsis, yet the action of doing so caused her discomfort. This balancing act is the nurse's actual skill; to connect with a patient and know how to ease suffering while achieving the greater good.

One of my favourite patient memories was of a sweet lady called Dotty. She lived in a side room to the main ward and managed, or so I thought, her hygiene needs herself and would always be very well-groomed with nice clothing and never without her lipstick on. However, she was psychotic and had auditory hallucinations, where she would hear voices in her head and have lovely conversations with herself. She always appeared happy, with a big smile on her face and would chuckle away while talking to the voices. She would walk up and down the L shaped corridors of the ward, often stopping to chat to the windows or singing a little ditty which she had made up herself. Her little song was infectious and would go "I am Dotty, and I'm a bit potty," sung in sequence with every step she took, repeatedly, and followed by a loud cackling laugh. After an eight-hour shift of hearing this tune hundreds of times, I couldn't get it out of my head, and I would want to commit murder. Her continuous loops of the ward made her particularly useful to the nursing staff and would be our third eye in spotting and reporting if ever a patient had fallen or needed our assistance.

One morning, as I was putting clean towels away in the linen room, Dotty approached me and asked if I could go to her room with her, as she had something for me. She scuttled off ahead to her room that was two doors down, and I followed on behind. I arrived at the tiny bedroom that contained a wardrobe, chair, and a single bed with a hand-crocheted bedspread, made by herself during occupational therapy visits. Her room was plain, with very few personal possessions on display; no photographs or memories of a previous life lived were visible.

As I entered her room, I saw her standing by her bed with a great big smile and poised with anticipation. She proudly presented me with a pretty, red, heart-shaped chocolate box. *How sweet*, I thought. She wanted to give me something special. As I thanked her, I opened the box of chocolates. An unusual smell hit me. *What is that smell?* I thought. I looked inside to see a layer of individually shaped chocolates and picked one out, ready to pop it into my mouth in a show of appreciation. As my hand approached my face, I instinctively went to smell that delightful aroma of chocolate, only to recognise the smell — of POO!

I retched internally and thought I was going to be sick. To

not offend Dotty, I hugged her with thanks and told her that I would eat them later with a cup of coffee in my break. She was delighted and squirmed with excitement. As soon as I was away from her sight, I threw them in the bin and immediately washed my hands. I couldn't believe that she'd given me a chocolate box full of poo, that she had lovingly moulded into heart shapes and prettily placed back inside the box. When I told the rest of the staff, they laughed so much. They then informed me that they'd received a few poo treats from Dotty during their time. They told me that she specialised in Malteser Russian roulette, rolling her poo into Malteser shaped balls and mixing them with the genuine chocolate balls. Nobody had ever seen her creating her gifts, nor did she ever show any signs of someone who was playing with poo. From that day on, I made a vow never to accept chocolates or sweets from a patient again.

On my last day, Joan called me to the office and told me that it was traditional for student nurses to buy cakes from the canteen on their final shift, for all the staff to share in their tea break. Of course, I said yes, after all, I was still terrified of her. Whatever Joan asked, I did, but I was beginning to warm towards her as she had taught me a lot. As I was about to leave to get the cakes, she added that she would like me to collect a long stand from Ward 14 on the way back, as they needed it that afternoon for a patient. At the canteen, I bought a mixture of cakes and a box of biscuits to say thank you to the staff and patients for putting up with me, and on the way back called into Ward 14.

I asked for the nurse in charge, and when the ward sister arrived, I informed her I was from Ward 15 and requested to ask for this specific piece of equipment as they needed it for the afternoon shift. She said, "Yes, of course, no problem. If you just wait there, I will sort it out for you," and off she went down the corridor to her office. After fifteen minutes of waiting, I began to think this was taking too long and that perhaps the Sister had become distracted and forgot.

I decided to go looking for the ward sister, who I found sitting in her office. I knocked on her door, and she shouted, "Enter!" I stood looking at her, hoping she would say what the delay was, but she just stared back at me blankly and said, "Can I help you?"

I said, "Excuse me, I have been here about fifteen minutes waiting for the long stand that I requested for Ward 15."

"Oh, yes, yes, of course, you did," she said, with a smile on her face. "Well, I think fifteen minutes seems about right for a long stand to me, don't you?" She began to laugh, but I didn't understand why she was laughing at first. Then it dawned on me. I suddenly felt a fool and realised that Ward 15 had sent me for a long stand, and that was what I well and truly got.

I thanked her for her participation in the prank and sheepishly walked back to Ward 15. On arriving through the door, a cheer greeted me and laughter as apparently, it was a traditional joke at the hospital for first-year student nurses. I took it all in good faith and enjoyed my last cup of tea and cake with the team. Once qualified, of course, I took great delight in carrying this tradition on with new student nurses. They fell for it every time, mainly because they were so eager to please, just like I had been.

PSYCHOSIS AND STIGMATA

*W*ard 12 was a mixed-sex acute assessment ward for patients under the age of sixty-five. I arrived there with a spring in my step as I was so eager to learn new skills for a different patient category. I was surprised to find many patients were out of bed in their night attire, drinking cups of tea and immersed in thick clouds of cigarette smoke. A young Hippy type of guy in his twenties flounced his way towards me. He grabbed my arm and spun me round to the music of 10CC on the radio. He sang along gently into my ear, "I'm not in love, don't forget it, it's just a silly phase I'm going through," while swaying me from side to side. He looked around the ward as if he were about to offer me a drug deal and whispered, "Morning nurse, you got any cigarettes I could have?"

"No, sorry love, I don't smoke," I replied.

With a big friendly grin on his face, he replied, "Bollocks! I don't believe you!" He spun me around, letting go of my hand as he curtsied and flounced back down the ward corridor, continuing to dance while looking for his next unsuspecting cigarette victim.

A few steps later, a young girl with bandages on both her

forearms stepped in front of me, blocking my way to the nursing office. Pretending to cry in a moany voice she said, "Nurse, I'm feeling very anxious after visiting Accident and Emergency last night to have my arms sutured, a cigarette would make me feel so much better."

I replied again, "Sorry, love, I don't smoke."

To which she replied in a raised sarcastic voice, "Well, that's not going to help me, is it Nurse?" and stormed off in a huff!

I hadn't even got to the ward office when I was stopped a third time by a young guy who put his arm around my shoulders and said in hushed tones, "Hello gorgeous! You got any fags I can buy from you? I can give you two pence a cigarette."

I began to think there was a bit of a theme emerging. Did I need to start smoking?

myself? Or did I just need to have cigarettes on me to share with the pleading patients? I replied politely once again, "Sorry, love, I can't help you because I don't smoke." He accepted my answer and sat down with his cup of tea and shared the last few puffs from another patient's cigarette.

Eventually, I managed to fight through the cigarette smoke and patients to get to the nursing office. I was greeted with enthusiasm by the nurses. Kath, the ward sister, said how happy she was to have another nurse on the ward today because it was a hectic day, as there were patients on one-to-one observation, and it was the Consultant's ward round. Tea and coffee were already sitting on a tray, so I helped myself to a coffee. I listened to the handover and took notes on each patient. It was utterly different to the type of handover on Ward 15 which used to comprise of 'the patient is a little confused, but ate and slept well', or 'the patient was bedridden and needed full nursing care,' or worst of all, a patient had sadly died during the shift.

The first patient report was about Tom, admitted early evening the day before. He had sat in a chair all night in a catatonic state and would require a gastric nasal tube fitted later in the day, allowing us to give nutrition and medication. Catatonic schizophrenia is a rare psychotic illness characterised by the patient's lack of movement, almost statue-like, and displays little communication. For example, if you lifted his arm upright into the air as if he were asking a question in class, his arm would stay in that position until you moved it back.

Melissa was a young lady who was suffering from depression and attention-seeking behaviour. She had cut her wrists again, apparently the third time that week. This time she had used a broken pen and had to go to the casualty department for sutures in her arms during the night.

Lesley was a young mum admitted during the previous evening from Jessops, the local maternity hospital. She had given birth to a baby boy five days ago and was diagnosed with Puerperal Psychosis, a psychotic illness brought on by the imbalance of hormones after childbirth. Delusions and hallucinations characterise it. She required one-to-one observation due to her paranoia and suicidal tendencies.

A middle-aged man called Bill had been awake all night, singing and dancing and talking nonstop, keeping most of the patients awake. He was diagnosed with Mania, a psychotic illness displaying great euphoria, overactivity, and grandiose delusional thoughts.

The handover continued, and we discussed and reported on many more patients, all with different psychiatric problems in various stages of recovery. I was fascinated and secretly excited because I had lectures about psychiatric illness in school but couldn't wait to learn about each patient and how they presented their unique condition.

Kath, the ward sister, decided I could work alongside her for my first shift. She said the best way for me to get to know the patients and routine was to help serve breakfast. As the patients came up to the breakfast trolly and stated what they wanted for breakfast, I introduced myself and asked them their names to put a face to the names from my handover notes. After the pleasantries of introduction, most of the patients asked the same question. Yes, you've guessed it, "HAVE YOU GOT A CIGARETTE NURSE?" It was like a long-play record on repeat, all the patients seemed obsessed with cigarettes, and it was beginning to get on my nerves.

In a side room off the main corridor so that she could be seen and observed by staff was Lesley. I asked her what she would like to eat for breakfast, but she didn't even look at me and only replied occasionally to other staff members. I decided to take her a couple of slices of toast, with a small pot of butter and jam. I tried to persuade her to eat as much as she could. But Lesley just stared at me, her face not depicting any emotion and didn't even attempt a mouthful. Kath had informed me that Lesley was paranoid, and she confirmed this behaviour by accusing me of poisoning her food.

I poured us both a cup of tea and joined her in her room. Lesley sat staring at me as I introduced myself; she intensely watched my every movement. I sipped my tea and observed that she was mirroring my actions when I took a sip of tea. I felt a little uncomfortable at her copycat behaviour and scared of what Lesley might do next, as I had never nursed anyone with psychosis. I was a little anxious she might throw the tea at me, but proud of myself that I had managed to get her to drink something.

Kath popped her head around the door and told me to go for my breakfast and that she would sit with Lesley until I returned. On my way to breakfast, I decided to call into the hospital shop to buy a packet of cigarettes and a box of matches. I had seen that when a patient was anxious, agitated or just bored, the magic cigarette did the trick to calm them, and most of the nurses had them in their pockets for that very reason. So, if I needed to fit into this community, it seemed that cigarettes were my key or currency. The shop was so tiny, situated on a corridor in the main building. It was fascinating; like Aladdin's cave in a matchbox, it had everything from clothes, drinks, sweets, snacks, fruit, toiletries, stationery, colouring books, newspapers, and magazines. Just about everything you could imagine or need was hanging from every wall, covering every surface in sight.

On my return, I proudly gave out my first cigarette to Melissa, who tried her luck, asking me again for a cigarette. I was expecting at least a "Thank you, nurse." What I received was sweet FA, not even a smile, just snatched out of my hand as she walked away. Sarcastically I shouted after her, "Melissa, a 'thank you, nurse' would have been a nice thing to say!" She didn't look back at me but gave me a two-fingered sign, accompanied by a big vocal raspberry as she walked into the garden.

I walked on to the ward a bit miffed at Melissa's attitude but put it out of my mind when I made my way to Lesley's room. It was apparent that she required some personal hygiene, as she hadn't bathed, cleaned her teeth, or washed her hair since the birth of her baby boy. Honestly, she was beginning to give off an unpleasant odour.

Kath beckoned me to step outside of Lesley's room and asked, "Are you confident enough to persuade Lesley to have a bath or at least a little wash?"

I said, "Yes, I'm willing to give it a go and would ask for help if I needed to."

Kath explained, "It would help if you tried to build a relationship with Lesley so she would begin to trust you. However, you need to keep a safe distance, never turn your back on her and ensure you have an escape route out of the bathroom if she becomes aggressive due to her paranoia."

So, armed with that information, I knocked on Lesley's door and asked if I could enter her room again. She nodded her head, but her facial expression never altered. It was vacant as if set in stone.

I sat with Lesley on her bed. I asked her, "How are you feeling about being transferred from the maternity hospital?"

Lesley sat staring at her hands, which she rubbed together ceremoniously in a set pattern, round and round as if giving them a good wash. "I'm not happy," she said, "and want to go home to be with my husband and baby, and don't understand my admittance to this loony bin."

"I understand," I said, "that you had been a little confused after the birth of your son and your admittance was for an assessment for us to help you become well enough so that you could return home as soon as possible. I'm a student nurse, and I'm here to help you today." She just stared at me. I could sense, looking into her eyes, she was suspicious and didn't believe me. I said, "How about I take you for a bath so you can have a lovely soak, and get you changed into some clean clothes?" She continued to stare at me, which was a little unnerving as I was unsure of what she was thinking. I continued, "If I were feeling unwell, or fed up, a bath always made me feel so much better and relaxed, so why not try to see if it helps, as I would be by your side to make sure you're safe."

Lesley sat twiddling her hands together for a few moments, then, much to my surprise, she said, "Yes, okay."

I collected her toiletries, sanitary pads and clean clothes and proceeded to the bathroom, linking Lesley's arm with mine to show her the way. Kath, the ward sister, gave me the thumbs-up and mouthed, "Well done," as we passed her on the way to the bathroom.

The bathroom was very spacious with one large window, a small sink in the corner and a long shelf full of clean towels, a laundry skip and a chair situated next to a large white Victorian bath. Lesley sat on the chair and started to undress out of her stained clothes. I had to turn my head discreetly so as not to inhale the smell of her body odour. I ran the bath and asked if she would like bubbles in the water, to my delight, she said yes. I had found in her toiletry bag one of my favourite bubble baths, Fenjal Bath Oil. As I poured the oil into the tub, I told her how much I loved the smell of Fenjel and inhaled the steam floating up from the bath passionately, she smiled and nodded her head and said, "Yes, me too."

At last, some type of response and communication from Lesley. I checked the water temperature and held onto Lesley's arm to steady her as she was a bit shaky getting into the bath. As she began to lower herself into it, she lost her balance and flew backwards. The water spilt out over the back and sides like a tsunami all over the floor. I jumped to my feet and quickly mopped it up with towels and put them in the linen skip, telling Lesley not to worry as it was my fault because I had filled the bath too full. I sat on the chair and let Lesley just enjoy her soak.

For the first time, she looked relaxed. I folded a towel into a pillow and placed it behind her head in the bath. She physically relaxed even more and closed her eyes. Her breasts were swollen and engorged, with milk seeping from her nipples, but sadly she could not draw the milk for her baby because of the medication she was taking for her psychosis. The drug would have transferred to the baby if she had breastfed, causing medical problems to the baby, so her milk had to dry up naturally. She laid for a few minutes just gently moving the water with her hands onto her body, smelling the fragrance of Fenjel on her hands. Abruptly, she started taking deep breaths and groaning loudly.

I sat upright on the chair, a little concerned, as I wasn't sure if it was the fact, she was enjoying the soak, or she was in distress. She made me jump as she sat up with a jolt, her eyes started rolling to the top of her head, and I swear her head seemed to go round and round like the girl from the Exorcist film. Lesley clung onto the bath sides, frantically moving her head from side to side and up and down. It was as if she was trying to force her eyes back to a normal position. Her groaning got louder and scarier. I had never witnessed anything like it; her eyes eventually refocused for a few seconds. I reassured her, telling her to try to keep calm and I would get someone to help. As I bent over, trying to feel for the plug, just in case she became unconscious and drowned, she grabbed me by the front of my uniform then pulled me with such strength and force that I lost my balance on the slippery floor and landed in the large bath with her! Water sloshed everywhere. I scrambled out as quickly as I had fallen in. I was soaking wet. I managed somehow to pull the plug out and shouted for help. It happened so fast; I was in total panic mode. Kath arrived within seconds.

We assisted Lesley out of the bath and wrapped her in a towel, she was shaking, terribly frightened and distressed. Lesley's eyes kept rolling upwards and stayed in that position; all I could see were the whites of her eyes. She was screaming, "Help me, God, please help me!" while clinging onto Kath's and my arms in fear.

Kath explained to me it was a rare side effect called Oculo-gyric Crisis from her psychotic medication. Therefore, Lesley's eyes involuntarily rolled out of control towards the top of her head.

Lesley said, "I thought the Devil had possessed me; that's why I grabbed you; because I was afraid of what was happening to me."

I reassured her that it was okay, not to worry about me and that Kath would get some medication to help her with these side effects.

Kath took Lesley to dry and dress her and gave her an injection to reduce the side effect of the antipsychotic drug. Once we had settled Lesley into her bed, Kath sent me back to the nurse's residence to change into a dry uniform and to come back on duty as soon as possible. I dried my hair with my hairdryer and tried to dry my shoes too, but they were still wet and made a squelchy, disgusting farting noise with every step I took.

I was a little apprehensive when I arrived back on the ward. I thought, *Bloody hell! I'm going to be in so much trouble for what happened in the bathroom.* However, nothing was further from the truth. Kath praised me and discussed how quickly and calmly I had responded, then explained how I could improve if there was ever a next time—for example, not getting too close to the patient in a crisis unless they were in danger. "I thought Lesley was in danger," I said, "as her eyes had begun to roll upwards, scaring the hell out of me, and I feared she might be starting with a fit and might drown. As I bent over to pull the plug to prevent Lesley from drowning, she had grabbed me with such strength, that I was surprised and lost my balance and fell into the bath."

Kath said, "Well, now you have explained what happened it seems you did the correct course of action to ensure her safety." She began to smirk, then burst into laughter and said, "Sorry for laughing, but you did look like a startled drowned rat!"

As PART of Lesley's medical plan, they had scheduled Electro Convulsive Therapy (ECT). I had heard such terrible stories about this treatment and how barbaric it had been in the past, so I was very anxious to go and witness Lesley having ECT.

Wearing her nightdress and dressing gown for comfort, she laid herself on the bed ready for her treatment, totally unfazed about what was about to happen to her. I was quite the opposite, concerned for her safety because of my fears of this treatment. I felt tears beginning to well up in my eyes as I held her hand and tried to reassure her with a smile that she would be okay. Her eyes locked with mine and didn't leave my gaze until they heavily sedated her. The doctor injected an anaesthetic and a muscle relaxant into her arm and placed an oxygen mask over her face. Electric conductors were placed on her temples and a mouth guard into her mouth to prevent her biting her tongue. I could feel my anxiety and emotions swelling as to what I might observe next. The doctor asked me to stand back from the bed while administrating a small electric current for only a few seconds through the electrodes.

Lesley bit down on her mouth guard and had a small convulsion that lasted for about ten seconds. Thankfully, it was far less invasive than I thought. I had imagined that she would be violently fitting for minutes, and the wards lights would dim as the current of electricity was released like in a scary movie. Once she was breathing on her own without the help of oxygen, Lesley remained asleep. I wheeled the bed to her bedroom and sat with her until she woke. Lesley recovered quickly, and surprisingly, was sitting up having a cup of tea in less than fifteen minutes. She had no recollection or side effects from the procedure, except a bit of a headache.

Lesley continued with her ECT treatments twice a week alongside her oral antipsychotic medication. Her mental state improved rapidly, and after eight ECT sessions, she became less paranoid and more communicative. After six weeks of nursing and treatment, Lesley was sent on home-leave for a weekend to ensure she could cope and was ready for discharge. Happily, it was successful and proceeded without any problems; her family were happy and confident to welcome Lesley back home. By the following week, Lesley was discharged from the ward to be with her husband and baby.

I realised that ECT was a successful treatment, and if I ever needed it myself in the future, I wouldn't hesitate to receive it as the results were quicker than just medication alone.

I missed Lesley as we had built a special relationship. I had nursed her every shift I worked on the ward. We had talked for hours and found we had a lot in common, especially in music, we were both avid ABBA fans and would sing along to the radio whenever they played them, much to the other patients' annoyance. A week later, Lesley arrived on the ward to show me her baby, George. She had been for an outpatient appointment to see the consultant and receive her final discharge papers. She gave me a huge hug and excitedly handed me a small present, and said, "This is a small thanks from me for your support and kindness, now open it up quickly! I can't wait to see your face!"

I opened the parcel to find a bottle of Fenjal bath oil and a card saying, *'Thank you for being there for me at the most frightening time in my life.'* Despite tears rolling down her cheeks, she burst into laughter and said, "Don't worry, Mel, this time you can enjoy a bath on your own. I won't be joining you!"

We sat chatting for five minutes while I had a cuddle from little George, he was such a beautiful happy baby, the spitting image of Lesley. I waved Lesley and baby George off as they walked toward the car park then returned to my duties on the ward.

While on a morning shift, the Ward Doctor arrived to refit a gastric nasal tube, to enable fluid, foods, and medications to be put directly into Tom's stomach. I sat comforting Tom and explained what procedure the doctor was performing, and why it was an essential part of his treatment. He didn't speak, resist, or move. He just stared straight ahead despite it being an uncomfortable procedure. It was extraordinary to observe his calmness as I felt I would have panicked if someone had tried to take a tube out of my nose, then pass another up my nose, passing down my throat into my stomach. Kath showed how to put the fluids via a syringe into the catheter and record it on his fluid balance chart. It was much easier than I had thought, so later that day, Kath observed me administering the liquid foods, and the medication, and then marked me as competent in my nurse training report. I sat reading the paper to Tom, as patients with this condition can hear and are aware of their surroundings but cannot move or communicate. So, explaining what I was doing and relaying local news was necessary to keep him in the here and now. Tom's catatonic condition continued for another week. We had to take him in a wheelchair to the bathroom to wash and dress him during this time. He was doubly incontinent and needed to wear a pad as he could not move himself to go to the toilet. Bowel movements and urine just passed involuntarily; he couldn't do anything about it.

Being aware of his situation must have been internally devastating and embarrassing for him. A week later, Tom slowly awakened from his catatonic state and then started to communicate, eat, and drink properly. He was a pleasant twenty-five-year-old man with a very gentle, calm manner. Tom was in a deluded state and genuinely believed that he was 'Jesus, the son of God'. He had a strange spiritual aura about him. When you talked to him, Tom made you feel at ease and so exceptional. He had long wavy dark brown hair, kind soft brown eyes and a beautiful radiating smile. When he touched my arm, he gave me goosebumps. Other staff told me they had the same experiences too. He looked like all the pictures I had ever seen of Jesus. Because he had so many similarities, I found his spiritual presence slightly frightening, yet compelling.

I walked on duty one afternoon to find a real buzz and atmosphere on the ward. The staff seemed over-excited at what they had witnessed. I couldn't wait to find out in the handover what had happened. The morning staff started the handover by excitedly stating that Tom had presented some unusual, exceptional symptoms, never seen before by any member of staff during their careers. He had signs of STIGMATA.

I had never heard the word stigmata before and embarrassingly had to ask what it meant. Fortunately for me, Anne, the young care assistant, didn't know the meaning either so, I didn't feel too much of a fool to have to have the word explained to me. The staff were waiting for the consultant to arrive and assess Tom and this unusual phenomenon. Kath had an instant camera and took some photos for photographic evidence of

Tom bleeding from the palms of his hands and soles of his feet. It was as if someone had nailed him to the cross. She took photos of his bleeding head, where blood dripped as if from the thorny crown. My God, it sounded unbelievable what the nurses had witnessed. Tom had been in the dayroom, sitting cross-legged on his chair meditating. Derek, the staff nurse, had sat next to Tom.

Derek witnessed the blood appearing and dripping out of the palms of Tom's hands. Derek checked that Tom wasn't holding a sharp object to cause this bleeding, but his hands were empty. He'd shouted to Kath to come and observe what he saw, as Tom's feet and head started to bleed too. Tom opened his eyes and looked up at the staff and said, "Do not be afraid! I am the son of God, Jesus Christ. I feel no distress or pain." They continued to observe him and contacted the consultant, who was off duty.

After the handover, the consultant stormed onto the ward and seemed angry and red-faced. I think he was angry he had been asked to come in at the weekend, as he had probably been playing golf as I took in his attire of baggy bright red tartan trousers, red and white large, checked shirt, and a tartan flat-cap. He stood with his hands on his hips, looked at Tom and huffed and puffed. He then scratched his forehead and shook his head. First, he lifted Tom's hands, one at a time, and examined them thoroughly, followed by his feet and head. After a few minutes he screwed his face up and shook his head again, he told the staff to meet him in the office.

As the office door closed, the consultant blasted them, blaming them for being unobservant at what had caused these injuries. He said that there was no such thing as Stigmata in his professional opinion, and that, in twenty-five years of being a Consultant Psychiatrist, he had never seen this happen before. He stated that the only explanation was that Tom must have self-harmed to act out his delusion of being Jesus. The staff were furious and strongly disagreed with him. They knew what they had seen, as Tom hadn't been left alone for a moment to self-harm, but the consultant refused to listen and dismissed everything the nurses said as total poppycock. He stormed out of the office and off the ward even more red-faced with anger. I guess you can't argue with a consultant as they believe they are like God most of the time. On this occasion, God trumped Jesus, game over. I thought the consultant was a horrid little man; I wouldn't say I liked his harsh attitude towards the staff or patients.

During a ward round where the doctors and consultant discussed and evaluated patients progress and treatment, I had observed his abrupt manner towards Melissa. He wrote 'CUT HERE' with a dotted line underneath the wording on her wrists. In his opinion, he said she was 'an attention-seeking, immature girl' with the weekly superficial cutting of her wrists. He said, "Next time, follow my instruction if you genuinely want to kill yourself and don't waste mine or the nurses time again." Today's behaviour just clarified my thoughts that he was a pompous, egotistical little man despite being a professional consultant.

Tom's bleeding continued only for a few hours and wasn't severe in blood loss. I cleaned and dressed the wounds as requested. The sores on his feet and hands were single punctures but hadn't gone entirely through to the other side of his skin, and his head wounds were just deep scratches. It certainly convinced me it was Stigmata, but what did I know? I was only eighteen years of age; I had little experience of life.

Tom's wounds healed over the next few weeks, and he became less delusional and more interactive. He continued to have an unusual spiritual aura about him that most of the staff continued to witness and sense. It was such a strange feeling of calmness when in his company and he instinctively knew if anything were bothering you; he would lend his ear to your troubles and give sound advice. Tom disbelievingly remembered that he had thought he was Jesus and still had the scars on his hands, feet, and head, but he couldn't explain how it happened or why. He was discharged home after five weeks in hospital but continued to attend as an outpatient. The hospital fully released him after another month. I am still confused at what I witnessed; did I honestly meet Jesus? It certainly felt like I did, or was I delusional, like him? Or had I been fooled by a conman? I guess I will never know. He remains a mystery of my nursing life, and I bet others who worked on the ward feel the same way too.

After weeks of buying cigarettes, I realised I wouldn't be able to eat for the next few months if I carried on buying twenty cigarettes a day to give to the patients. I decided to contact my Dad to send his old cigarette roller to me. I purchased papers, tips, and tobacco to roll my own, which cost less than half the price of a packet of cigarettes.

Rolling cigarettes was a skill my dad taught me at the tender age of ten for pocket money. I got ten pence a week for rolling him twenty cigarettes a day before I went to bed, so he had them ready for work early next morning. He kept his cigarette equipment in a small wooden bureau. I would pull up my chair, sit there in my nightdress, up to his bureau, then sit rolling away in his machine, swinging my legs, and placing each cigarette in line with tips at the top into his silver ornate cigarette box. I just loved the smell of tobacco and was very skilled at rolling perfect cigarettes. When Dad died in 1994, I kept his bureau, and to this day, when I open the lid, I can smell fifty years of tobacco. I sit and inhale happy childhood memories of rolling the cigarettes. Some people would class it as childhood slave labour, but I would call it an unknowing skill I needed to learn to aid my future as a psychiatric nurse.

HEARTBREAK AND FLOWERS

*M*y next ward was at the Sheffield Royal
Infirmary. All Psychiatric nurses had to learn
general nursing skills, as psychiatric patients also suffered from
medical illnesses as well as their psychiatric ones. I arrived at
6.45 am feeling a little apprehensive as other students had told
me that the general nurses tended to look down their noses at
psychiatric nurses. They believed that psychiatric nurses were
not real nurses and inferior, yet I felt we were superior because
we nursed, both body and mind. My shift started at 7 am, and I
wanted to be timely to give a good impression. As I entered the
ward, a distinct smell of disinfectant hit my nostrils—pristinely
made beds with matching top bed covers and curtains met my
eyes. I was greeted by the ward sister, Pam, who welcomed me
to the ward and explained I would be under her charge. She
asked me if I knew the necessary nursing skills to take vital
signs such as temperature, pulse, respiration, and blood pressure. I informed her that I had been signed off competent in all
these tasks of nursing.

The first patient I looked after was a young eighteen-year-
old girl called Mandy. I was to take and record all her vital

signs. She had been admitted presenting abdominal pain and bloating, and was waiting to go to the theatre to explore her abdomen. She told me she was terrified as her mum had died in her twenties of bowel cancer not long after Mandy had been born. She believed she could be next to die. I tried my best to reassure her, but she just cried inconsolably and didn't want to let go of my hand. The ward sister asked if I would like to escort Mandy to the theatre and watch the operation to gain experience. I jumped at the chance as I had never seen a medical procedure before.

I collected her notes and held Mandy's hand, or should I say she held onto mine so tight that my fingers turned white. The hospital porter arrived to push the bed to the lift and down to the theatre. We squeezed into the tiny lift which could only house the bed and me tight right in the corner. The porter had to run down the stairs to meet us as a patient had to be with a nurse, and it was his job to push the bed around the hospital. On opening the lift doors, I could see we were in the bowels of the hospital, it had peeling cream paint flaking from every wall, with hundreds of wires hanging in uniformed lines on the walls and ceiling. Despite all these wires, the area remained dimly lit, and I could hear a distinct humming noise from a boiler room in the opposite direction. It felt stuffy and smelt very fusty as there were no windows or ventilation. For a hospital, I didn't think it looked very hygienic.

We wheeled Mandy into the theatre, which was incredibly bright compared to the corridor we had just walked through, as the theatre had huge, frosted windows letting sunlight stream in and many theatre lights. It was a bit of a shock for my eyes to try and adjust. The consultant and team were all dressed in clinical overalls and masks and kindly helped me to put on my sterile overall over my uniform and handed me a surgical mask. The consultant was friendly and reassuring towards Mandy, which enabled her to let go of my hand and grab his. Bless her, she was terrified and visibly shook and cried. He explained what the operation involved and reassured her she was in his safe hands while placing the syringe into her canular. He asked her to count backwards from ten. By count number six, she became drowsy, and by four, she was fast asleep.

The anaesthetist placed a black rubber rimmed mask over her mouth and nose, while the theatre nurses lifted her gown, and put two sterile green sheets over her abdomen. The consultant was eager for me, as a student nurse, to get closer to the action as possible so that he could explain the operation and his findings. He even asked me to pull a small wooden box beside him to stand on, so I could look over his shoulder to get a better view of the operation. I was so hot, flustered, and nervous. I feared I would fall off the box and cause a calamity of some kind, like falling into the trolly full of surgical instruments or worse, onto the patient. He asked for a scalpel, and a nurse handed it to him. I cringed as he made his first incision into Mandy's belly, cutting it from belly button to the pubic line.

A horrid potent smell, like rotten flesh, immediately filled the theatre. Everyone made a gasping noise because despite wearing a mask, the smell was nauseating. I thought I was going to be sick, but just managed to hold myself together. The consultant began to move her intestine through the gap in her belly then decided to cut across to get better access. Her belly now resembled the top of a hot cross bun. The intestines looked pink, greenish, and white with thickened areas. There was so much intestine, and I was amazed when he told me that a human being has over fifteen feet in length of small and large intestine combined. I didn't know if the smell and appearance were typical or not, but soon realised it wasn't, when the consultant shook his head and said, "Oh, dear, how tragic! Poor lady."

He explained that Mandy was riddled with cancer in her intestines, and showed me the widespread areas that displayed it. He placed the intestines back into the abdomen and began to close the wound with sutures. He explained there was nothing more they could do for Mandy except make her comfortable for the few weeks she may have left. How could this happen to such a young woman in the prime of her life? I naively thought that cancer only happened to older people. Everyone became noticeably quiet and subdued in the theatre at the realisation that Mandy had only a little time left. People think that the traumas of their work harden nurses, but this proved that we were all human and genuinely filled with emotion and grief at this tragic news.

My shift finished before Mandy woke from her anaesthetic. I had to phone Steve to collect me from the hospital as I felt my legs wouldn't hold me up to get on the bus. I felt so sad and queasy at this experience; it had knocked me for six. I cried in Steve's arms, heartbroken at this diagnosis for Mandy. I couldn't give him details because of confidentiality but told him she was a young girl six months younger than me. I couldn't imagine dealing with this diagnosis at that age. I didn't want to face Mandy the next day but knew I would have to grow up and be there for her, as that was my job. I would have to be brave and learn the skills to deal with this. After all, I was sure there would be more tragedy to come later in my career.

On arrival on the ward the next day, I observed that Mandy's bed was empty. I presumed she must have been moved nearer to the nursing station for closer observations during the night or even to intensive care because of the severity of her surgery and diagnosis. The handover began with the sad news of Mandy's death during the night. She had only lived ten hours after her operation and had drifted away peacefully, never regaining consciousness. Which I felt was a blessing for her. I was in total shock, as were many of the nursing team. After a few deep breaths, I told myself to be brave and get on with it. I learned a skill to hide my emotions, as I knew many more patients needed me that shift.

∼

MY NEXT PATIENT allocation was Joan, a forty-year-old Irish mum of two children, complete with big smiles, gorgeous thick red hair, and a lilting Irish accent. Admitted with chest pains and breathing problems a week prior, she was now eagerly waiting for her test results, of bloods, X-ray, and a biopsy of the lungs.

The ward sister, a group of trainee doctors and I waited inside the drawn curtains around the bed for the consultant to arrive to give Joan her diagnosis. What a character the consultant looked when he arrived on the ward. He was small, with a shiny bald head, wearing a black suit, big red thick-rimmed glasses and a red dicky-bow with white spots. I tried not to smirk or burst into laughter as I thought that at any moment, he would take out of his pocket a red nose and his bow tie would spin around. I even wondered if he worked for the circus as a clown on his day off. I couldn't stop staring at him and tried to stifle my smile by biting my lips. One of the doctors gave me a friendly nudge and discreetly shook his head as if to say, I know what you're thinking, but don't say or do anything.

Consultant Coco-the-clown weakly shook Joan's hand and said, "Good morning, Mrs James, I am your medical consultant. I have received all your test results today, and I'm afraid you have terminal inoperable lung cancer." There was a long, unhealthy pause by everyone as we digested his words. "Do you have any questions?" he asked.

Joan's beautiful smile had disappeared. She stared blankly at him in total shock. He'd delivered the tragic news so matter of fact, without empathy, or compassion, just totally clinically.

Eventually, she found her voice and asked, "How long do I have to live? As I have twin girls aged seven and I need to—"

The consultant rudely cut her sentence short and replied, "I'm not sure how long you have, but probably months. The ward sister will discuss with you your palliative care later." He shook her hand and left to talk to the next patient in the next bed with the ward sister and the doctors following behind.

I remained with a very shocked and distraught Joan. She put her head in her hands and began to sob. I sat on her bed and tried to comfort her. I put my arm around her and gently rubbed her back up and down with my hand. She lifted her head and looked at me in disbelief and said, "How the hell do I tell my husband and girls? How do I tell my dear Mum? What the hell has just happened to me? Please tell me it's a nightmare, and I will wake up."

I could only mutely shake my head. After about ten minutes of trying to console Joan, the ward sister came back and saw me sitting on the bed with her. She shouted at me, "Get off the patient's bed, you're not allowed to sit on patients' beds. Get off at once!"

I looked at her in disbelief. *Really?* I thought, *This isn't the time to criticize me while trying to console and reassure Joan after her devastating diagnosis,* as I reluctantly did as instructed.

Joan said, "I really wish I could have a cigarette right now; I really need a cigarette please." She looked at the ward sister and said, "Can the nurse take me outside so I can smoke, please, so I can try and take in what the consultant has just told me?"

Sternly, the sister said, "Certainly not, why don't you have a bath instead; that might help."

When the sister had left her bedside, I winked at Joan and said, "Come on, love, and have a soak in the bath, and bring your cigarettes with you in your toilet bag, so the sister doesn't see them."

Joan was so grateful and followed me to the bathroom. She

undressed silently and in slow motion as if time had stood still in her world. Once in the bath, I opened the window and let her light her first cigarette. She laid back in the bubbled bath and sobbed buckets between each drag of her cigarette and said, "Why me? I'm too young to die. I have things I want to do in my life. I'm not ready yet."

I sympathetically listened.

The first cigarette didn't last long, as she took huge drags as if trying to numb the pain with the nicotine. She dipped the butt-end in the water to put it out and asked me to pass her another cigarette. As I lit her second cigarette, she inhaled her first breath so deeply she nearly coughed her guts up. When she finished her coughing fit, she burst into laughter and said, "Here I am dying, and yet I bloody well nearly killed myself from a coughing fit. I truly needed that cigarette, nurse, thank you so much for allowing me to smoke." Joan lay back as if in ecstasy, puffing her cigarette in silence. I just sat quietly, letting her absorb her bad news.

Unexpectedly, the bathroom area's outer door opened, and I grabbed the cigarette out of Joan's hand into mine. The sister popped her head around the door to see if we were okay. She looked at me in disbelief and was furious when she saw the lit cigarette in my hand. "How dare you smoke in front of a patient, and on duty! How dare you behave in such an unprofessional manner. Put it out at once, and when you have finished helping Joan to bathe come to my office."

She flounced out as quickly as she had flounced in leaving me to think, *Oh shit, that's me in the doghouse again*, as she'd already told me off for sitting on Joan's bed. I let Joan soak a little longer and told her not to worry or rush. I distinctly knew another telling off was coming, and Joan needed time to absorb her diagnosis first. I helped Joan get ready into her clean nightdress. She was so apologetic and wanted to come clean to the ward sister as she didn't want to get me in any trouble because of her. I insisted Joan didn't because that would be both of us being in the sister's bad books. After all, it was me who had suggested she bring her cigarettes to the bathroom, so she agreed to keep quiet.

I knocked at Sister's door.

Her stern voice came through the door. "Enter!"

I entered and stood opposite her at the desk. She immediately ripped into me, saying what a disappointment I was, about my lack of professionalism, and obeying rules. I only listened and took whatever she said, because, in my head, I knew I had behaved empathetically toward Joan. To me, that was more important. It was what she had needed mentally to cope with her devastating news at that time, and, after all, a cigarette wasn't going to make any difference to her medical condition in the short term. Sister ended her rant with, "I have reported you to your tutor at the school of nursing. I have arranged for you to go at 9 am tomorrow and don't be surprised, young lady, at the outcome. As they may remove you off your course permanently and it's nobody's fault but your own. Twice I have had to speak to you today about breaking ward rules. They must always be adhered to for continuity and safety of patient care."

I was dismissed and sent home. Oh God, had I just blown it? Had my principles and kindness just ended my career? In bed that night, I tossed and turned and thought about what I would say and how I could defend my actions, and not get Joan into any trouble as she had enough to cope with. However, I knew in my heart that I would do it all over again whatever the consequences of tomorrow faced with the same scenario.

THE TUTOR WAS WAITING for me as I arrived at 8.55 am. I followed him into the office, where he directed me to sit in the chair opposite him. The tutor started the conversation by saying he had read the sister's report of my behaviour and was extremely disappointed, as he expected better from me. He continued, "Before you try to explain to me with a lie what you think I want to hear, remember I know you, young lady, and I know you don't smoke. So, it's in your best interest to tell me the whole truth, okay?"

I decided to tell the truth as I had never been particularly good at lying. I explained how Joan's consultant had told her so coldly and matter of fact her devastating diagnosis. At that time, even though cigarettes probably caused her cancer, to me, a cigarette was her only cure to deal with the situation; to help her digest the tragic information before she told her family. I described Joan laying in the bath sobbing and smoking, and on hearing the door of the bathroom open, how I had panicked and taken the cigarette out of her hand, so she didn't get into trouble, as she had been through enough mentally that day. I pretended it was my cigarette and took the blame.

He sat back in his chair, silently, and visibly thought about this predicament. "I should reprimand you for your unprofessional conduct because rules are rules. However, occasionally breaking the rules are justified, and yesterday, I think, was a day to break those rules. In actuality, I would go as far as to say it was a day to rip up the rule book and put it in the bin. I bloody well agree with you and would have probably done the same thing. What shocking lack of compassion and empathy for Joan by the medical team. Don't worry, Mel. I will report to the ward sister that I gave you a verbal warning and recorded it on your file." I looked at him in shock as I didn't want a bad record on my file. He then smiled and said, "Don't worry, I will rip up this complaint of behaviour, no evidence, no case to answer, no record on your file. Once again, broken rules are for the greater good. My advice to you, if ever there is a next time, is don't get caught. What you did is what psychiatric nursing is all about. Well done, you. I think that Joan must have been incredibly grateful for your kind actions." He escorted me to the door and shook my hand and squeezed it as if acknowledging my kindness. I left the school of nursing with a great sense of relief. I couldn't wait to get back to work and make a difference in patients' lives.

I returned to the medical ward that afternoon to find that they were discharging Joan home to be with her family to start her palliative care. She was so relieved to see me walk onto the ward again because she thought they had sacked me. She gave me the biggest hug and said, "You're how nurses should be. Promise me you won't change to be like some of the rest," as she gave the sister a sidewards glance and nod. I promised her I would always try to be true to myself and do my best.

Later that afternoon, a bouquet of flowers arrived on the ward, and the ward sister called me into her office again. Her face was like a stewed prune. *Oh god, what have I done wrong now?* I thought. Sister sat back in her leather chair and said, "Nurse! It seems to me that you want to flaunt all the rules to annoy the hell out of me." She handed me the flowers and said, "These are for you."

I looked at the message on the card, and it said, *you're a one in a million angel. We will never forget your kindness. Thank you, Joan, and family.* I have got to be honest I felt like putting two fingers up to the ward sister, but I think my smug expression said it all. As I left the office, I glanced back at her; she was smiling and shaking her head.

I was beginning to enjoy my time on this medical ward. I even started to like the ward sister, despite her giving me a hard time and not such pleasant jobs like cleaning the dirty bedpans, but hey, someone had to do it, and after all, I was the student nurse. It was all about learning new skills, good or bad. I even managed to keep out of further trouble.

On my last shift, they admitted a lady called Daisy for assessment with breathing difficulties and chest pain. I was to take and record her vital signs. Respirations should be around sixteen to twenty breaths per minute, and hers were thirty-five. A typical pulse should be about sixty to eighty beats per minute, but hers was racing at one hundred and ten. I could see her pulse in her neck veins pounding. Her eyes seemed to bulge out of their sockets because of the fear and distress she was feeling. I sat with her for a few minutes, holding and stroking her hand, trying to get her to relax and breathe slower because anxiety can cause raised results with vital signs. She remained terrified and gripped my hand so hard her long painted nails indented into my skin. No wonder nurses used a lot of hand cream, as their hands received abuse every day by anxious patients.

As I sat and comforted Daisy, I looked up to see the handsome junior doctor, Billy, enter the curtained bed area. He gently pulled the curtains closed behind him. I visually absorbed him in slow motion. DING! DONG! He was bloody gorgeous; tall, dark, and handsome, with smoky brown twinkling eyes and long eyelashes. He smelt divine and looked incredibly sexy in his pristine white coat. He blew my senses, causing me to be breathless myself as my heart raced. He was like a doctor in the movies that every woman would swoon over. I watched his every move as he listened to Daisy's chest and took some blood for analysis. I thought, *Oh my goodness, you could practise your bedside manner and examine me any time, Doctor Hot and Sexy,* and hoped I hadn't just said it out loud. He looked at me and smiled his heart-melting smile, as he seemed aware of what his presence was doing to me. I could feel myself blushing, but I still couldn't take my eyes off him just yet. There was a moment as our eyes stared at one another, it was if we telepathically transferred lustful thoughts to each other. I'm sure he was reading my mind, and I sensed he liked it as he sexily smirked and raised an eyebrow at me as he left me with Daisy. My God, I was in Love and Lust. Daisy, between gasps of breath, said, "I think he likes you, Nurse." Eventually, Daisy relaxed and fell asleep, enabling me to now deal with my other allocated patients and try and get my flustered imagination grounded, as it had just been in a turmoil full of naughty, naughty thoughts.

After an hour or so, Daisy shouted, "Nurse, help me!" and was clutching her chest in pain and gasping for breath. Doctor Billy and I pulled the screens around her bed. I held her hand to try and comfort her and told her to try and slow her breathing down, breathing slowly in sync with her to try and get her to follow my lead. The doctor took his stethoscope from his neck and placed it on her chest. Abruptly, Daisy coughed, and projectile bright red blood flew out of her mouth, hitting Billy on his white doctor's coat. I will never forget the fear in Daisy's face, as she witnessed all the blood coming from her mouth and nose. Blood continued to spurt out her mouth and nose with every heartbeat. Billy took it all in his stride as blood splattered everywhere. He shouted to the ward sister to bring the crash trolly and to ring for the crash team.

We tried to lay Daisy on her side, so she did not choke. However, it was difficult as Daisy's blood continued to splatter all over the walls, curtains, bed, Billy, and me. It was like a scene in a horror movie at a brutal massacre. Within ten seconds, she fell into unconsciousness; after twenty seconds, Daisy took her last breath and died. The whole episode had taken less than a minute. Her skin was now as white as driven snow, and her face despite being blood-stained, now looked at peace. Billy and I both froze to the spot, just looking at each other, feeling helpless and in total shock. The ward sister suggested that we shower in the staff changing rooms and change our uniforms. The consultant and crash team arrived to take over and record the incident of sudden death. The cleaning team closely followed them to put screens around the area, take the curtains down, strip and disinfect the bed, and mop the floor area free from the blood.

I couldn't speak or move. I just stared at poor Daisy, thinking, *what the hell just happened to her?* Sister pulled all the curtains around all the other patients' beds so they couldn't see the bloody mess we were in and escorted Billy and me to the male and female staff shower unit.

I took off my sodden blood-stained uniform and looked in the mirror above the sink. Blood heavily splattered my face, hair, and nurses cap, and my underwear had gone from white to red. I stripped naked and stood in the shower, silently in disbelief, as the hot water flushed the blood from my face. I washed my hair and skin frantically to get every drop of blood off me. I watched and thought, *That's Daisy's life swilling down that drain.* The ward sister brought me a clean uniform from the hospital store to change into, but I had to go underwear-less as I had thrown my bra and pants in the bin. I knew I would never be able to wear them again.

I surprisingly saw Sister's caring side come out as she sat beside me, comforting me. I still could hardly speak. I didn't know how to begin or what to say. I felt in a daze. She gently brushed and blew my hair dry with one of the wall hairdryers, as I sat hunched up on a chair. The Sister informed me that I had to come back to the ward, as there were still things to sort out. "You must write a report about the incident with Daisy."

Back on the ward, Billy arrived, looking red-eyed; it was apparent he had been traumatised and had cried too. They brought drinks of sweet tea with brandy, which was a cure for a shock in those days. We wrote our reports and then were instructed to leave our shifts early. We left the ward together, with Billy's arm around my shoulders in solidarity and comfort. All thoughts of lust and passion had disappeared.

Outside, we both decided we needed a large, strong drink; the stronger, the better. The pub was only a few hundred yards away, but it seemed to take ages to walk there. It was a proper old man's drinking pub, with years of dirt, grime, and cigarette smoke, with two old blokes watching horse racing on the TV.

We sat in the corner, alone, after ordering two double brandies. At first, we sat in silence and downed the brandies in one swig after chinking the glasses together. We toasted to us, and the sad loss of Daisy.

Billy looked at me and asked if I wanted another double for the road. I nodded, and he ordered two more double brandies. Slowly, we began to open up to each other. "Well, that was a hell of a day, probably the worst in my whole career," said Billy.

I agreed and said, "It was truly surreal, and a tragic way to die! It has made me question whether I am cut out to be a nurse."

Billy reassured me that I was a good nurse and not to let this experience put me off nursing. I learned from Billy that Daisy had suffered from a ruptured thoracic aortic aneurysm, which she could never have survived.

We sat for a few hours, chatting into the early evening, and drank many more double brandies. It was apparent we needed to get drunk, laugh and shelve the trauma of that day. The only way we could cope was to drink ourselves into a stupor. I don't remember saying goodbye to Billy, or getting back to the nurses' residence. All I do know is that I woke up in the early hours of the morning with a hangover from hell and felt sick. Every time I closed my eyes to try and fall back asleep, I replayed in my mind repeatedly the events of the day before. Next morning, I hoped that I would enjoy Billy's company again soon, but sadly, our paths never crossed again.

OUT OF UNIFORM

Alcohol became one of my coping mechanisms, alongside my best friend, chocolate. It seemed my episode with Pernod and blackcurrant on my first date with Steve a year ago, thankfully did not put me off alcohol after all. Most weekends, other nurses and I living in residence would have a party — just for parties' sake. I guess it was because most of us were immature teenager's, discovering first-time freedom from our parents, as we grew into adulthood. We would collect a kitty together on a party night and buy the alcohol from the staff social club as it was much cheaper than the supermarket. As long as they brought drinks, we invited anyone and everyone from the hospital. We would dance and sing along to the music playing from a little record player in the corner of the lounge. It would only allow us to play the maximum of six single records at a time. It was a bit of a pain in the arse changing them every ten minutes, so we thought it excellent when the new 'NOW' LPs, with twelve or more songs of the most up to date chart music from different artists, were introduced into the seventies. There was something for everyone's musical taste. The little record player could only take two LPs at a time, as the records were so heavy, but they lasted around half an hour each side, which was less annoying.

The parties were a recipe for disaster because of the amount of alcohol we all drank. It often caused disagreements, arguing, scuffles and fights. It was usually over something trivial, like someone had taken their drink by mistake, or tried to chat up their girlfriend while they had popped to the loo. Nine times out of ten, the situation calmed down quickly. After all, we were all training to be psychiatric nurses to have the skills to calm things down. On the rare occasion, usually, if someone were too drunk, a fight would get out of hand — a bit of pushing and shoving, followed by a broken window or door as they threw someone out for being too drunk or gobby. The next morning, when the warden, Annie, asked us all how the window broke, and who might be responsible, of course, none of us had been there, seen anything or knew anything about the breakage. She would roll her eyes and say, "It must have been the hospital fairies again." If we had given her names, they would have been liable to pay for the breakage. Annie wasn't stupid; she knew who was at the parties; she knew who the usual suspects were because she sometimes joined us and partied the night away. She was just going through the motions of being the warden and filling in a report for a replacement.

Our parties became the talk of the area, and the local professional footballers from Sheffield Wednesday football club would drink in the hospital social club and join us all at our parties. God, they were handsome guys, fit, sexy, wearing expensive suits and aftershave. The reason we loved them joining us was the fact they brought Champagne. I had never had Champagne before, and I began to get a taste for it. I loved how the bubbles would tickle my nose when I took a sip. It made me feel very sophisticated as I sipped it from a beer glass. Sadly, on a student nurse wage, I could never afford to buy it for myself, but thankfully the footballers kept us stocked at every party. Mostly if it were a Saturday night and they had won a game. They would party until the early hours and eventually crash out on anyone's bedroom floor or with one of the nurses. We all kept their secrets because it wasn't a kiss and tell society. We respected their privacy. We just liked the endless supply of Champagne and their company as they were fun and charismatic, with incredible muscly thighs. But, boy, I could tell some stories about some footballers in their youth and before they became famous, but my lips remain sealed.

LIVING in the hospital grounds meant we would get regular visitors from the long-stay wards, patients asking for cigarettes, treats or cups of tea or coffee. They were like our extended family who we cared about very much. I remember a patient called Harold; he would call most days asking for a cigarette and a coffee. He always brought his mug just in case he got lucky. On one occasion, I had run out of coffee and milk, so I was unable to make him a cup, but he took his cigarette from me and put it behind his ear for later as he was already smoking, and said, "Don't worry nurse," and scuttled off down the drive. Fifteen minutes later, he returned and knocked on my door again. He had brought me a large jar of instant coffee and a bottle of milk, stating he had bought them from the shop for me. The cheeky sod told me how much I owed him. I rounded up the payment for more than it was and gladly gave it to him because it saved me going out to the shop later. He said, "Any time you need anything, nurse, then let me know, I can go and get it for you."

Naïvely, I said, "Okay, thank you." Over the weeks, I observed that he provided a little shopping and errand service for most nurses. It kept him in the supply of extra cigarettes and kept him busy.

One afternoon, when I was in the local shop buying a few bits for myself, I saw Harold doing a shop for someone else. He was wearing an oversized grey overcoat with large pockets. I noticed he behaved a little bit suspicious by looking around to see if anyone was near him. I watched him from a distance; to my disbelief, I saw him stuff a bottle of shampoo into one of his pockets. He followed it with a small jar of coffee and some sweets. He was carrying a shopping basket, and placed a packet of biscuits into it, then made his way to the till. He paid for the biscuits and walked out without paying for the other items in his pockets. I was astonished, I couldn't believe I just had witnessed him stealing from the shop, but of course, I said nothing to the shop owner as I didn't want to get him in trouble. It did make me genuinely concerned, and question myself had he paid for the things he brought to my room or had he stolen them too.

The next day, I bumped into Harold on the corridor in the hospital. "Good afternoon nurse, you got a cigarette for me?" He said in his usually cheeky-chappy manner.

I gave him a disapproving look, and I told him, "No, not this time because I'm not happy with you." I went on to explain what I had seen the day before. He looked puzzled by my attitude and answer, as he knew generally, I was a soft touch when it came to doling cigarettes out. I told him I had seen him stealing from the local shop. He stood tall and seemed proud of his achievements and grinned.

He said, "Don't worry, nurse, they know I steal from them, but they are afraid of stopping me because they think I'm a psycho-nutter. I shop for all you nurses because you're all so kind to me," and gave me a cheeky wink. How could I argue with that sweet answer, but I did tell him that he should stop stealing because generally, people's luck ran out and eventually, they got caught. Cheekily, he replied, "No, not me, nurse. I've had years of practice. I'm a professional at stealing; they will never catch me." He must have been making a fortune from all the nurses, while the shop made a loss. He was the hospital's loveable rogue, The Middlewood Artful Dodger.

Steve enjoyed visiting me when off duty. My room was our private place to get to know each other — if you know what I mean. Steve still lived at home with his mum and dad, and they were extremely strict. He was not allowed to stay out late, or stay with me overnight, despite him being twenty years of age. My room became our love pad. What they didn't know or see, didn't hurt them. He always caught the 7 pm bus from his home and would be at my room by 7.30 pm, so at 6.45 pm, I would get showered, put on my sexy underwear, covered by my silky, sexy short black dressing gown, apply my makeup and blow-dry my hair. In my bedroom was a wardrobe vanity unit, which when opened, the middle had a sink, mirror, and drawers, very practical for small rooms.

I remember one particular evening. I got back from the shower unit, wearing only a towel. I opened the wardrobe door, so I could clean my teeth and apply my makeup. Bloody hell, I had the shock of my life. Steve leapt out of the sink unit, frightening me half to death. He had arrived early and hid in the wardrobe; he loved to torment me and make me jump. I screamed, and my towel dropped to the floor, much to Steve's delight. He grabbed the towel as I frantically tried to grab it back, he flicked my arse with it and chased me around my tiny room. I squealed with excitement and anticipation as he pushed me onto my bed. He tickled and kissed me passionately. You can guess what happened next (Nudge, nudge, wink, wink). We never did get to the staff social club that night, we had much more exciting things to do, and he had a lot of making up to me for scaring me half to death.

HALLUCINATING WITH WOLVES

I lived with two girls at the residence, who asked me if I would like to move with them into a four-bedroomed house that belonged to the hospital. It was just ten minutes away from the hospital by bus. It would mean we could have more independence, and break away from all the parties as it was beginning to take its toll on me — drinking many evenings until the early hours, then showering and changing into my uniform to be back on the wards for 6 am. As a young nineteen-year-old, I could easily manage sleep deprivation, but I was beginning to get black bags under my eyes, and I found it hard to study for my end of first-year exams. I decided moving the following month with them to the house was a good idea if I was ever going to get to my second year in nursing. I do believe that my liver would have packed its own bags and left me if I hadn't made that decision.

Two weeks before I moved into the new house of residence, I woke up one morning with a terrible headache, extremely hot and flushed and felt so dizzy and weak. I knew I couldn't go into work in that state. So, I phoned the ward to say sorry I was feeling unwell, and I couldn't work my shift. I tried to take my

74

silk nightdress off, now stuck to my body with sweat. It felt cold and wet as I peeled it upwards off my body, not a pleasant sensation. I washed my face and body in the tiny sink with cold water to cool myself down and got back on top of my bed naked, with a cold flannel on my head. I tossed and turned because I was so hot and irritable, but eventually, I must have fallen asleep for a few hours.

Abruptly, my eyes opened. I realised I had an unusually high temperature and visibly drenched with sweat. I also felt disoriented and confused as to where I was. I could hear a frantic scratching noise at my bedroom door and couldn't understand what it could be. I tried to ignore it because I didn't want to get out of my bed, but the scratching got louder and began to irritate me. I managed to drag myself to the door, still naked and opened the door only an inch to see who it was. It burst open and in came five big grey wolves, all snapping and snarling at me. I was terrified. I ran and jumped onto my bed, scuttling right to the headboard screaming, but they followed me to the end of the bed, still snapping and snarling continuously at my ankles.

They smelled of a wet dog after rolling in a dead animal; it was disgusting and made me retch. I was bewildered, I couldn't work out what was happening to me. Where the hell had they come from? As there weren't any wolves in Sheffield to my knowledge. What were they doing in my room? I threw my slippers at them and screeched, "Leave me alone, get away from me!" but they came closer, snarling and growling with their mouths dripping with saliva from their long pink tongues and sharp teeth. They had menacing light blue eyes fixed on me. I believed they were going to eat me alive.

I ran to the window which had a small outside balcony, thinking I could escape the wolves, they followed me. I could feel their warm breath on me, as they snapped at my ankles. I jumped over the step and onto the three-foot-wide balcony, screaming at the top of my voice, "Help me! Help me, somebody please help me!" I hoped someone would come and save me. If not, I would have to jump to the ground below if they made a full attack. The wolves kept snarling at me at the window, but the rail kept them away. They jumped up and put their front paws on the rail as if willing me to jump. I looked at the drop to the ground below and knew I would probably severely injure myself, but there was no other option: either get savaged or jump, as I believed they were preparing to pounce.

I began counting down to make my jump on the count of three. Unexpectedly, a doctor from the wards and Annie, the warden, arrived in my room. They calmly asked me to stop where I was, and not to jump as, by now, I had straddled my leg over the railings of the balcony to jump. They gently coaxed me to step back into my bedroom and sat me on the bed. I was terrified and hysterically shaking and crying. "Where have the wolves gone?" I asked as I looked around the room frantically. They had just disappeared. Paul, the doctor, held my hand and reassured me that I was safe, and I was okay, and to take deep breaths to help control my breathing. He assured me that the wolves had gone and wouldn't be back. I was trembling and sweating, and my heart was pounding out of my chest. Annie wiped my forehead with the cold, wet flannel.

After a little while, I began to calm down. Annie helped me into a clean nightdress as I was embarrassingly still naked. I hadn't even realised because of my fear. Dr Paul gave me two paracetamols and a Valium injection to help keep me calm. I lay awake, disturbed, and convinced that the wolves would return. I just kept going over and over in my head what had happened. Annie sat on the bed and stroked my hair until I eventually settled back to sleep.

When I woke the next morning, Annie was still by my side, fast asleep in the chair and snoring like a pig. She must have stayed with me all night. I gently woke her and thanked her for remaining with me. I didn't dare ask about the wolves, because I felt embarrassed that I had caused so much trouble the day before. Annie was so sympathetic and gave me a reassuring hug. She explained that Paul, the doctor, had left some medication to take while still feeling ill. She made me a slice of toast and orange juice to help me digest my medication, and within minutes, I had fallen back to sleep. I stayed in bed for four days with a fever, muscle and head pain and malaise. I was checked on daily by my new friend, Dr Paul, and Annie. I slowly began to improve.

During one visit by Paul, he explained he had been working on a ward opposite the nurse's residence. He saw me trying to jump from the balcony naked and desperately screaming for help. He ran to the nurse's residence and bumped into Annie, who had heard the commotion. They ran up to my room, hoping they would be in time to prevent me from jumping. I was unsure why I had behaved as I did and explained to Paul that I did see the wolves but felt a fool because nobody believed me. In turn, he explained to me why I had behaved as I did and what had been wrong with me. I was in total disbelief at what he told me.

No, I hadn't been taking drugs or got drunk. No, I wasn't attention-seeking, but what I did have was the 1977 Russian flu, which was at epidemic levels and had, like COVID-19, originated from China and carried over to the UK from Russia. Allegedly, it affected only people under the age of twenty-five; this was because people who had a similar flu virus in 1957 had antibodies, giving most of the over twenty-five-year-olds immunity. This Russian flu caused me to display psychotic symptoms from an excessively high temperature from the flu virus. The wolves that seemed so real to me were, in fact, terrifying hallucinations. I had suffered from all the clinical types of hallucinations. They were: Visual – because I could visually see the wolves. Tactile – because I had felt their breath and saliva on my legs. Auditory – because I could hear them snarling and growling, and finally, Olfactory – because I could smell their disgusting breath and fur.

My God, those hallucinations were frightening; to this day, I can see them and the incident in my mind as if it was an actual vivid memory of reality. This experience helped me in the future to understand patients suffering from hallucinations and how terrifying it could be for them. I could truly empathise and reassure them that it would pass, that I believed what they could see, hear, or touch, and how real it seemed to them. I could explain that I genuinely understood as I too had these hallucination symptoms in the past. Hallucinations are not always traumatic, or frightening; some patients can see or hear amusing, funny things which are much easier to deal with. I wish I had seen fairies in my bedroom instead of wolves because the hallucinations had truly frightened me enough to want to jump for my life. My life could have ended there and then all because of the Russian flu.

FEAR OF THE YORKSHIRE RIPPER

*J*n my second year of nursing (now wearing a blue belt), I lived in the new hospital house a few miles from the hospital with my two friends, Joyce, and Jill. I now had to drag myself out of bed an hour earlier, because of the walk to the bus stop. Getting up at an earlier time didn't bother me, it seems my first year of alcohol and lack of sleep had given me enough stamina and practice. What did bother me – in fact, freaked me out – was the ten-minute walk to the bus stop to wait for the bus.

The Yorkshire Ripper was on his prowl to find and murder women between 1975 to 1981 in the South Yorkshire area. I was genuinely terrified at the thought of bumping into him on the streets in the dark. The hospital and TV had warned us to keep safe and be vigilant and stay in two's if possible. In fact, the hospital had a few phone calls to say one of the nurses could be the next victim. They were hoaxes of course, but we didn't know that at the time, it just fuelled the fear. If my friends were on a different shift to me, I would have to walk for ten minutes alone to the bus stop at 5 am. I made sure to prepare in the event I ever met him. I had a Yorkshire Ripper defence kit in my large handbag. It consisted of a big can of hairspray to spray into his eyes, a whistle which my dad gave me to blow if I was fearful, waking up the entire neighbourhood, and a medium-sized sharp knife to threaten him if he came near me, which, in fact, I kept in my coat pocket for easy reach. The large bag itself was long-handled and was full of other girly rubbish too. It was heavy enough for me to get a good swing of the bag and knock him stone-cold out with one blow. I even practised my swing at home. I was so competent that I could have been an Olympic hammer thrower.

Most mornings a guy used to say hello and walk to the same bus stop as me. I was very suspicious of him because I had seen a few photo fit drawings on TV and a description of what the Yorkshire Ripper might look like. They informed us he was tall, dark-haired with a beard and had a northeast accent. The guy walking to the bus stop with me matched all these features. The news played a tape sent by the Yorkshire Ripper to the investigating officer taunting him, saying, "You will never catch me, Jack," in a Geordie accent. I nicknamed this man who walked to the bus stop 'Bus stop guy', as I was never brave enough to ask him his name. He always walked on the opposite side of the road from me, because, previously, I warned him I was afraid of him because he could be the Yorkshire Ripper.

I even showed him my knife from my coat pocket to show him I meant business. He looked shocked and put his hands up in defence, but said he fully understood my fear and knew why. He always said, "Good morning," and obliged as asked by keeping his distance to make me feel safe. Despite his actions, I still didn't feel safe or trust him. I was always suspicious. He carried a big Adidas sports bag, which only fed my imagination, convincing me he had all his killing equipment inside. He chatted about his work as a chef at a factory canteen. Also, about his family and his music likes and dislikes. I only minimally answered, so I didn't get drawn into the conversation. All the time he talked to me, I suspiciously thought, *He's trying to get me to relax in his company, then when I'm relaxed and off guard he will attack me.*

It was a hell of a way to start a morning, total fear, and exaggerated alertness like I had drunk twenty cups of coffee. Strangely, he never talked about the Yorkshire Ripper, despite it being all over the TV and radio, and the topic of conversation on everyone's lips. Women all over Yorkshire were genuinely terrified of being out alone. Everyone I knew had a theory about who he was, and where he lived, which only fed my vivid imagination more. At the bus stop, he would stand at one side and me the other. I never took my eyes off him until I got onto the bus. Then I could relax a little and breathe normally again instead of nearly hyperventilating. Maybe this standing opposite ends of the bus stop and street was my practice run for the Coronavirus two meters safe distancing for the future. I cried with relief the night the Police caught the Yorkshire Ripper; they found him in Sheffield with a lady of the night in a dark alleyway. Steve and I had passed the entrance of that alleyway only an hour before, on our way to the Red Cross HQ only five hundred yards away. I freaked out at the thought I had been so close to the Yorkshire Ripper on that night.

THE YORKSHIRE RIPPER was arrested on the 2nd of January 1981, late at night after being stopped by a probationary police officer. He had observed the Yorkshire Ripper had false number plates on his car. The police took him to Dewsbury police station, where they questioned him about the number plates and the fact, he had so many characteristics of the Yorkshire Ripper, except he had a Yorkshire accent, not a Geordie one. They eventually proved the Geordie accent to be a hoax. What sort of sick person does that? taking the investigation off-track, causing more young women to be attacked and murdered.

The following day, they decided to search the scene where he was arrested and found he had abandoned a hammer and rope in the grass after telling police he needed a pee at the scene before getting into the police car. My God, the prostitute must have thought how lucky she had been not to be his next victim, a few minutes later it could have been a different story. They also found a knife in the cistern of the toilet he visited in the Police station. Calmly, he admitted to all his attacks and murders, describing how he had murdered each woman. Later in the week, the Yorkshire Ripper stated that God had sent him to get rid of prostitutes and claimed diminished responsibility.

After a lengthy trial at the Old Baily, he was found guilty and convicted of thirteen cases of murder and given twenty concurrent life sentences. I was so relieved that at last, I could go out unafraid that I might be his next victim. The morning after the Yorkshire Ripper conviction, 'Bus stop guy' asked, "Is it now okay to walk together?" He introduced himself as Ted. Of course, I said yes, and hugged him to thank him for being so kind to me and my imagination. I told him that I would always know him as 'Bus stop guy.' He reaffirmed that I did the right thing about keeping a distance and staying vigilant. He laughed and told me he swore my hair stood up on end with fear every morning.

I told him he was probably right, but it might also have something to do with the copious amounts of hairspray I sprayed to keep my fine hair in place. He told me the thought of walking to the bus stop was fearful for him too because he had encountered a blonde female nutcase carrying a knife on the loose. I was puzzled at first, thinking that I hadn't heard anything about this woman, then I realised he was talking about me, and we both laughed and I apologised. During our conversation at the bus stop, Ted told me that two years before they arrested the Ripper, he had, in fact, been detained for questioning because he had the accent and the look of the photofit of the Ripper. Police were questioning thousands of men up and down the country with the same description as the Yorkshire Ripper. Christ, if he had told me that before, I would have had a heart attack thinking there's no smoke without fire. Women of England could now feel safe and get on with a typical life for the first time in five years.

THE CURRENCY OF SEX AND CIGARETTES

*O*n my next ward, we worked a three-shift system, mornings, afternoons, and nights. Don't know who on earth thought that these shifts worked well for nurses on a six-week cycle, as it played havoc with my social life, sex life and sleep pattern. The night shifts I found the hardest to keep awake. You would think it easy for me because of partying in my first year and getting only a few hours' sleep each night. I honestly found it hard to keep my eyes open, especially the witching hours of 2 until 4 am.

On my first night shift on duty, I was awake at least twelve hours before I went to work, and a minimum of twenty-two hours before I got back into my bed. I got the best sleep ever after that first shift because I was so exhausted. I would often wake still in my uniform sprawled out on the top of my bed because I had just opened my door and dived onto my bed, too tired to undress. I decided to learn new skills to keep me awake in-between the nursing care of the patients. I learned how to play cards, scrabble and to knit.

My first knitting experience was a jumper for Steve to wear at work to keep him warm. He worked for British Rail as an electrician, often outside and laying on cold floors to do his job. Sadie, the SEN, showed great patience with me. Firstly, teaching me how to cast on, knit one and pearl one and casting off. I was slow, but surprisingly, I soon got the hang of it. Our next shift together she said, "Tonight's the night, Nanny the knitter," (her new nickname for me) and presented to me a knitting pattern for a plain V neck men's jumper.

After a few more nights of practice knitting squares, I decided to go shopping for some brown wool and correct sized needles at our local haberdashery shop. I was so excited to start to knit the jumper on my next night duty. I cast on my stitches and decided to make it a bit bigger than the pattern said by adding about twenty stitches across and twenty extra rows; this was because my beloved Steve had a long broad back with his 6ft 4-inch frame. Each night I worked I would knit line after line, lose count of the lines and check and double-check, it drove me crazy and Sadie even crazier, as I eventually passed it to her in frustration to check it for me.

Sadie eventually gave me a piece of paper and told me to write down the number of lines I was supposed to knit, then cross it off the piece of paper once I had finished it, which would enable me to keep track of the lines easier than counting in my head. This system was a game-changer and allowed me to knit more of the jumper nightly, instead of frustratingly counting and double counting and driving her, and me, insane.

Sadie showed me how to shape and cast off the back. The V's front was more complicated, but I did complete it after a few night shifts. However, I forgot to make it as long as the back; I was so busy concentrating on the V of the neck. Next task was the sleeves. Somehow, I managed to get one sleeve three inches longer than the other due to lack of concentration. I didn't notice until I had cast off and placed them side by side. I guess this must have been done on my first night on duty, when sleep deprived. I sewed the jumper together. What a bloody mess it looked, but I was still proud of my first effort and determined to give it to Steve as a surprise.

My next night off duty, I waited for Steve to visit me at the hospital house. I wrapped the jumper up in decorative paper and presented it to him as he walked through the door. He opened the present with excitement, but his face soon altered as he tried the jumper on. We both hysterically laughed at this monstrosity of a jumper. It was buttock-length at the back and just below waist at the front. His right sleeve was above his wrist and his left sleeve down to his knuckles. It also looked like a family of moths had moved in; there were many holes where I had dropped stitches.

Nevertheless, after all the laughter, he kissed me and said, "It's the thought that counts, and I will wear it with pride that my girlfriend put love, time and effort into making it for me." He took it home and wore it at work the next day under his overalls to keep warm. That indeed must have been love on his behalf. Or was it the fact he was scared I might knit him another jumper to replace it?

BEING A LONG STAY WARD, it was a home for patients who had been in the hospital for many years. The patients were institutionalised and unable to live in the community. Many of them had been in the Asylum since they were teenagers; some because they had genuine psychiatric or medical illnesses, or trauma like experiences of the war on the front line, or during the bombings. However, sadly, some because something had happened in their life that society didn't accept. Such as unmarried teenage pregnancy or abuse. Long-stay patients were my favourite type of patient because they were such unusual, unique characters.

A typical night shift began with helping everyone get washed and ready for bed. The patients waited by the kitchen as we served hot chocolate and biscuits from a trolly, followed by a medication round. All the patients knew the routine and would queue in an orderly fashion. Usually, patients would take themselves off to bed after their last cigarette of the night within an hour or so. We would take it in turns to check the patients hourly, ensuring they were all settled and sleeping. At midnight we would get big bowls of hot water and disinfectant and wash down all the chairs, tables, and the floor with a disinfectant in the day areas and bathrooms; this was to ensure the cleanliness of the wards, as at night there wasn't a cleaning service. We opened the windows so the smell of the strong industrial disinfectant could escape, as some nights it seemed so strong my eyes would weep. We washed the night crockery and put tea bags in the teapots on the breakfast trolley alongside the crockery and utensils. By the time we had completed these tasks, it was around 2 am. We checked on all the patients again.

One night I remember checking the patients at around 3 am, and all were sleeping like babies. It was a quiet night, so I decided to continue knitting my scarf, which I had started the night before. I heard a bang of a door in the bedroom area and decided to investigate. Yellowish glowing night lights dimly lit the room, but one's eyes adapted to see in the dark easily. I looked closely at each patient to ensure they were breathing, and sleeping and safe and secure in their beds. I noticed that little Gertrude's bed was empty, and the fire escape door was wide open to the cold hospital grounds.

The ward wasn't one of the locked ones, and the fire escape was just an unlocked door with a fire escape sign attached to the door. Most of the patients were free to walk around the hospital and grounds from this ward and venture into the local community, but obviously, it wasn't safe in the middle of the night.

Gertrude (or as we called her, Gerty) had been a little more confused than usual because she had been diagnosed with a urine infection that week. A urinary tract infection (UTI) often causes the elderly to become confused. In the past few days, Gerty had shown confusion and disorientation, so I was concerned she was missing, and for her safety, raised the alarm. After an initial search of the ward, we realised she wasn't on the ward and must have gone out the fire escape into the cold night. Guess who got the short straw? Me, of course. With another student nurse called Sarah, who was working on the ward next door. The nurse in charge issued us two torches, two blankets and hospital capes to wear over our uniforms. We looked like caped crusaders being thrust out into the night to save the world.

Gerty was a tiny, frail lady in her late seventies with a long medical history of anxiety. Most of the day, she would sit in a chair, rocking and rubbing her hands together in a circular movement. Or she would walk up and down the corridors of the hospital, talking to herself. Occasionally, popping out for a walk in the grounds. They admitted her to the old asylum in 1920 because she had accused her brother of beating her on several occasions after he had come back from the horrors of the first world war.

She couldn't take any more of his daily beatings, so she ran away from home at the tender age of sixteen. After a few days missing, the police found her living on the streets. Reluctantly, the police brought her back home. She told the police why she had left home and even showed them her bruising all over her body. When questioned by the police, her brother denied his abuse towards his sister and stated that she had always been a bit of a crazy girl, making up stories about people, and getting into trouble. He told them that Gerty needed locking up because it was all in her head, she was a bit of a nutcase. The police believed him, so she was diagnosed with insanity and admitted to hospital. In those days, her treatments were heavy sedation, Electro Convulsive Therapy (ECT), and the use of straitjackets to restrain her when she became agitated and tried to leave the hospital.

Psychiatry was very barbaric in those days, and psychiatrists believed people could be possessed by the devil, causing insanity. As a young, innocent girl of sixteen years of age, Gerty must have been extremely frightened. No wonder she suffered from chronic anxiety; she had been through so much in her life.

It was a freezing winter's night. Gerty was only wearing a cotton nightdress and probably no footwear, so quickly finding her was critical as she could easily suffer from hypothermia. It would have been quicker for us to split up to look for her. However, new rules because of the Yorkshire Ripper meant we always had to be in two's, and to be honest, in an old Victorian Asylum and its spooky grounds, I would not have wanted to search or be on my own anyway.

Sarah and I linked arms and walked through the grounds, shouting Gerty's name, then stood in silence to listen. All we could hear was the wind whistling through the trees and bushes, and the owls hooting as if answering us back, and the shadows seemed to be following us. By now we were more than afraid and kept having fits of hysterical giggling, purely to cope with the fright. Methodically, we continued our search of every square inch of the grounds. We checked outbuildings and the copse of trees and bushes. We also shouted her name and shone the torch at anything we saw or heard. Unexpectedly, we could hear crying coming from under a bush, a whimpering noise.

We slowly walked closer and held onto each other for support. We crouched by the bush and shone the torch a little closer to see if it was Gerty. We could see a dark figure with two beady red eyes looking back at us. We bent down closer, telling Gerty not to be afraid and not worry, as we're there to help her out. Abruptly, a frightened fox leapt from under the bush, squealing like a baby, and scampered away. We fell back on our backsides and nearly shit ourselves as neither of us had realised wild foxes lived in the grounds as we had never seen one before. We scrambled up onto our feet and pulled ourselves together and continued our search towards the church, which was the last building on our list we needed to search.

As Gerty had been missing an hour already, we were beginning to become genuinely concerned. We were freezing despite wearing our capes, so Gerty must have been hypothermic being slipper-less and in her nightdress. The area around the church was eerie and pitch black as it had no street lighting, just the glow from our torches and a little moonlight. Our grip onto each other got even tighter, and our inappropriate giggling got louder. I tried the door of the church, thankfully it was locked. Which meant we didn't have to look inside the church, as we were becoming more frightened by the minute and screamed at the slightest noise. As we left the church, we got more desperate to find her. So, we both decided we would shout her name even louder.

"GERTY!"

We then listened again for an answer.

Remarkably, a small, frail voice answered, "HELLO!"

Sarah and I jumped out of our skins and hung onto each other even tighter. We shone our torches left and right. We found little Gerty wearing a thin blue cotton nighty, curled up on an ice-cold stone slab by the side entrance to the church. We helped her onto her feet and wrapped her in the blankets. She was so cold to touch, visibly shivering, and her teeth chattered. Hurriedly, between us, we carried her back to the ward, me holding under her arms and Sarah the legs. Despite her frail, small body, she seemed incredibly heavy to carry. We nearly dropped her a few times. Bless her; she was afraid and confused. She was shouting for her mother. However, thankfully, confused or not, she was alive.

Eventually, after ten minutes of carrying her, we arrived back on the ward. We gave her some hot chocolate and put on a clean nightdress, dressing gown, fluffy slippers and a blanket around her legs and shoulders to keep her warm. The nurse in charge phoned the on-call doctor to assess her for hypothermia or any other injury she might have sustained. Even though she was a tiny, frail old lady, she was as strong as a bull. She was examined by the doctor and remarkably given the all-clear, not even a scratch on her frail body. Within an hour of finding Gerty, she was tucked up, back in her bed and fast asleep, none the worse for her adventure of the night. They left Sarah and me to shiver and try to get the mud off our nursing shoes with hand towels while drinking a coffee. Unfortunately, we received instruction from the nurse in charge to get back to work soon after that. Not a thank you or well-done forthcoming, as if our efforts meant nothing. Oh, the glamour of nursing and our actions.

ADA WAS A LARGER-THAN-LIFE character of the ward and adored by all the staff. Ada arrived when she was a young girl aged about eighteen years of age because she had severe epilepsy. She was more than sixty years of age now, so had spent the best part of forty years in this hospital. Ada was a small and dumpy lady, with a big round face and facial hair that the bearded lady at a funfair would be proud of. She used to comb her dark brown hair off her face, which made her face look even rounder. Unfortunately, because of Ada's medication for many years, her stomach distended to the point that it made her look more than nine months pregnant with twins. She would waddle from side to side, stroking her belly like a heavily pregnant woman does naturally. She was a chain smoker, so her twenty cigarettes per day allocation would only last until after breakfast, then she would be on the scrounge and on a mission to get more cigarettes to support her fifty plus a day habit.

She would follow you around the ward asking for cigarettes and would do anything she could to get them. 'Can I help you make the bed, nurse?', 'Can I make you a cup of tea, nurse?', 'Can I go to the shop for you, nurse?' All followed by, 'Can you give me a cigarette, nurse?' Of course, I always had my roll-ups in my nurse's uniform pocket, but I would only give her one or two throughout my shift because, to be honest, even if I gave her all my cigarettes on the day, she would want more. Equally, she pestered all the other staff and anyone who walked onto the ward, like porters', doctors', and visitors. She was relentless, but had a charm about her that nobody could resist her pleas. I often wondered if I left her in a room full of cigarettes, how many would she smoke in a day. My guess was hundreds until she ran out of puff.

Ada's party piece, performed every day, was to sing her favourite song she had learned from a TV advert to enable her to maintain her cigarette habit. She would stand tall as if on a theatre stage, beat out the tune's beat on her belly like a drum, and sing the Toblerone chocolate bar song. The one that begins, *Toblerone, out on it's own.*

At the end of her performance, she would curtsy and give a beautiful grin. We would cheer, "More, more." Sometimes she would succumb to our encore and sing it twice. She, of course, eventually asked the million-pound question, "Can I have a cigarette, nurse?"

Everyone continued to cheer and clap as we handed her one or two cigarettes. How could we not reward her for such a reasonable effort? We never got tired of her daily performance, and I learned a party piece of my own, the words and tune to the Toblerone song too.

Once she had fleeced all the nurses for cigarettes, she would then go on another mission to obtain cigarettes to keep her habit going. SEXUAL FAVOURS!

Yes, you read it correctly. Sexual favours for other patients were her secret side-line. She even had a tariff for her services: five cigarettes for full sex; five cigarettes for a blow job; three cigarettes for a wank; one cigarette for a kiss; one cigarette for a feel of her boobs. She openly told me her tariff, during a conversation one afternoon. I thought she was joking as Ada had a great sense of humour.

One morning after breakfast, as I made the beds down in the female dormitory, I heard giggling and groaning from a side room. I peered into it to find Ada in a compromising position, with her legs splayed in the air, and a male companion with his arse jiggling up and down, having full-blown sex. I was shocked and clumsily said, "Oh, sorry Ada," closing the side room door behind me.

She replied, "Just a minute, nurse. We haven't finished yet. Can you give us ten minutes and come back later to change the bed?"

I was so shocked at her answer but saw the funny side of her cheeky attitude and the audacity that she was expecting me to change the bed that she had been shagging in only minutes before. Once she had finished her sex session, she walked out of the side room, pulled her dress into place and counted her five cigarettes. She gave me a naughty wink and grinned like a Cheshire cat. I just smiled at her and shook my head in disbelief at her proud behaviour. My eyes had been well and truly opened wide to the ins and outs of patient life. We never spoke about the incident, and I never told a soul until now.

MAKING AN ENEMY

The tutors assigned a specific assessment at the end of each year of training for student nurses. Due to my contracting the Russian flu at the end of my first year, they postponed my assessment. The assessment of the first-year nurse, was to provide total personal care of a patient. At the beginning of the first few weeks of my second year, I had to complete this assessment. I had chosen Thomas, who was an old, regimented army guy with dementia. He was only in his early seventies. Within a timespan of two years, he had gone from an exceptionally healthy, fit, athletic man to a very frail, confused, forgetful, agitated man who could not attend to his personal needs, walk, or communicate much. The medical team seemed to think his dementia was multi-infarct dementia caused by drinking excessive amounts of alcohol during his army days; this was causing mini strokes called Trans-ischemic attacks (TIAs). It was the culture to drink heavily with his team-mates. I suppose it was a coping mechanism to help filter out the trauma of war and disasters.

On the morning of my assessment, the tutor from the school of nursing joined me. He was my least favourite tutor. I had met him a few times inside and outside of work and disliked him immensely. He was small, big-headed, and a slimy character that most of the female nurses disliked as he was arrogant and a bit too touchy-feely for my liking. He thought himself God's gift to women and was very derogatory towards them, too, a textbook chauvinistic pig. But I would have to smile and be pleasant to him and try to get through my assessment and not let his attitude affect my performance.

My assessment started at 7 am after the night staff handover; I took specific notes about Thomas. Like how he had slept the night before, his physical and mental well-being, checked his charts to observe when he last received pressure area care and fluids input and output.

With a gentle manner and smile, I gently woke Thomas and explained I was his nurse for the shift and that I was there to help him have a wash and make him comfortable. I introduced him to the tutor, stated that I was being assessed and hoped he didn't mind. He just smiled and nodded as he didn't communicate much, and he didn't understand or comprehend what I was saying to him. I collected a trolley and placed a half-filled bowl of hot water onto it. I had learned my lesson from my first day in nursing by not filling it too high. I set three flannels, one for his face and neck, one for his body and legs and the last for his bottom and genital area onto the trolley. Next, I added a hand towel for his face and hands, and two bath towels; one for all his body and the other to cover his dignity.

HE DIDN'T WEAR PYJAMAS, as nightshirts were preferred when nursing a patient in bed, especially if they had a catheter, because threading the bag and tubes into pyjama bottoms of a confused patient who grabbed and resisted was like an extreme task from the Krypton Factor game show.

I emptied Thomas's catheter bag of urine, measured and

recorded the amount on his charts. I washed his face and hands and upper body; this was the easy bit as Thomas cooperated with gentle coaxing and explanation. However, when I attempted to wash his legs, genitals, and bottom area, he became uncooperative and aggressive despite explaining what I was trying to do to him. He shouted and hit out at me, swearing, calling me a whore; thank God he wasn't wearing his teeth, because he tried to bite me, gumming me half to death in the process. His biting didn't hurt but left red marks on my hands and arms.

I stopped and tried to calm him down by reassuring and explaining to him in a gentle, calm voice that I was his nurse and was here to wash him before his breakfast. He calmed down a little, and I would then try cleaning him a little bit more. Slowly and gently was the best way forward. Some days, Thomas would be cooperative, but today of all days, he was at his worst. He was very agitated, confused, and he made it clear he didn't like me today. I think it was because as well as talking to him, I was answering the questions from the tutor. But, unfortunately, I had to carry on and finish his personal care.

I asked the tutor if he would mind helping me, but he replied, "NO! Just imagine I'm not here."

I pulled the cot sides up for safety and ensured that Thomas was covered with a sheet to respect his dignity. I looked for Pat, the ward sister, to help me with the last bit of his personal care, as it was apparent, he needed two nurses to accomplish the task. Eventually, after an hour of battling with Thomas, we had managed to wash and dress him, attend to his catheter, pressure area care and give him a wet shave, which he always loved and never resisted.

The next job I hated the most, was cleaning his false teeth and placing them in his mouth. You couldn't just give the teeth to Thomas for him to put in himself, as he would try and eat them or throw them at me because he had no idea what they were. So, after explaining to Thomas that I would place his teeth in his mouth, I opened his mouth gently. After a count of 3-2-1, I popped in his top teeth. My brave fingers had to be in and out his mouth like the SAS on a mission. I repeated the same manoeuvre for the bottom teeth, which was even more difficult as he bit down with his top set, trying to bite me. This time I was successful and I managed to keep all my fingers intact in the process.

My next task was to help feed Thomas his porridge and give his morning medication, of which the tutor asked many questions: 'What category of food was porridge?', 'What were the medications Thomas was taking?', 'What were they used for?', 'What were the dosages and side effects?' and 'What type of dementia did he have?'. Plus, hundreds of more questions quickly fired at me, like he was a quiz host with a stopwatch. I handed over to Pat, so I could have my well-deserved breakfast and study up on anything else I may get asked about Thomas. I returned to the ward and continued pressure area care. I emptied the catheter bag again and fed Thomas his lunch of shepherd's pie with peas, and jelly and ice cream, followed by his lunchtime medication and wrote in his nursing notes my observations for the end of shift.

After six hours of nursing, the assessment came to an end. I could breathe a sigh of relief as it's quite stressful being watched on every turn and move you make. After fifteen minutes, the tutor asked me to meet him in the office to discuss my assessment; I asked Pat, the ward sister, to join me to give me support. After all, it was my first assessment, and I was a little nervous. She gave me her thumbs-up before we walked into the office and whispered, "It's in the bag, Mel. Don't worry. You were fantastic."

I sat opposite the tutor at the table and felt quietly confident and proud of myself, despite it being difficult at times due to Thomas being confused and unpredictable. He sat back in his chair, looked straight at me with an emotionless face and said, "I'm very disappointed to tell you that you have failed your assessment this time, but you will have the opportunity next week to do it all again."

You could have knocked me off my chair with a feather. I was stunned. I thought I had done well. I did not expect this result at all, neither did Pat; she let out a gasp and looked disbelievingly at me, then at him. He smirked as if enjoying his decision and started to put his papers back into his briefcase. Simultaneously, Pat and I asked him why I had failed. He took out his notes from his briefcase and proceeded to read me the list.

He stated coldly, "Firstly, when you introduced yourself to Thomas, you didn't say your name, just that you were his nurse; you need to be more personal so that he can identify you. Secondly, you left the patient alone to get another member of staff when he became uncooperative. Thirdly, you failed to place a lid over the jug of clean drinking water. Fourthly, you didn't offer another choice of breakfast when other patients did have a choice. And finally, you failed to give medication six-hourly, as prescribed."

I was in total shock. Surely these were not grounds for failure. I instantly answered these failures with a defensive attitude and tone. "Firstly, I didn't say my name because he wouldn't remember it, as too much information and words confuse him, but he does understand the word nurse, and identifies it with the uniform, which I re-enforced to him throughout my delivery of care. So, I don't think that classed as a fail." I took a calming breath, "Secondly, I left Thomas for twenty seconds in a secure cot-sided bed to get help from the ward sister. You were there by his side, so I thought he was safe; I didn't feel he was in any danger, and don't see how I could have done it any other way apart from bellowing for a nurse, which would have been very unprofessional of me. So, I don't think that was a failure.

98

Thirdly, I agree I forgot to put a lid over the water. That was a lack of concentration, but hardly a life and death situation. Plus, the water gets changed every two hours, so I don't think that requires a failure either."

I glared at the assessor. "Fourthly, I didn't offer a choice of breakfast because Thomas has always had porridge for the last forty years of his life; it is his favourite, and he doesn't handle change very well as it causes him to be anxious and aggressive. Also, his wife had asked us to make sure we continued while he was in the hospital. It's in his nursing notes as his breakfast routine, of which I followed. If it had been another patient, I would have offered them a choice. Maybe if you were unsure, you should have asked why he was having porridge because you did ask what category of food the porridge was. I could have answered the reason why and showed you in his care plan. I thought you would have read the nursing care plan and observed I followed it. So, I don't think this was a fail." By now, my hands shook in rage and nerves. "The reason Thomas was not given medication precisely at 6-hour intervals was that the Pharmacy was late in delivering his new medication to the ward. I looked at his chart; he received it only ten minutes late. I didn't see a problem with that as there has to be some flexibility when administering drugs. Such as a 2 pm drug round would take thirty minutes to complete, so the first patient would get theirs at 2 pm and the last patient about 2.30 pm and usually in alphabetical order, so they received it at the same time each shift. It's standard practice, so I didn't think that was a failure either."

He just shrugged his shoulders as if he couldn't give a damn, and stated it was his final decision. He said, "I'm failing you, and that's that. You will get reassessed next week; I will rearrange it and let you know the date."

He couldn't look me in the eye, and displayed his usual cocky attitude. I could see he was enjoying his decision more by the minute. It was apparent he didn't like me, and I knew the reason why, but I didn't think he would stoop so low to bring a personal issue to a professional assessment. At first, I was afraid to speak. I thought about it for a few minutes and, eventually decided I didn't have anything to lose. I would say what I felt and knew he would not like me bringing what had happened months before to the table. I put my hands on my hips and said, "I take it, the real reason you have failed me today is the fact that I gave you the knockback at a party. You know the party I'm talking about, the one where you told me you wanted to fuck me and tried to push your hands up my dress and into my pants when we were dancing. My friends saw you perving over me, and they made fun of you when you tried your inappropriate manoeuvre. I pushed you away, telling you I wasn't interested and to stop as I didn't fancy you because you were far too old for me, it was unprofessional, and my boyfriend wouldn't be happy if he found out. We were laughing at your pathetic proposition, so you grabbed your coat and told me I would regret laughing at you, and stormed out the door, drunk, angry, and humiliated. I take it today is your way of paying me back for saying NO."

He stopped, dead in his tracks, and looked at me with his eyes wide open. He became red-faced and flustered and couldn't speak. He knew I was right. The fact I had said it in front of Pat, the ward sister, seemed to anger him even more. I could see it in his face. I said, "I don't mind retaking the assessment as it's good experience and practice for me, but I would be asking for a different assessor because I don't trust you."

Pat, now angry herself, said, "I should put a formal complaint about him into the school of nursing about his behaviour, if I were you, as I disagree with his decision and behaviour." She went on to state, "You are a very competent student nurse, and they were not elements of failure for nursing."

He just glared at Pat, "Keep your bloody nose out of my business." He still couldn't look at me; he only collected his coat and briefcase and left.

I shouted after him, "That's it, little man, you run away, you're nothing but a bully." I was angry and upset at him for bringing his grievances to my assessment. Still, I knew reporting him would probably be disbelieved, and I would get a reputation for being a trouble causer, which might cause more harm than good for the future in nursing. So, I did nothing, kept quiet—much to Pat's frustration.

A week later, I was reassessed by the head tutor who had interviewed me regarding the cigarette incident at the general hospital. He assessed me and passed me with flying colours and stated he was extremely impressed at my professionalism. He told me he had seen the report from my previous assessment and couldn't understand why he had failed me on the points recorded because they were minimal and didn't class as a fail. He stated that because he was head of the school of nursing, he would investigate. I didn't say why or what had happened at the party to him. However, I knew the real reason he failed me, and I thought I would let him sweat, thinking he might get found out. Unfortunately, our paths would cross further on in my career and not surprisingly, he would continue to hold a grudge.

SKILLS THAT CHANGED MY LIFE

My next placement was at a day centre for patients who required specialist treatments, such as cognitive behavioural therapy, relaxation therapy, and hypnosis.

In her early fifties, Betty was a lady who suffered from an obsessive-compulsive disorder (OCD), classed as an anxiety disorder. People with this condition experience a range of recurring and intrusive thoughts, obsessions, ideas, or actions. These urges are so strong. They drive the sufferer to do repeatable things to alleviate painful emotions and unwanted thoughts. When it becomes so severe, it takes over their daily life.

Betty's specific obsessive-compulsive behaviour stemmed from the fear of contamination from germs or viruses. She had spent the past six months progressively getting worse, as her washing and cleaning routine took over her daily life, so she was referred to the day centre for treatment by her GP.

Her condition had started while she was on holiday in Spain with her husband and three teenage boys. She became ill and needed hospitalisation for a few days, after contracting viral gastroenteritis, which caused severe diarrhoea and vomiting.

The Spanish doctor informed her that she had acquired it from food prepared by someone affected by a virus or touched a surface contaminated by poor sanitation. He explained that the area's most likely to be affected were toilet handles, doorknobs, light switches, all types of surfaces and eating utensils. He then stressed the importance of washing her hands and wiping surfaces regularly to prevent her from passing it on to anyone else in her family; this is where the seed set into her mind, and her obsession began.

When Betty arrived in her little red Mini car at the day centre for the first time on a Monday morning, I watched her through the window. She stepped out of the vehicle wearing jeans and a t-shirt covered by a long-handled huge cloth bag diagonally draped across her chest down to her hip. Betty walked to open the boot of the car and took out a second similar cloth bag. She pulled out a washing up liquid bottle filled with fluid and a towel from this second bag. She placed the towel under her arm, poured the diluted washing up liquid into her hands, and rubbed her hands together vigorously. She made sure to wash them thoroughly. This procedure lasted at least five minutes, and she kept looking at her watch as if timing this procedure. She dried her hands on the towel, placed the towel and washing up liquid back in the bag, and discarded it into the car's boot. She closed the car's boot with her elbow, so her hands didn't touch the car again.

The day centre manager, Judith, asked me to meet Betty and fill in the nursing notes for her admission. Betty walked through the already opened front door with a sideways crab-like movement, so as not to touch any part of the door or frame. She held her hands and arms in front of her chest. Like a surgeon would once he'd gloved for surgery. I introduced myself and asked her to follow me to the office to fill in her nursing notes before the psychiatrist assessed her to prescribe her treatment plan. Betty followed me up the beautiful, large sweeping staircase. Unusually, she walked in the middle of the stairs very slowly and precisely, so as not to touch the bannister or walls at any point. She stood waiting for me to open the nursing office door and entered through the door sideways again. I asked Betty to take a seat.

She fidgeted a little, and looked around her immediate area, then reluctantly sat down on the chair, but always ensured her hands didn't touch any part of it. All this time, she'd kept her bag across her chest and her hands in front. I asked Betty if she would like to put her bag on the chair or desk, but she declined and looked horrified at my suggestion. Betty was easy to assess as she was very friendly, cooperative, and informative about her illness despite her anxieties. After the assessment, I asked if she would like a drink of tea or coffee, before seeing the consultant. Betty said, "I'd love a cup of coffee, but would have to make it myself," which I thought strange but told her to follow me to the kitchen. I showed her where everything was and stood back and observed; this is where I learned her illness's severe gravity.

Betty asked me to turn on the hot water tap and took out of her large cloth bag, a small bar of soap and a small towel and rewashed her hands for at least five minutes. I could see that she had a ritual into how she washed her hands. She rubbed her palms together first, then around the back of the hands. Then in-between the fingers. She rubbed up the arm to the elbow and, finally, around and around each hand again, then rinsed under hot water. She repeated it five times. Eventually, she stopped and dried her hands and asked me to turn the tap off.

Betty then asked me to pull two paper towels out of the dispenser and put them in the bin, which I did curiously. She asked, "Can you run the hot water tap for me again?" as she took three more paper towels with her forefinger and thumb and wet them in hot water and wiped the surface of the kitchen unit. Again, Betty repeated this five times. She took five more hand towels and placed them on the cleaned work surface. Betty took her mug out of her bag, a brown paper bag with a small jar of coffee, sugar sachets, and a teaspoon and placed them on the paper towels. "Can you pull the lever on the geyser to let the boiling water flow?" I did so, and she counted under her breath to five. She scalded her mug under the geyser, repeated it five times and placed it on the clean paper towels.

Betty then opened her coffee jar and put a teaspoonful of coffee and the sugar sachet contents into the mug. She asked me to pull down the geyser lever again to allow the scalding water to flow, counted under her breath to five once more, and then filled her mug with the water. After fifteen minutes of her ritual of washing, wiping, and scalding, she was ready to drink her coffee. I had never seen anything like this before, her hands were red raw from all the washing, and I became exhausted at just watching her rituals. Betty explained, "Everything I do creates more anxiety." Her illness seemed to imprison her, it had completely taken over her life, and there seemed no escape from this behaviour.

The consultant arrived and introduced himself to Betty and put his hand out for a handshake, but Betty recoiled and said, "Do you mind if I don't shake your hand? Please don't think me rude."

There was a moment of silence, and then he said, "Yes, of course, no problem, please follow me to my office."

I didn't receive an invite to his psychiatric assessment but read the notes after. It stated that for the first few days we would allow Betty to behave as she did now with all her compulsions and rituals, but everything that she did had to be recorded in detail so he could prescribe a program of treatment.

BECAUSE BETTY HAD SO many issues when washing, eating, going to the toilet and mixing with people, we had to take it in turns of a two-hour window of observing and recording and two hours off where another nurse would take over. I had the 2 pm to 4 pm shift. Betty had about finished her lunch. I observed that she had her plate and mug that she had bought in with her. Betty was wearing a pair of white gloves to eat her sandwich and crisps. Now I understood why she had to carry a big cotton bag; everything she needed for the day was in that bag to prevent contamination. So far, I had personally witnessed her use soap, a towel, coffee, sugar, a mug, a spoon, a plate, a sandwich, a packet of crisps and a pair of white gloves. Goodness knows what else was inside it.

She carried the plate and emptied the crisp packet and crumbs into a bin, opening it with a foot pedal. She put the plate, spoon and mug into the sink and asked me to turn on the hot water geyser so it could scald the crockery. She took off her gloves, placed them in another brown paper bag and placed them into the cloth bag. Out came the soap and towel from the magic Mary Poppins bag, and she started her ritual and compulsive behaviour all over again. It was so frustrating for me to watch; the time that the most straightforward task took was overwhelming, but worst of all, draining and exhausting for Betty. She was completely aware of how time-consuming everything she did was, and kept tearfully apologising for her actions.

Betty stated she needed the toilet. I apologised for following her to the loo because I had to assess her every ritual and movement. I waited outside the cubicle door to give Betty some privacy. Betty said, "Thank you, nurse, but it's okay, the consultant has explained to me that you nurses need to watch my every move to understand me and my illness."

I heard her peeing from a standing position, then a rustle as she dug in her bag, I presumed it was for a toilet roll. I imagined that to use one that someone else may have touched would freak her out. She then came out of the cubical using her elbows and arms bent up in front of her body to ensure she didn't touch it. She didn't flush the toilet, so I did it for her, knowing that it might trigger a whole cleaning frenzy. She thanked me and walked over to the sink and asked me to turn on the hot tap for her as she got her soap and towel out of her bag. Bless her. The handwashing ritual started all over again. By the time she had finished, it was 3.30 pm, so we sat in the day room chatting about her family and how her illness had become so debilitating. It was a chance for me to get to know her, and her, me.

Before we knew it, was home time for Betty. She said goodbye and thanked me for being so kind with her and walked to the front door. As she did so, she took her car keys from her bag and squeezed out the door sideways in her distinctive crab-like move. When she got to her car, she immediately opened the boot with the key and got out the bag with the washing up liquid bottle and towel to enable her to wash her hands five times before getting into the car to drive home. I had never seen a patient with OCD before; it seemed so tiring for her. It interfered with every aspect of her life; I had never realised how debilitating this cruel uncontrollable behaviour was until now.

After a few days of assessing Betty, we had a team meeting to report all that we had observed to the consultant Psychiatrist.

We mentioned Betty's ritual hand and arm washing with her own soap and towels, which caused her hands to be red and sore. Her relentless cleaning of surfaces, crockery, and utensils to prevent cross-contamination. The avoidance of touch with her hands to avoid cross-contamination. The relevance and obsession with the number five. Betty chose the number five for every action like washing hands five times, counting to five minutes, allowing the geyser to flow free from germs for five seconds, five paper towels at a time and so the list went on. We discovered that the number five became vital because she had five members in her immediate family, Betty, her husband and three teenage boys. Betty suffered from delusional thoughts. She thought that doing her action five times or counting to five would prevent her family from becoming ill. If Betty didn't do it, her anxiety became overwhelming and thought they might become seriously ill and die, so felt compelled to carry out her rituals to keep them safe. The compulsory use of her own crockery and utensils because she didn't trust that someone else could clean thoroughly like her, and they would become contaminated, and in turn contaminate her.

That led her to make and eat food prepared only by herself, because others may be affected and contaminate her via the food. Her toilet routine and use of a toilet roll she bought because contamination of the toilet area, especially the toilet roll, was touched by other hands. I didn't witness this personally, but she told me she used five sheets at a time to wipe herself. She carried homemade cloth bags, a different one every day. She made these bags to ensure she had the things she required to keep her safe. She had made nine in total, one for day-to-day use to carry her belongings, one in the car with her hand washing items, and a spare bag inside her daily bag if her outer part of her bag got contaminated. Betty washed all the clothes she had worn and the bags at the end of each day. All five times. Finally, she had chronic anxiety and tearfulness if her rituals were disturbed and felt compelled to start the process all over again.

After the discussion, a plan of care was devised to follow for eight weeks and then review.

We were to reduce the amount of handwashing with the use of behavioural therapy and hypnosis. Betty would receive a prescription for anti-anxiety and anti-depressant medication, as well as some hand barrier cream. She would also receive relaxation and visualisation therapy and daily reflection sessions at the end of each day. It was all so new to me, but I enjoyed watching all the treatments and learning the skills to practice myself. It intrigued me how successful the treatments were, even though it was a slowly-slowly approach to improve her condition.

On week three, Betty continued to improve slowly. She had got her hand washing and rituals down to three times from five. After observing and being trained by Judith, the day centre manager, it was my first time to work independently with Betty to get her rituals from three down to two that week. I was very anxious but confident at my ability to succeed. I felt confident when Betty started any of her rituals. I reminded her that she had done well the previous weeks in getting to the number three and reinforced that no contamination had occurred to her, or any family members. Therefore, it wasn't necessary to count to three today, only to two.

When she finished her ritual at number two, I asked her to stop. I praised her when she had stopped and asked her to tell me how she felt at that moment. You visually could see her shaking and struggling to stop and wanting to carry on with her rituals. There was indeed an inner battle with her thoughts to carry on, but she genuinely wanted to get back to her everyday life free from these rituals and delusional thoughts to keep her family safe. We took deep breaths together and reiterated that nothing would happen to her family if she stopped at two as nothing had done before reducing from five times to four then to three and now to two. This exercise was for every action she did during the day, such as counting, washing, and wiping. So, required one-to-one observation and nursing. Betty was still allowed to use all her own things as we had to tackle the ritual first. Other aspects of her complex illness would naturally disappear with the ritual, or we would tackle it separately. Betty explained how she had felt at the end of each day; sometimes, she felt proud of managing it and was euphoric when achieving her goal. Other times, she would be too anxious and would be physically fighting herself not to stop while in floods of tears.

When Betty became severely anxious, I would take her to the

relaxation room, a dark room with a warm glow from a purple light, and lavender smelling candles, and a tape that played gentle, relaxing music to perform relaxation therapy. Betty laid on the bed covered with a sheet, which she had brought with her in her bag. The session would start after I put the 'do not disturb' sign up and shut the door. Once Betty was comfortable on the bed, I spoke in a soft, calm voice and joined in with her breathing to get a specific rhythm together. Each time she breathed in I asked her to smell the lavender in the air and listen to the music, making herself feel more relaxed, and imagine she was sinking into a soft fluffy duvet or floating on water. I then asked her to take a deep breath and clench her jaw together, squint her eyes tight and hold for a few seconds then release the breath, pushing the stress out from the jaw and eyes. We repeated this three times.

The second stage was to take a deep breath in and hunch her shoulders, right up towards her ears and clench her fists and then relax on the breath out; we repeated this three times. This routine continued with different body areas — holding the stomach, clenching the buttock muscles, pointing the toes and leg muscles like a ballerina until she felt relaxed. I continued to ask her to breathe naturally, to smell the lavender and listen to the music for ten breaths, and to sense her body feeling lighter and lighter with every breath she took.

I would then introduce visualisation therapy. In a previous session, Betty had chosen a walk in the woods which she loved near to where she lived. I asked her to visualise her favourite place and take a walk through the woods. Observe what she could see, such as the different coloured leaves on the trees, the blue-sky peeping through the trees, the water flowing in the brook, the bluebells hidden next to the trees and the morning dew glistening on the spiders' webs. Then asked her what she could smell, such as damp moss and flowers. Then what she could feel. Such as the warmth of the sun on her face and the breeze on her skin. Finally, to listen to what she could hear, like the water over pebbles in the brook and birds singing in the trees.

I asked Betty to lay for a while in her happy place and enjoy this feeling of tranquillity and calmness. She said, "I feel so relaxed using visualisation."

"Good," I encouraged. I then explained that when Betty became anxious and wanted to continue a ritual, she should close her eyes for a moment and try to visit this happy place in her mind and take slow deep breaths, as this would help her calm her anxiety.

Betty thought she would never get better and was angry at herself for the slow progress she thought she was making. I reinforced that she was achieving all her goals set for her eight-week program. Her hands were less red and sore. Betty looked physically more relaxed, and her sense of humour developed and took the Mickey out of herself often. She would say, "What's in my magic bag for lunch today," and pretend to be a magician taking a rabbit out of a hat, when in fact it was just a sandwich out of a bag. Betty was so grateful for the nursing care and therapy we had provided. She said that during her most challenging treatment, she had felt safe in our hands. Trust between therapist and patient is so important to enable success. Some days Betty found it hard to keep herself positive, but she got there in the end with our skills and help.

By week eight, Betty was now free from all her rituals, no more counting, washing, and wiping. We had worked with her to eat foods prepared by someone else, even though the hospital food wasn't the nicest, and for her to eat off the day centre crockery and use the utensils too. But the cherry on the cake was when we bought fish and chips and ate them out of the paper using just our fingers to eat. Seeing Betty lick her fingers and enjoy her food without thinking of her past rituals was an incredible sight. Who would have thought that possible eight weeks ago?

The magic bags were a thing of the past. She informed us that she had burned them all in a bin in the garden. Betty couldn't believe how much time she had back in her life. At home, she now managed to get back a normal relationship with her family and was ready to go back to work as a senior shop assistant in a notable local department store. The thought of handling money from the public would have sent her into a frenzy before, but now Betty couldn't wait to see her friends and customers. She was ready for life to throw everything at her again.

On her last day at the day centre, Betty made a Victoria sponge cake for us all to share with her last cup of coffee, which she even let me make her. It was tearful as she thanked us all for helping her back to her normal self, as before she had felt total despair, anxiety, and hopelessness and at times felt like suicide was her only way out of OCD. To watch Betty, leave the day centre by opening the doors with her hands, kissing us all goodbye and getting straight into her beautiful red Mini car without a hand wash in view was a complete contrast from her first day of attending the day centre. It was a privilege to nurse Betty and learn so many skills I would use the rest of my life in and outside of work.

MY YEARLY ASSESSMENT as a second-year student was a drugs assessment. I chose to take it at the day centre, and luckily for me, Judith was a qualified assessor.

I spent days revising all the drugs in the trolley and learning their names. I sometimes had difficulty getting my Yorkshire dialect around some names, and I'm sure I didn't pronounce them correctly, as a Yorkshire accent has a very rounded tone. I also studied what side effects to expect and an explanation of the symptoms, and what drug couldn't be taken alongside another drug because it would cause serious complications. I also learned how to store, and administer drugs in the form of liquid, tablet, capsule or injection and the recording of the drugs administered to the patient. The whole assessment would take about two hours.

On the morning of my assessment, I was so nervous, especially since the knock to my confidence by failing my first-year exam the first time around. But Judith was so lovely and made me a coffee before we started and told me not to worry as she knew I knew my stuff and to put the experience where it belonged — in the past. The techniques I had learned for anxiety indeed came in to play that morning. Judith started the assessment by telling me she would choose just four drugs out of the trolly. They were Valium, Amitriptyline, Lactulose and Ferrous sulphate. I began to give my knowledge of each drug.

The next stage of the assessment was to take the drug round and identify the correct patient, correct drug, and correct dose. I then observed the drug-taking and recorded it on the drug chart for all twelve patients' lunchtime medication. My last task was to give an injection to Peter, an elderly gentleman. He had an iron injection because he had difficulty swallowing oral medication; at times, he would discard his medication in the bin to sabotage his treatment.

I prepared a sterile trolly and sterile tray with the ampule of Ferrous sulphate, a green-tipped needle, a 5 ml syringe, two antiseptic sealed wipes, a plaster, and a pair of tweezers and a red pen; this was the injection tray in the 1970s. You might wonder why a red pen and a pair of tweezers? It was in case the needle broke if a patient moved when being injected. The red pen was to draw around the area where the needle had snapped, and the tweezers were to try and pull the needle out. Nowadays, it's a kidney-shaped cardboard receptacle with the injection placed inside, already drawn up and no emergency equipment if the needle broke.

Peter came into the clinic room and laid on his belly on a bed with his pants pulled halfway down his bum. I washed my hands thoroughly with Hibiscrub, an antiseptic wash, which, for your information only, was fantastic for cleaning up jewellery, especially diamonds; they gleamed, sparkled, and dazzled. I checked Peter was the correct patient, but the cheeky monkey decided to try and be funny and said, "I might not be Peter. I could be Alan or even Harold."

I said, "Really? Peter, this is not the time to do this when I'm in the middle of an assessment."

He laughed his head off and said, "Of course, lass, you know who I am. I'm Peter, the love of your life," and blew me a kiss. He was showing off. I could have strangled him, but I continued to smile through my gritted teeth.

Judith said, "I'm satisfied that it's Peter," and gave Peter a friendly nudge. She then told him to behave himself as he wasn't helping me.

I checked the dosage on the chart of the medication and cross-checked it on the vial, they matched. I placed the needle onto the syringe, snapped off the end of the vial and drew up the thick syrupy brown liquid medication into it. I ensured there was no air bubbles in the syringe by flicking my forefinger at the top of the syringe until the bubbles dispersed. I then tore the sterile wipe swab open and wiped Peter's buttock in the upper outer quadrant area; this was the correct area I had to dart my needle into to avoid the sciatic nerve. Verbally, I prepared Peter by stating, "On the count of three, I'm going to put the needle into your left cheek of your bum. Keep still. It might sting a little bit, but it'll pass."

Peter said, "Yeah, lass, you get on with torturing me. I know you love it," and laughed again.

"Right, on the count of three - one, two," I said. At the count of two, I put the injection into the upper outer quadrant of his left buttock and shouted, "180!" like a darts player shouting as he hit a triple sixty.

Judith and I laughed, while Peter shouted, "Ow!"

I pulled back slightly on the plunger to ensure there wasn't any blood in the syringe, which would indicate I had hit a blood vessel. Thankfully, there wasn't, so I slowly pressed the thick liquid into the buttock. It only took a few seconds. I took the needle out and placed it into the tray and wiped the area with an antiseptic wipe and placed the plaster on top of the injection site. *Phew, thank God for that,* I thought.

Peter sat up on the edge of the bed and said, "I've got a bone to pick with you, lass. You didn't put the injection in at the count of three. Why?" I explained that usually, the patient clenched their buttock when anticipating the arrival of the needle, which caused the muscle to harden. So, putting it in at the count of two, the muscle was softer and less painful. Peter said, "Oh, you're a darling, you think of everything," and gave me a peck on the cheek.

I returned the trolly to the clinic room and disposed of the needle, vial, tweezers and syringe in the sharps box and threw the plaster cover and swabs in the clinical waste bin. I put the red pen in the stationery draw. I washed the trolly down with sterilising spray. That was my second assessment over and done with. I just needed to know now if I had passed or not.

Judith said, "Coffee time, I think, don't you, Mel?" Parched with anxiety, I welcomed this plan. Honestly, a brandy chaser would have gone well with it too. Judith sat with me and said, "Time for the results." She did the noise and action of a drum roll. "Of course, you've passed your assessment, Mel. You were great; you were knowledgeable about your drugs, you adminis- tered them according to legislation, and you were caring and amusing with Peter. You helped him relax, as we both know he's a scaredy-cat when it comes to injections." I breathed a big sigh of relief because I could now enter my third year as a student nurse and gain my red belt. I became more and more confident at my job because of all the learning experiences other nurses and patients had given me. I loved it.

STEVE and I were feeling happy in our relationship and decided to book our first holiday together in July 1979. We looked in the local newspaper and saw an advert for Sunny Side guest house in Great Yarmouth. The price was right, and the guest house's position was just off the promenade, as we didn't want to hear too much noise from the fair attractions and penny slots. We had never spent a whole night together because Steve's parents were strict and old fashioned in the fact, they believed you didn't sleep together until your wedding night.

LITTLE WHITE LIES

The advert stated you had to provide the linen for the beds, can you imagine that now? We phoned and booked a double room but told his mum and dad it was two single rooms because they wouldn't have let Steve come on holiday despite him being twenty-two years of age. Steve's mum said, "I will give you the sheets for your holiday, and wash them when you return," as if giving a subtle warning to not engage in any funny business.

Steve and I looked at each other and tried not to smirk as we knew we couldn't use those sheets as it was a double bed, but we had to go along with the little white lie. So, on the morning of our trip, we met at the train station. We had two small cases for a week's holiday, more like hand luggage for Easy Jet nowadays, and a small carrier bag with his mum's sheets. But in my case, I had the double sheets. They took up so much room I had to take a few tops out of my case to fit them in.

We bought two teas and a few sandwiches and crisps, the ones with the blue bag of salt in them and boarded the train. We chatted and held hands all the way there. We were so excited about this new venture, but the real excitement was sleeping together without the fear of getting found out. I remember one evening while at Steve's house, his mum and dad went to the pub for a few hours in the evening. As soon as they left, Steve and I stripped naked and started to make love in front of the fire on a soft furry rug. After ten minutes we heard the key in the door, then a knock. Thankfully, we had pulled the latch down. To our horror, it was his dad; he had forgotten his wallet. We jumped up and hurriedly put our clothes back on. When Steve went to open the door, I noticed my bra still on the floor. So, I hid it under a cushion. His dad walked into the lounge. As his dad looked for his wallet, he lifted the cushion where I had hidden my bra. To my horror, he found it and threw it at me and said, "I presume this is yours." He then continued to look in the lounge to find his wallet. He left the house again, and Steve and I fell about laughing, but I couldn't stay until they got back as I was so embarrassed.

His mum said to me a few weeks later, "I hope you and our Steven are not having sex." I was so shocked at her statement. I thought we had got away with it and went bright red. She said, "You must save yourself for whenever you decide to get married."

"Oh, of course not, Mrs Baker," I said. "What sort of girl do you think I am?" I had my fingers crossed behind my back, of course.

"Well, I hope you're a good girl, cos our Steven's not like that. Don't you lead him astray; he's a good lad."

How I didn't laugh out loud, I don't know, because I knew exactly how precious her boy Steven was, he could be a very naughty boy at times.

When we arrived at the guest house, Steve had to sign the register on behalf of the two of us. It was so different in the seventies; a man signed for everything. The guest house looked clean and tidy in reception and had a little corner bar in the lounge. We received the rules of the house: No excessive noise or music in the room. We were to be back in the guest house by 10.30 pm as they locked the doors. There was no tab at the bar; drinks had to be paid for when ordered. Also, no external visitors allowed in the hotel or rooms. We agreed to the terms and conditions then were shown to our room, which was up three flights of stairs. I wasn't prepared for the room with a view as advertised.

My God, the room was so small, with the smallest double bed I had seen in my life. Steve would only just about get his size 13 feet in the bed, never mind about the rest of him. God knew where I would sleep. It had a small cracked single window with the view onto another hotel, with curtains far too small for the frame that hung on for dear life. That wasn't all. It had a tiny sink in the corner with a mirror above it, a small single wardrobe, and a chair. If that disappointment of the room wasn't enough, worse was to come. We didn't realise that we had to share a bathroom with the rest of the floor.

When we saw the bathroom, I took a sharp intake of breath. It was a bit of a shock. I looked at Steve with my arms folded across my chest and said, "No way am I getting in that bath." It was disgusting, with brown stains and scum around the bath. The toilet wasn't much better and had a loose toilet seat. The loo paper was that waxy square sheet in a box, no way I was using that on my delicate bum. Unfortunately, there was no alternative. We had to use the bathroom; it was a case of use it or not wash for a week.

My first journey out of the hotel was to the small supermarket at the end of the road to buy disinfectant, bleach, potscrubbers, cloths, rubber gloves and soft toilet rolls. I scrubbed the bathroom from top to bottom. Thankfully, there wasn't any other guest on our floor, so we had sole use of the bathroom, and I kept it as clean as possible. After my moaning and scrubbing of the bathroom, Steve grabbed me, threw me on the bed and kissed me. We laid there and looked around the room, and laughed at the fact we had paid good money to stay in a mucky dismal shoebox for a week. It was like staying at Fawlty Towers. But we didn't care because we were together and that's all that mattered.

We walked on the promenade and laid on the beach most days, where we snored to the sound of the waves, neither of us wearing sunscreen. People never did on English holidays as sunscreen was for if you went abroad. Well, we looked like a right pair of lobsters by the end of the week. We hated the fairground rides as we both felt sick on anything that moved, especially with a round and round motion, but we loved the dodgems. We would get in our cars, the bleep would sound, and Steve would set off chasing me. I would squeal when he bumped into me, but he would get the grump on if I chased and crashed into him; telling me I was too aggressive and not playing the game fair.

Our favourite pastime was the penny slots. We would get a bag of two pence pieces and walk around stalking all the penny slots, seeing which seemed ready to drop its wealth. Some days the slots were kind to us, and we won most of our money back, but other days despite them hanging dangerously at the tipping point, our money would disappear sideways. I would then pretend to trip into Steve's arms accidentally on purpose and give the slots a knock. The money would fall out as winnings, and the kiosk man would give us a dirty look. I would give my innocent butter-wouldn't-melt-in-my-mouth look. It worked every time, and he would smile back at me and shake his head.

At night, we didn't eat in the guest house. We bought fish and chips, or pie and chips and sat on a bench as we looked out to sea and took in the night air and atmosphere of a typical seaside town. Slowly, arm in arm, we would walk back to the hotel, undress each other with a knowing glint in our eyes, and make love. I loved waking up next to Steve all snuggled up together, hoping we would make love again before breakfast.

After all, we had to build up an appetite to devour two fried eggs, two rashes of bacon, two sausages, tomatoes, beans and mushrooms and enough toast and tea to sink a battleship.

On our last day, we realised we hadn't used the single sheets his mum had given us to use in our supposedly single beds. They were still in the bag. So, we took my double sheets off and put the four single sheets on and rolled about again, doing what courting couples do best. We had to make them look slept in, or we might be in big trouble when we got home if his mum suspected we had slept together.

As the time to departure loomed, we became quiet and a little sad, because we had had a wonderful time. We got to know each other and loved the thought of us and what our future held. We would now have to wait a whole year to go on holiday again, but hopefully next time somewhere a little better than Sunnyside guest house. We'd bought rubbish seaside presents, a vase saying Great Yarmouth for his mum and a keyring for his dad, but the best gift was a photo of Steve and me inside a small red tube key ring, great memories.

THE ART OF SPYING

Only one more year to my final exams, time was passing so quickly, it hadn't seemed two minutes since I started my first ward. This final year determined whether I would be able to take charge of a ward confidently.

Due to his institutionalisation and aggressive behaviour in prison, they admitted Eric, a man in his late forties, to the ward. They'd arrested him in his early twenties because he'd arrived home one night to see his petite mother being raped by his drunken, aggressive father on the kitchen table. She had screamed for help. Eric witnessed his father slap his mother, saw red, and grabbed his father and punched him with one blow to the chin. His father fell to the floor and hit his head, splitting it wide open on the edge of the fireplace and died.

Eric never forgot the sound of his father's head hitting the floor. He said it was like a coconut being cracked open. He was arrested for the murder and given a sentence of twenty-five years. Eric developed anger problems while in prison because of the aggression shown to him by other inmates, and the fact he, for hours on end, remained in lock-up. It sent him, in his words, "Stir crazy." The doctors heavily sedated him because of his frustrations and aggression for years in prison. At the end of his sentence, they assessed him and found him unfit to return into the community due to his institutionalisation. Therefore, they discharged him to our psychiatric hospital for continued care instead.

The more I got to know Eric, the more I developed a soft spot for him. He was a tall, well built, muscled guy, a bit like the strongest man at a fair who hit the bell with a hammer. But really, he was a gentle giant, a pussy cat, with the vulnerability of a lost soul. He displayed anger issues and learnt behaviour when trying to cope with his frustrations. He would shout and hit the walls with his fists, but never a person. He threw chairs and turned over coffee tables if the mood took him, which was a little scary for other patients and us.

I observed that before he showed signs of aggression, he would clench his fists by his side and repeatedly say, "I'm going up the pole, Nurse. I'm going up the bloody pole," and a few minutes later he would erupt. It was like frustration caused the anger to build up then he would explode in a fit of aggression.

During my shift, I liked to sit with Eric when I'd completed all the physical nursing. I would ask him about his past, and he told me he used to be a coal merchant, delivering coal to people's houses. He was an uneducated man as he had to leave school at the age of fourteen to help provide money to his mother for food. His father was a layabout drunk, who spent most of his money on drink. He told me often he and his mum would go hungry when he was growing up. He and his child-hood sweetheart, Lucy, had become engaged before the murder, but sadly she abandoned him after his incarceration. He had tried writing many letters to her, but the letters were all sent back unopened, which saddened Eric. His mother had been loyal to him and visited twice a week until she died two years before his release. Eric was always very tearful when he talked about his mother, saying what a sweet, loving lady she was, but sadly had a horrible life of poverty and being bullied and beaten by his drunken father. He told me he didn't mean to kill his father, only to get him off his mother to get her to safety.

One afternoon Eric started shouting because another patient had knocked into his chair when he was sleeping after his lunch. He shouted, "I'm going to bloody kill you when I get my hands on you!" The other patient ran for his life, as Eric was a big bloke with a booming voice. Eric continued, "I'm going up the pole, Nurse. I'm going up the bloody pole."

I grabbed hold of Eric by the arm and said in a calm voice and manner, "Eric, come and sit with me in the quiet room so we can talk and try and calm you down. You don't need to throw anything today."

He stopped dead in his tracks and looked shocked at me because usually people were afraid of his booming voice or shouted back at him, telling him to shut up and calm down. He took my hand very gently into his. I must admit I was a bit afraid at what he might do next, but he said, "Okay," and we walked together holding hands, and he stopped shouting.

I asked him, "Why do you always shout, 'I'm going up the pole,' when you're angry?"

He said, "I picked this up from the wardens in prison. If I ever became aggressive, they would shout to other wardens to get the injections to sedate me cos I was going up the pole. However, I don't know why I say it. It just describes that feeling of rage and frustration I feel."

After ten minutes, he was calm and enjoying my company, especially holding my hand. Sometimes people forget that we all need human contact, kindness, and touch, as it is human nature, and releases endorphins to make us happy. For years, Eric hadn't had that closeness of touch from another human being. Even when his mother visited him in prison, they denied his right to hug her. So, holding his hand for the first time in years, felt secure and calming, which helped me develop a plan of care.

I said to Eric, "Whenever you feel the anger surfacing or the feeling of going up the pole, as you call it, you should come and find another nurse or me for us to sit in the quiet room with you undisturbed so that you could calm your anger."

A few hours later he did just that. For no reason at all, he became angry and frustrated. He shouted, "I'm going up the pole, Nurse!" His eyes locked with mine and he came over to me. I put my hand out, and he took it, and we walked out while he was still shouting. It was still his learnt behaviour from the prison days.

"Eric, you will give me a headache if you carry on shouting," I said as we sat down on the chairs still holding hands.

He apologised. His shouting instantly stopped, but his irritability was still visible, his legs trembled, and his face grimaced. Eric sensitively stroked my hand with his thumb and said, "You have such warm hands, Nurse; they make me feel loved."

Anyone who knows me now will tell you I always have hot hands. Patients always found them comforting. "What's made you angry now?" I asked.

He said, "I don't know, it's this anger, it just rumbles up from my belly into my chest, and I must let it out, I can't control it."

I thought I would practice some of the behavioural therapy I had learned in the day centre. I asked him, "Before you went to prison, did you have a favourite place where you enjoyed the feeling of relaxation?"

He sat silent for a while as if searching for a memory from a long time ago. "I loved going down to the river to fish in the early evenings before the sun set."

"Okay," I said. "Can you close your eyes and visualise it for me now, and tell me what you see?"

A small smile graced his face. "Yes, it's beautiful—big trees blowing in the breeze. I can hear the sound of water flowing on the pebbles in the river. Hear the birds in the tree and the smell of the riverbank." It was thrilling to see this calming response.

Later, I discussed my idea with the nursing team, and they agreed it would be worth trying to see if we could reduce his aggression. Every time he had his going up the pole moment, he would try to stop and find another nurse or me and sit in the quiet room to enable him to think about his relaxing place. It didn't work every time but at least seven times out of ten, which was a massive improvement, and his learned behaviour was beginning to subside. Getting to know Eric more as the weeks went by, I discovered that Eric loved singing as he had been in his local church choir, but sadly he hadn't sung since before being sent to prison. He had a beautifully rich baritone voice. So, we encouraged him to sing after tea with a few other patients who loved singing too. It was like an afternoon at the music hall. Eric's favourite song was *Daisy* because his mum used to sing it. Forty years on, I still know all the words to this song. The singing and a little ballroom dancing to music were excellent stress relief and made them all happier than looking at the four walls or TV.

Nora was another patient I adored because she was such a character. She was a tiny, cuddly lady aged around sixty years of age. Nora wore jam-jar-bottom round glasses and had rosy red cheeks, big blue eyes, and pure white short, curly permed hair. I always told her she looked like Mrs Santa, Santa's wife, which always made her chuckle.

Nora's admittance to the hospital was just after the war with schizophrenia. It was a type of schizophrenia that was caused by syphilis. She believed and told everyone she was a spy for the English government and had secret powers to allow her to spy on the Germans, Russians, and any one of whom she was suspicious. She was happy in her little world, but we never saw any behaviour to show her acting out her delusions of being a spy except occasionally she would talk into her hand. Not that there were covert radios in those days. Nora spent her days' knitting, sewing, and watching TV. The poor posture of sitting and knitting over the many years caused her to have a curvature of the upper spine, causing her chin to rest on her chest.

One afternoon, Nora stated she didn't feel well. She looked more flushed than her usual red cheeks, so I took her temperature to discover it was 40 degrees Centigrade. The ward doctor, James, listened to her chest and stated she had a chest infection and wanted her to go for an X-ray at the general hospital. I was to escort her as a third-year student nurse. I was now competent to nurse and escort patients without supervision.

I helped Nora with her coat, and she winced as I helped her put it over her shoulders. She said, "I'm okay, nurse, don't worry. I'm just a bit under the weather, and I'm sure I don't need all this fuss of being taken to the hospital."

Eventually, after persuasion from her favourite doctor, she agreed to go to the hospital. She insisted on bringing her big red tartan shopping bag, with all her wool and needles for knitting. Admittedly, she refused to leave without it. Allegedly, it helped her spy, so of course, it had to come too.

I helped Nora take her clothes off at the hospital and put her into a hospital gown for the chest X-ray. Being a psychiatric patient, she always had to be supervised when in the general hospital by a psychiatric nurse. I couldn't understand why, as Nora was a little dear old lady, very cooperative and gentle. They insisted she required this amount of supervision because it was policy. Once gowned, I too had to be by her side wearing a heavy protection tabard while she had the X-ray. The technician said, "On the count of three, I want you to hold your breath, and keep holding until I say you can breathe again."

I told Nora to smile, for the camera, and of course, followed his instruction by holding my breath too, going bog-eyed to make Nora laugh. He took two or three X-rays of her chest and asked us to wait until he had examined her X-rays. The technician seemed to be in his booth longer than usual, making me a little concerned there was something seriously wrong. Eventually, after ten minutes, he came out, scratching and shaking his head, and looked perplexed. He asked me, "Do you know this patient well?"

"Yes," I said. "I've been nursing Nora a few months now. Why?" He tried to tell me something but got tongue-tied. "What's wrong?" I asked. He beckoned me into the X-ray kiosk and pointed to the X-rays lit up on the wall.

MY GOD, I was as shocked and as tongue-tied as he. The X-rays displayed hundreds of fine white lines, pins and sewing needles all over her chest. He said, "Do you mind if I take further X-rays of her body, as I'm intrigued to see if she has more?"

Of course, I said yes, as I was as curious as he was to what he might find. After an hour of X-rays, he asked me to come into the kiosk again. Holy shit! Every X-ray showed hundreds of more needles of different shapes and sizes all over her body. She even had a thin long knitting needle under the lower left arm. I was so shocked at what I was seeing. Not one part of her body was free from needles. Nora must have inserted them all herself, but the question I wanted to ask was why?

The technician decided to inform the head of the X-ray department to discuss his findings. He arrived and had to sit down when he saw all the X-rays, he kept rubbing his bald head and said, "Unbelievable, unbelievable. How the hell is this lady still alive, I've never in my life seen anything like this before." He picked up the phone and said, "I must inform the consultant of these unusual X-rays. He will be amazed as we are."

I helped Nora dress back into her clothes and took her to the canteen for a well-deserved cup of tea and cake, while they wrote the report. I sipped my tea, thinking of how I could approach the question of why she had needles over her entire body. Nora looked up from her cream bun and said, "You want to know about the needles, don't you?"

My God, it was as if she had read my mind.

Her explanation was priceless. She put her hand over her mouth, looked around to make sure no one could hear her and whispered, "Come closer," so she could tell me her secret story. "You see, Nurse, all the needles help me spy on people. The government contacted me and told me to insert a specific needle in my head, which would enable me to spy on whoever they instructed me to spy on. They contacted me on my first day in the hospital in 1948 and every day since. Every time they tell me who I must spy on, I receive instruction to place a needle into my body, enabling me to listen to their conversations and watch their every move. The government can listen in to any conversations by tuning into my needles."

Horrified but intrigued, I asked, "Is every needle linked to someone you've been spying on?"

"Yes, of course, Nurse, and I know you won't tell anyone because I spied on you last week and you're not a spy, so I know I can trust and tell you anything."

I looked at Nora in total disbelief and asked her if she remembered where she positioned my needle in her body. She looked around the canteen and made sure we weren't overheard and told me, "It's in my left thigh, just above my knee." She took my hand to let me feel it. I could feel a fine hard line about two inches long just under her skin. It seemed weird that she'd inserted a needle because of me, it made me shudder at just the thought. I was shocked at how long this delusion of spying had gone on for; unbelievably, over thirty years. We knew she thought she was a spy but knew nothing about the needles as they were invisible on the surface of her skin, and she had never displayed any injury, discomfort, or infection.

The medical consultant arrived to examine the X-rays and

stated it was impossible to remove the needles; they were too deeply embedded. To remove hundreds would probably kill her, as some were in her brain and liver and vagina. Nora was so relieved that they would not remove the needles because she could continue her mission for the government.

I arrived back on the ward with the X-rays and a report from the consultant. Everyone was in total shock when I read the report and told them about our adventure. Not one member of staff had ever noticed the loss of needles or Nora inserting them into herself. Some nurses had nursed Nora for many years and had never suspected a thing. Nora spent a week taking antibiotics for a chest infection, and they changed her care plan to keep all needles in the office and sign them in and out at the end of each day when Nora used them for her sewing or knitting.

Thank goodness Nora got a chest infection, or we would have never been any wiser about her hundreds of inserted needles. The doctors were baffled how she had escaped getting sepsis or any other serious illness. It was a miracle she survived and, believe it or not; she lived for another ten years.

THE MEMORY GAME

My last ward as a third-year student was a short stay assessment ward; this was where I would take my last assessment — management of the ward for a full shift. It meant once qualified, I could walk onto any ward and competently take charge.

Eddie was the charge nurse, a lovely gentle middle-aged guy, with a very caring and empathetic demeanour towards both staff and patients. But he also was strict and organised. Eddie loved training student nurses and was very enthusiastic about training you to the highest standard. He had the reputation of being the best of the best. I was so excited to learn and be on his team. He had one distinct behaviour, for which everyone in the hospital best knew him.

Eddie was called the Dymo tape king. He was obsessed with the stuff. Dymo tape was a plastic strip put into a small handheld label printing machine that could type the letters to make a label. You would then cut it off and take the sticky plastic off the back and stick it on anything. But Eddie took it to another level. Every book, file, draw, cupboard, and even doors had a Dymo label, all colour coordinated for different sections. Red for the office, blue for the clinical room, yellow for the bathroom and green for the kitchen. Would you believe that the box that housed the Dymo tape machine had a Dymo label on it saying 'Dymo tape', yet the box showed a picture of the machine and displayed in big one-inch letters the word DYMO TAPE? I swear he had an obsession regarding this stuff. I guess if you stood still long enough next to him, you would be Dymo taped too. The machine was glued to his hand, or so I thought, as he never seemed to be without it. He was like a cowboy ready for action in a shootout in the wild west.

My first morning on duty, Eddie asked me to work with him alone to assess how competent I was, and what I needed to improve on to go out into the world as a staff nurse. We encouraged patients to get up for breakfast and wash and help them make their beds. He felt it essential that they took pride in themselves and surroundings, no matter how mentally ill they were, as he stated a clean body and environment, promotes motivation, and a healthy mind.

At 9 am a new admission was due on the ward, a forty-five-year-old man called Peter, and that's all the information I had on him. Eddie wanted me to admit him to the ward, assess his nursing needs, attend his medical assessment with the ward doctor and for me to write the nursing care plan. All with the supervision of Eddie taking notes of my every move and instruction.

Peter arrived on the ward escorted by two plain clothed police officers, which was very unusual. I had never experienced that before in my nurse training. He was very smartly dressed, in a suit and blue shirt but no tie. He carried a small sports bag and looked very subdued and hung his head down, not giving anyone eye contact. I introduced myself and Eddie to him and asked him to come to another office, where we would assess him. He just looked up and nodded. I asked another staff member to make a tray of tea and coffee for us, so we could relax before I assessed him.

My first question to help break the ice was, "Would you like tea or coffee, Peter?"

However, he answered in an irritated, sarcastic voice, "I don't know, as I don't know what I drink or even if I have milk or sugar. Don't you know I have lost my memory?"

What a strange thing to say, so I pressed on and said, "Well, what shall I pour you? Tea or coffee?"

He said, "I will try coffee with some milk." I made the coffee and handed it to Peter. He took one sip and said, "Mmmm, this is going to need some sugar," and he put two teaspoonfuls into his cup and stirred it very loudly.

One of the police officers said that they'd arrested Peter because he was a suspect in stealing money from his works office, the sum of £10,000.00. Since his arrest in the town centre, he had stated he knew nothing about the burglary and appeared to have lost his memory, unable to say who he was or where he was.

I didn't know what to say to that but said to Peter, "Well, you're in the right place for us to help you find your memory again."

Eddie nodded approvingly at my answer, but I felt it was a stupid thing to say. I conjured up in my mind an image of me looking under the bed and miraculously finding it. I think I was nervous and felt a little out of my depth with this situation. I had assessed many patients before, but never anyone arrested by the police or claimed he had total memory loss.

How the hell was I going to assess him if he had no memory? Indeed, he wouldn't be able to answer any of my questions. But after our coffee and chit chat, I began my assessment.

Peter answered, "I don't know," to every question. He didn't know his name, where he lived, or if he had a family. He continuously looked at the policemen as if for help with the answers.

Thankfully, the police could answer some of my questions but only the basics, like his full name and address, date of birth, his next of kin, his wife and his two teenage girls' names, and his employment as a finance officer at a local firm in Sheffield. So, I did as much as I could under the circumstances and said I would come back later to see if he remembered any more. Fortunately, I would communicate with his wife and GP later to get any medical history.

When I returned to ask him more questions, he seemed irritated that I wouldn't leave him alone. "For God's sake, is this necessary? Go and do your questions with someone else."

I explained that it was my job, and the more I knew about him, the better nursing care we could provide. My first question was, "Why do you think they admitted you to the hospital?"

He said, "I felt depressed and very anxious, and devastated I had lost my memory. It caused me to feel suicidal."

I asked him, "Do you have any idea as to why you had lost your memory?"

"Of course," he said very sarcastically. "I DON'T KNOW!"

He didn't like being questioned and was becoming more irritated the more I asked. I observed that all his actions were wildly exaggerated. It was as if he played a part on the stage – the way he hung his head, holding it in his hands; his lack of eye contact, and the way his feet dragged as he walked hunched over as if his memory loss made him forget how to walk correctly. His huge sighs while he hit his head with his hands and shouted, "Why can't I remember anything?" and "Oh, God, please help me," and looked to see our reactions.

Peter was shown to his bedroom and asked to unpack his bag, which had only a stale sandwich, some Benson and Hedges cigarettes and a lighter, his blue tie, his wallet with a business card and a photograph of his family and a few quid in it. I asked him about his wife and children, but of course, he looked at me arrogantly and said, "I keep on telling you, I don't remember anything. I don't recognise them. I keep on telling you, but you're not listening; you must be stupid."

I ignored his rude comment and carried on writing my notes, but glared and raised my eyebrow at him, so he knew I wasn't impressed with his outburst. I left Peter on his bed to rest and took his tie and lighter for safekeeping, as he could use them in a suicide attempt.

In the staff office, the police, consultant, and Eddie waited for me to discuss more.

The police officers stated they believed he was faking his depression and memory loss as there was lots of evidence of his involvement with the money's theft at his office. However, they hadn't found the money yet. He had left work yesterday afternoon, at 2 pm, and remained unseen until 9 pm, where he was discovered at a pub in Sheffield town centre. He had told the landlord that he didn't know who, or where he was, and thought he had lost his memory. He begged the landlord to help him because he was frightened. The landlord then rang the police as he worried about him because he had told him he wanted to kill himself. The police arrived at the bar and instantly recognised Peter; they had attended a briefing that afternoon about Peter as a missing person, and suspect in the burglary of the £10,000.00. The police took Peter to the station for questioning. A police doctor assessed his mental state and authorised the admission to a psychiatric hospital the following day for a full assessment before they could thoroughly interview him about the theft.

Eddie and I discussed a care plan we wanted to implement. We wanted to give one-to-one observation because of his suicidal tendencies. We also wanted to observe his mental state and behaviour and record it on a chart hourly. Later, introduce his family after a few days to see if he recognised them. Then review his plan of care after three days. The consultant psychiatrist agreed with the nursing plan. It was decided at this moment in time not to give any medication for depression or anxiety, only to observe his behaviour for a few days.

In the first few hours, Peter kept himself to himself, and didn't mix with other patients or staff. He just sat in the ward's day area, reading a daily newspaper, and smoking his cigarettes. I observed him at a distance just a few seats away, pretending to read a magazine without his knowledge that I was assessing his behaviour; this was so his behaviour could be as natural as possible. Eddie was sitting opposite me, assessing me as I assessed Peter. It seemed a bizarre triangle of assessment.

Peter had a good appetite and made a choice of what he wanted for lunch, and when the auxiliary asked if he wanted tea or coffee this time, he said confidently, "A coffee, please, milk and two sugars."

Eddie and I locked eyes and gave each other a knowing look. So, was his memory coming back? Or, before, had he played a game in front of the Police?

After lunch, Peter continued sitting in the day area alone, but I observed that an ABBA song, Voulez-vous, came on the radio, and from behind his newspaper he was singing along and tapping his feet. The behaviour of looking depressed and anxious, and dragging his feet seemed to have subsided.

Julie was a blonde, flirty glamour puss, suffering from Mania. She was overly chatty and over excitable. After dancing around the day room to ABBA, Julie sat herself down at Peter's side, nearly falling on top of him. "Hello," she said. "I'm Julie, don't you just love ABBA?"

Peter's eyes lit up as this blonde bombshell sat beside him. He answered, "Yes, I love their songs too."

"What's your favourite?" she asked Peter.

He replied, "Dancing Queen, a bit like you were a few minutes ago," and flirted back at Julie with a nudge and naughty smile.

"Oh, mine too. I love that song," said Julie and began singing it at the top of her voice. They continued chatting for about thirty minutes, or should I say Julie talked without drawing breath, and he listened and nodded a lot.

I recorded my observations and handed them over to the afternoon staff, who would continue to observe Peter's behaviour throughout their shift too.

The next morning, in the night staff handover, they stated that Peter had been chatty to other patients. However, when the staff talked to him, his body language completely changed from looking happy and chatty to depressed and anxious. He then stated how horrid it was not able to remember anything.

During the night, Peter's wife Brenda had brought some clothes and toiletries and left them at the hospital reception. However, she didn't come onto the ward to see Peter as the Police had requested that she not contact him until they gave her permission, because of the investigation. I collected his case from reception and woke Peter at 8.30 am.

He stretched and opened his eyes and pulled his top sheet over his head and said, "Oh God, help me, please, I still can't remember anything."

"Your wife brought you a case of clean clothes and toiletries," I said.

Peter pulled the sheet from his face and looked shocked. "Is she still here, on the ward?" he asked.

"No," I said. "You're not allowed visitors just yet."

He seemed to breathe a sigh of relief.

After breakfast, Peter sat in the lounge reading the the local evening newspaper from the night before. It had a small article about the burglary on the front page. Of course, we left it out deliberately for him to find and see if he reacted. I stayed in the ward office and observed him through the window. He read the paper from the back sports page forwards. At one point, he sat bolt upright in his chair and seemed to be paying particular attention to the front page. He put the paper down on the chair next to him and sat silently rubbing his forehead and looked very anxious. After about fifteen minutes, he got up and walked down to the end of the corridor, where the communal phone was. I walked down to him and asked, "Are you okay? Do you need any help with anything?"

"No, thank you, Nurse. I just needed a break from the main ward as that Julie can be full-on, she is driving me mad with her constant chatter."

In fact, Julie was on her bed, resting, and hadn't been near him for a few hours. I agreed with him that she could become tiresome and reminded him that he couldn't leave the ward. He leaned on the wall and said, "I will be back in a minute, after a bit. I need to take a few moments to myself."

I nodded and walked away, but on turning the corner of the corridor, out of Peter's sight, I stood and listened.

He picked up the phone and dialled a number, as if from memory. I waited to listen to his telephone conversation but could not hear any part of the conversation because he was whispering. The phone call lasted less than a few minutes. I heard him say, "Bye love," and put the phone down. He walked back onto the main ward area, looking extremely worried. I recorded his behaviour in his nursing notes and discussed with Eddie what had just happened. How did he know who to phone? How did he know the phone number without looking it up if he had memory problems? We were beginning to doubt his diagnosis of depression and anxiety and memory loss. But as nurses, we had to be non-judgemental and continue to nurse him but report his behaviour to the consultant, who, in turn, would contact the police.

Later that morning, the consultant asked Peter if his memory was improving and about his mood and suicidal thoughts. Peter replied he felt no better. In fact, he was now worse, because this place was driving him crazy, watching all the nutters on the ward. The consultant was not best pleased with this remark and reminded him it was a hospital for people with mental health problems. After all, that was why they admitted him to the ward; to assess his mental health. Peter just shrugged his shoulders and looked pissed off.

That afternoon, the police had arranged with the nursing staff for Peter's wife and two girls to visit the ward, but to not look straight at him at first and let the staff take them to Peter, so the nursing staff could assess if he identified them. At 2 pm, Peter's wife walked through the door of the day area. Peter looked up and stood to his feet for a second as if recognising her, then realised his mistake and sat down and picked his paper up again and hid behind it. Eddie introduced his wife to Peter, and he burst into tears. He shouted, "Why can't I remember you? I'm so sorry. Please forgive me." It appeared all overly dramatic.

Eddie asked me to show them to the other interview room so they could be alone to talk. I stood outside the door but didn't listen to their conversation, but could hear and see them hugging and crying.

When his wife, Brenda, left the ward, she and her daughters were distraught at seeing Peter in this unusual predicament. Peter went to his bedroom and seemed preoccupied with his thoughts and didn't want to chat with anyone. I took him a mug of coffee and sat beside him with mine.

Peter started to cry, this time inconsolably. He didn't want to talk about his visit from his family or the loss of his memory. He just buried his head into his pillow and sobbed. It was the first time I observed his emotions as genuine.

Two hours later, plain-clothed detectives arrived on the ward. They had come to arrest Peter, as more evidence had come to light that he was the main suspect of the burglary at his place of work. I asked Peter to come to the consultant's office to speak to the consultant. He followed me and appeared shocked when the consultant introduced him to the two detectives. He said, "I know why you're here." He listened to what they had to say to him and agreed to go to the Police station for questioning voluntarily. It was all done very discreetly, not to upset Peter, or to cause suspicion to any other patient.

A few weeks later, the police informed us that Peter had confessed to pretending his memory loss to cover up the theft of the money he had stolen. Allegedly, he was having an affair with his secretary, and he had stolen the money so he could start a new life with his mistress in Spain. Well, he certainly got a new life, but not with his mistress; a new life supplied by her Majesty, the queen.

AFTER TEN WEEKS of working with Eddie, I had developed newfound confidence. I had learned so much from different experiences, patients, and treatments. It was now time to do my final assessment—total daily management of the ward. Eddie had let me take charge of the ward and manage it throughout the shifts for the previous two weeks to practice for my assessment, but still under his supervision. It was bizarre, on the morning of my assessment, I wasn't nervous or anxious as I had been before. Eddie had prepared me well, and I was overly excited to get it over and done with because it was my twenty-first birthday the following week and I had some serious partying to do.

The night staff gave the handover about the patients during the night. I then allocated the staff to individual patients for their shift and wrote on the board who I'd allocated them to, making it straightforward for me to follow. While the staff were attending to the patients' needs, I checked and recorded all the fire escapes and fire equipment to ensure that everything was correct, and the ward was safe in the event of a fire. I organised the ward round with the consultant and doctors and reviewed every patient's condition, progress, and problems. I ensured that any medication changes were prescribed and signed for by the doctors and sent the prescription cards to the pharmacy, who would deliver them back to us on the ward by 2 pm. I also updated any care plans for the nursing staff to follow after the ward round. I gave both morning and lunchtime medication. Eddie, to my surprise, asked about legislation, and about every bloody drug in the trolley. I ensured the staff had staggered meal breaks, so the staff covered the ward sufficiently and safely. I checked the medical room for equipment and ordered more equipment where necessary, plus checked the oxygen cylinders were full and in working order. I checked all the equipment on the emergency drug trolly, which was for use in the case of cardiac arrest, and other medical emergencies.

There was no planned admission or discharge of a patient on this day, so I got off lightly, or I would have had to organise that too.

After lunch, each staff member gave me a report about each patient, so I was equipped with up-to-date information to hand over to the afternoon staff. After the handover, Eddie said this was the end of my management assessment and took me to another room to discuss his finding.

"How do you think you did, Mel?" Eddie asked.

I replied, "I'm confident in my actions and management of the ward and enjoyed the experience."

Eddie then congratulated me and said, "You have passed your assessment. I have observed that you are a very competent nurse, with excellent management skills." He smiled as he said, "I'm proud to have worked with you and would love to keep you on my ward once you're qualified."

I was thrilled as I wanted to work with Eddie and his team. I wanted to make a difference in psychiatric nursing, and couldn't wait to return after my two weeks off the ward. The first week was for a holiday, which tied in beautifully with my birthday, and the second week was to revise and take my final exam on the 3rd of October 1979, to become a registered mental health nurse RMN. I would work with Eddie until I received my exam results, then I would be allocated as a newly qualified staff nurse wherever the hospital needed me. Unfortunately, you couldn't choose where you wanted to work, or I would have wanted to stay where I was, but I lived in hope as Eddie had stated he wanted me to work on his ward as a staff nurse, and would put in a request to the powers above him.

BIRTHDAY PROPOSAL

The morning of my twenty-first birthday, Steve and I were up at the hospital staff social club putting up balloons and 21st birthday banners. Thankfully, the social club bar staff said they would arrange the buffet for fifty quid, the usual stuff of sausage rolls, sandwiches, crisps, and other party rubbish. The catering staff made a square chocolate cake iced with white and chocolate piped fondant icing, with a silver 21st birthday banner on the top. We had to rearrange the tables as I had ordered a DJ, and we needed lots of room for dancing because dancing was still my passion. Before we left the tatty social club, it looked pretty with balloons and banners strategically placed around the room and paper tablecloths on the tables. Steve took me home to get ready for my party, and he went home to change too. I had bought myself a beautiful turquoise blue silk trouser suit from a little boutique in town, and new white platform shoes and a matching small white handbag. I thought I looked very glam, probably a bit too much glam for a staff social club, but who cared, it was my birthday.

Steve picked me up at 6 pm to take me to the party. He took one look at me, smiled, and said, "Whit woo, look at you. You look gorgeous," and kissed me. Well, that was the only compliment that mattered to me today.

At 7 pm, lots of friends arrived at the party bearing gifts. I had never had so many presents or flowers in my life, and I'm sure I could have opened a florist stall. I was genuinely shocked. Steve had to put them all in a storeroom for safekeeping. The DJ started up his music, I, of course, was first on the dance floor and danced the night away to the Bee Gees, Roxy Music, ABBA, Gloria Gaynor, Donna Summers, Human League and many more artists. At 9 pm the professional footballers from Sheffield Wednesday arrived, bearing their usual gift of champagne. We all cheered and cracked a couple of bottles open. By now, we were all a little drunk. So, when the DJ put on *Oops Upside Your Head,* everyone dived onto the dance floor. We had to do the routine to the music. It was so funny as we were all rolling about laughing, and I'm sure the DJ put it on twice as it seemed to last forever. My new suit was now filthy, but I didn't care.

At 11 pm we began to wind down the party, as it could only go on until 11.30 pm because the club was in the middle of the hospital grounds, and we didn't want to disturb the patients. Thankfully, the bar staff said they would clean everything away, so all I had to do was thank everybody for coming and collect my flowers and presents. Steve took me to the house with my housemates. We had just opened more champagne when the door flew open and in walked about twenty or more partygoers, insisting we carried on partying. Next, the footballers arrived, which Steve loved because he was a big fan of their team, and he loved chatting with his football heroes. It was nearly midnight, and Steve said, "We have been so busy today, I haven't had time to give you your present."

It had never crossed my mind because I had a lovely busy day. He led me upstairs, sat me on the bed and presented me with a small box wrapped in silver paper and pink bow. I opened it to find a silver watch with a heart face. It was so beautiful; no one had bought me such a beautiful gift, ever. He took my head in his hands and kissed me and said, "This is a special piece of jewellery for you to wear with a heart because I love you, and, if you're a good girl, I will buy you a piece of jewellery for your left hand at Christmas." He then stroked my wedding ring finger.

What? What had just happened?

"Was this a proposal?" I asked Steve.

He said, "Yes, love." He was smiling, but embarrassingly blushing.

I was about to ask him why there was no bent knee or no question, "Will you marry me?" when my friends banged on the door and said, "Come on, lets party, plenty time for you two to shag later."

I think Steve thought he had been saved by the bell so as not to get on his bended knee. But of course, I said yes, and gave him a passionate kiss. What a memorable twenty-first birthday it had turned out to be.

We returned downstairs to the party and announced our engagement. Everyone was delighted for us and made a toast. Steve had to leave at 1.30 am because his mum and dad wanted him home before 2 am. I kissed him goodbye and carried on partying, dancing, and drinking. An hour later, suddenly, I was lifted off my feet by the footballers and given the bumps, all bloody twenty-one of them. My head was spinning, and I felt sick. When they finished, I ran up the stairs to the bathroom to be sick. Of course, it had nothing to do with the large volumes of alcohol I had drunk all day and evening; it was definitely the bumps. I laid sprawled out around the toilet seat, feeling very dizzy. The bathroom was spinning. My friends decided to put me to bed, and that was the last thing I remembered about that fantastic day.

The next morning, I awoke, feeling very groggy. I could hardly open my eyes. As I stretched out, yawning, I could feel someone in bed with me. I opened my eyes to find a naked man I had never met before laying by my side. I looked under the covers and hoped I had my nighty on. To my shock and horror, I was completely naked too. I laid there in total shock for a few moments, trying to remember anything, but nothing came into my mind. The naked guy stretched and opened his eyes, looked at me, and said, "Morning, sexy."

I shouted, "Who the hell are you? And what are you doing in my bed?"

He said, "I'm Dave, and I presume we slept together last night," giving me a cheeky wink. He then dared to say, "Who are you?"

I screamed at him, "I'm Mel, I live here, and it was my party. I don't even know you, so how did you get to my party? And why are you in my bloody bed?"

He stared at me and said, "I followed everyone from the club and crashed the party."

Now I was outraged and told him to get out of my bed. He sat up in bed and said, "Calm down drama queen and keep your hair on."

I was not best pleased with his reaction.

As he sat up to get out of bed, two of my friends came in.

One of them said, "What the hell are you doing with a man in your bed, Mel?"

"I thought you got engaged last night?" said the other. "What will Steve say?"

I burst into tears and begged them not to tell Steve because I didn't know what had happened. All I could remember was having the bumps and being put to bed after I had been sick, then waking up next to this moron; a guy who I had never clapped eyes on before.

My friends looked at each other and started to laugh.

"What's so bloody funny?" I said?

"After you had been sick and crashed out, we took your

clothes off and put you to bed," the first one said. "But at the end of the party, we found this guy, Dave, on the stairs, very drunk."

"So, we stripped him and put him in bed with you as a joke," said the other.

I was absolutely fuming at their actions because I didn't remember anything. I didn't even know if we had had any sexual encounters or not, and what would Steve say if he found out? They told me they had phoned Steve and explained what they had done, and he was on his way.

Oh my God! What was I going to do?

I shouted, "Get out and go home, Dave, now. Steve's a big guy, and he will kill you."

Dave didn't need asking twice. He shot out of bed, put his clothes on in record time and was out of the house within minutes.

Steve arrived about twenty minutes later. I was waiting for him in my bedroom, terrified that he would finish with me. But instead, Steve was a gentleman and told me not to worry as he had been told by the so-called friends what they had done and gave me a great big cuddle. He still looked a bit worried and preoccupied in his facial expressions, so I didn't believe him. "I'm so sorry, Steve. I can see you're not happy with me, but seriously, I didn't know anything."

He then sat by my side and took my hand and told me he was upset because he had to tell me that my young nephew, Adam, who was about six years old had fallen down the staircase and had landed on his head on a tiled floor. They had rushed him to the hospital; he was conscious but had fractured his skull and had a concussion. Adam had asked me to go to him. I washed and dressed quickly, and Steve took me to the hospital to visit him. Fortunately, he made a full recovery.

What a traumatic yet exciting weekend it had been. For many reasons, I certainly wouldn't ever forget my twenty-first birthday, that's for sure.

I DID IT MY WAY

*M*y final exams were only a week away, so I decided to buckle down and put every waking hour into revision. I didn't revise books like most people, as I hated reading. All because of an incident in my childhood.

At six years old, my male schoolteacher asked every child, in turn, to stand beside him at his desk to read to him. I hated it and would pray he wouldn't shout my name. I used to stand as far away from him as possible, but he pulled me close by my waist, stating he would not bite me. He had terrible breath and stunk of cigarette smoke. When I started to read his hand would travel from my waist to my thigh and stroke gently up and down my outer thigh. After a few minutes of reading, he would slide his hand up my thigh and slip his hand into the back of my knickers and stroke the cheek of my bum. I used to stand rigid and entirely still. I found it hard to read because I didn't like his hand on my bum cheek. I couldn't concentrate and would try to skip words from the book to get to the end quicker, but it would only extend my reading time as he showed me the words that I had missed. I used to feel sick and burst into tears, but he made me finish my reading before letting me go back to my desk.

At six years old, I didn't realise that it was wrong for him to do this. I just knew I didn't like the feeling of dread it gave me and began to hate reading. This hatred of reading books continued for the rest of my life. I could never concentrate and take in what the words were saying, and continued to skip words. I learned everything either parrot-fashion or by listening to tapes. For all my CSEs and O levels and other exams, I developed a Melanie way of learning that worked for me, by getting my friend to read to my tape recorder to listen while sitting on my bed, feeling relaxed. For my final nursing exams, my way of learning was that I identified each illness from a patient I had nursed with that condition. For example, I remembered Betty for OCD; it was all there in my mind, every sign and symptom, and all her treatments.

On the morning of my finals, I felt very nauseous due to anxiety, as I was aware that the past three years of training had led to this very moment. The whole class seemed noticeably quiet and subdued as we sat down at our desks, ready to start the exam. The tutor gave out the papers, placing them upside down on our desks. He asked us not to look. At 9 am, he said, "Turn your papers over and start; you have three hours to answer questions from part A and part B."

I took a deep breath. I turned the paper over and read it from beginning to end and wrote myself notes on a spare bit of paper to refer to it later. I was pleasantly surprised by the questions. The night before, I had revised all the patients with these illnesses on this same paper. I couldn't believe my luck. I used my new Parker pen, a twenty-first birthday present from my mum, and steadily and accurately began to answer the questions. My head was down, and my brain was in the zone.

The three hours flew by. I finished at 11.45 am, which gave me time to reread and add to my answers before the tutor shouted, "Stop and put your pens down; the exam is now over!" I was happy with my answers and walked out of the room feeling quietly confident. Big mistake, because once we were all in the pub, celebrating the end of our training, I realised everyone had different views on how we should have answered the questions. Doubt now crept into my mind. I now wasn't so confident with my answers. After a few more wines, I thought, *What the hell, there's nothing I can do about it now, and if I fail, I will have a chance to retake the exam.* I had six weeks to worry about it, as the letter would arrive around mid-November.

DIAMOND RINGS AND AGGRESSION

During those six weeks of waiting for my results, I worked on Eddie's ward and learned even more. He was an encyclopaedia of knowledge. During the night, a twenty-five-year-old lady called Jennifer had been admitted, displaying psychotic behaviour and aggression.

Reading Jennifer's notes, she thought her husband was having an affair, and she had threatened to chop his cock off during a heated argument. He thought it was just her temper talking, but when he woke in the middle of the night, he found her bent over him with a pair of scissors in her hand about to do the deed. It was sheer luck he woke at that time, he pushed her off balance and managed to escape out of the bedroom window and out into the street.

She completely lost her temper and smashed up her bedroom in an uncontrollable rage and ran down the street after him and screamed, "I'm going to kill you, you bastard."

The neighbours, who were terrified of her behaviour, called the police.

Her actions were totally out of control. She smashed her husband's car by kicking and punching it and scratched 'Bastard' on the car's bonnet with the scissors. When the police arrived, she became verbally and physically aggressive towards them and threatened to kill herself if they arrested her. They had to tackle her and take away the scissors. She was arrested and taken to the police station, where a police Doctor assessed her mental state. He found Jennifer uncooperative; she fought the officers, screamed and spat, out of control, and tried to injure herself by bashing her head on the wall. She said voices told her to attack her husband and smash up the house, but then said that even if the voices hadn't told her to, she would have done it anyway because he was a cheating bastard. The Doctor felt it unsafe for her to stay at the police station and put her on a Section of the Mental Health Act because she refused to come into the hospital voluntarily for assessment.

Once admitted to the ward in the early hours of the morning, Jennifer's behaviour didn't improve. She kept climbing onto the bed, jumping up and down, then onto the bedside cupboard, before jumping off deliberately into the wall so that she could cause injury to herself. She even took the belt from her trousers and placed it around her neck to hang herself. She continued to scream, biting and kicking. It took several night-staff to restrain and sedate her to protect her from herself. The staff had decided to put her in a side room as she was disturbing all the other patients. For her safety, they equipped it with only a mattress and sheets on the floor. They changed her clothes to just a cotton nightdress and allocated a nurse for observing her on a one-on-one basis through the observation hatch of the door. All night she swore and screamed; she was relentless, she didn't tire, but did lose her voice a little because of the screaming and shouting. After the morning handover, Eddie asked me to sit outside her room from 7.30 am until 10 am and observe her behaviour and attend to her nursing needs. I would be relieved by another member of staff at 10 am.

Jenny seemed to be incredibly angry with life and was

verbally and physically aggressive towards all of us. I introduced myself to Jennifer, stating I was one of the nurses looking after her today. She spat through the hatch and said, "What are you looking at, fat bitch."

I said, "That's a charming greeting, Jennifer. I'm here to keep an eye on you for your safety, seeing as you tried to injure yourself last night."

Oh boy, she wasn't best pleased with my smart-arse answer and paced up and down her room, like a caged animal, and screamed, "Bitch. Fucking bitch, I'm going to kill you."

We kept the door locked because she had wrestled with a nurse trying to open it earlier to give her breakfast.

"Open the door, blonde bitch," she shouted through the observation hole of the door and banged relentlessly with her fists, which were now becoming black and blue with bruises.

First, I ignored her behaviour because if you answered her, she became even wilder. But after half an hour of relentless shouting and banging on the door, I thought, *I've got nothing to lose. Okay, let's have a go at talking to her and see if I can calm her down.* I asked Jennifer, "Would you like a cold drink?" as I could hear that her voice was getting weaker with all her shouting and screaming.

She replied, "Go fuck yourself."

I said, "I'm thirsty, so I'm having a cold glass of orange squash. Are you sure you wouldn't like me to get you one too while I'm in the kitchen?"

"Do what you like, bitch," she answered.

I took that as a yes and got two drinks, one for her and one for me. It was like she was trying to shock me with her behaviour, but I kept calm. I knocked on her door and asked politely and calmly for Jennifer to sit on her mattress so that I could bring her orange juice into her room. Surprisingly, she did as I asked. Tom, the staff nurse, unlocked her door and stayed there as back up in the event she became aggressive again. I walked in nervously. I thought to myself, *This is where she jumps on me or throws the drink over me*, so I was mentally prepared to run. However, Jennifer took her drink and downed it in one. She was so thirsty. I asked her, "Do you want mine too, seeing as you are so thirsty?"

She replied, "Yes, please."

I passed it to her from Tom, and this too was downed in one. I walked out the room backwards, in case she decided to attack me, but she just sat on the mattress looking utterly exhausted. Once out the room and the door locked, I suggested she might like to rest, seeing as she had been up all night. It was like all the aggression and fight was at last out of her body. She curled up on the mattress and fell asleep within seconds as her head touched the mattress. I sat observing her from outside the room as she slept, she looked so peaceful, not like the raging bull she had been for the few hours previously. I handed over to Tom for a while and spent time with other patients needing my help. At noon, I returned to the side room. Jennifer was still sleeping.

I think she was exhausted. At 1 pm, she woke from her beauty sleep. She shouted, "Nurse, I need the loo."

Due to her previous behaviour of hurting herself, I got a commode for her to use. Strangely, she cooperated again and used the commode and said, "Thank you," very politely. All this time I'm thinking, *She's up to something. She's trying to get me into a false sense of security, any minute now she will kick off, and I will be her next victim.* She didn't; she remained calm and laid back on her mattress and closed her eyes. At 2 pm, my shift ended, and I thankfully handed her over to another nurse. It's quite nerve-racking when you're trying to anticipate a patient's next move when they are unpredictable and aggressive. I won't lie to you; it's frightening and challenging because there is no rule book. You have to try your best because what works for one patient might not work for another.

The next day was a Saturday; a special Saturday for me. I

was going to meet Steve in Sheffield town centre to choose my engagement ring after my shift. I was on cloud nine and extremely excited at the thought of choosing my ring. That's all I could think about; what shape, what stone, what design.

Once again, I was to nurse Jennifer one-to-one from 8 am until 10 am, then from noon till 2 pm. At 8 am, Jennifer was only just waking. She'd had a terrible night again, shouting and hitting the doors and walls of her room. They gave her sedation to calm her at 2 am, and by 3 am she had fallen asleep until now. I greeted Jennifer, "Good morning, how are you feeling today? I bet you feel a bit better after your sleep."

"Go and fuck yourself."

I let Jennifer wake up gradually, as she must have felt groggy with all the sedation, she had received over the past two days. I took her some toast and orange juice into her room. I didn't even have to give her the drill of sitting on her mattress; she just did it and said, "Thank you," for her breakfast. She was so unpredictable, one minute up and aggressive, the next nice and calm, a bit of a Jekyll and Hyde character. Of course, I didn't trust her and left her room backwards again to ensure my safety.

Once she had finished her breakfast, she tapped lightly on the door and asked if she could have a bath and promised to behave herself. I asked Eddie what he thought, and he agreed that there had been some improvement in her behaviour, so if I prepared a bath for her, we would jointly take her to the bath-room for her bath. Simultaneously, other staff members would change the bedding, wipe the mattress and mop the floor, so it was clean for her to return. I asked Jennifer to come with Eddie and me to the bathroom, holding out my arm for her to link. She fully cooperated but was very wobbly on her feet due to the medication. She looked so vulnerable and frail. I nearly felt sorry for her. I washed her beautiful thick brown hair while she laid in the bath.

I could see she enjoyed her soak, so I put some more hot water in to warm the bath up for a little longer. After about fifteen minutes, I informed her, "Just five more minutes. Then I'm afraid you must get out."

She nodded and laid back and enjoyed her soak. When the five minutes were up, I asked her to get out of the bath, and I pulled the plug to drain the water. Well, as if by magic, the verbally aggressive Jennifer returned. "You're a bitch! A big, fat, blonde bitch! Why can't I just stay here? I'm not doing any harm, and you're not in charge of my life, bitch. Now fuck off." She then spat at me. She gripped onto the side of the bath and refused to let go.

Typical Mel wanted to shout at her and tell her to stop misbehaving and get out of the bloody bath now, but nurse Mel couldn't. I said calmly, "Now, Jennifer, let's not start all this shouting and being uncooperative again, you were doing so well, and there are other patients that need to use this bathroom." I didn't force her out of the bath but just waited patiently. She stared menacingly and pulled faces at me. I continued to wait in silence, trying to get her to do it herself as I didn't want to have to force her out of the bath.

Eventually, after a ten-minute stare-off, she started to feel cold in the empty bath and got out reluctantly, still giving me the evil eye. Eddie was close by me but didn't intervene while I passed her a towel and nightdress I had warmed on the radiator. Jennifer smiled and said, "Ohhh, thank you; the towel is so soft and warm."

We walked her the few yards to her bedroom arm in arm, without incident, but suddenly she started to kick off again. She grabbed my hair and pulled it hard. Eddie grabbed her by the waist and tried to pull her off me, but she wasn't going to let go before she had pulled out a few handfuls of my hair. Two other staff members came from behind and lifted her legs off the ground, causing her to feel off-balance; this made her let go of my hair because she thought she was falling forward flat on her face. So, she put her hands out to protect her fall.

I pretended it didn't bother me, as I had been taught by Eddie to never, ever show a patient fear, or they would take advantage of you. After a struggle, we managed to get her back to her room and locked the door behind her. I was so glad to go on my break and shed a few tears after rubbing my scalp because it hurt. Thirty minutes later, I was back on the ward, but it wasn't my time to be with Jennifer so I could catch up with my other jobs and patients. Honestly, I enjoyed the rest away from her for a few hours.

At noon, it was my turn again. I wasn't looking forward to it, but it was my job, and you couldn't discriminate against any patient no matter what happened. Jennifer was sleeping like a baby again; in fact, she snored her head off due to sedation to prevent more outbursts for her safety. Tom and I stood, quietly talking, for ten minutes outside her door. I excitedly whispered to Tom that I was going to choose my engagement ring in town with Steve after work. He was excited for me because he too had just got engaged the month before. Tom also had bought a flat just ten minutes' walk from the hospital and had set a date for the following June to marry. "My God, Tom, you're well organised," I said, as Steve and I hadn't even thought that far ahead, but I knew I wanted a May wedding because of the blossom on the trees in the church grounds. We had a lot of saving up and organising to do before setting a date.

Jennifer banged on the door, which made us both jump a few feet in the air. "I want a drink, Nurse. I'm so thirsty. Please, please get me a drink. I promise I will be good, Mel. Please get me a drink," she deliberately fluttered her eyelashes. She repeated, "Pretty, please..."

Undoubtedly, the medication and shouting had caused the thirst. I asked, "What would you like to drink, Jennifer?"

She replied in a sarcastic voice, "Champagne, of course, so

we can celebrate you getting your fucking engagement ring today."

Oh, hell! She had been listening to our conversation, what was she going to do with that information in her mind? I laughed and said, "Sorry, love, this five-star ward has just run out of champagne, but I can get you squash or lemonade, madam."

She laughed at my answer and opted for the lemonade.

I spoke to Eddie, and he said, "I think we should have a team of nurses waiting outside the room in case she becomes aggressive again. But are you happy, Mel, to take it into her or shall I get another nurse to take over?"

"No, it's okay. I will go in as you have taught me never to show fear and I'm not going to let Jennifer see I'm bloody well terrified of her."

So, we set up a plan of action.

I returned to her room and asked Jennifer to sit on the mattress so I could enter the room, she said, "Okay," and sat on the mattress. Another nurse unlocked the door, and I walked tentatively into her room, followed behind by four other nursing staff who stood at the door. I gave her the lemonade, and she said, "Thank you," and smiled. I walked back slowly towards the door, not taking my eyes off her for a second. I could sense an atmosphere between us.

Abruptly, Jennifer leapt to her feet and threw the lemonade at my face, calling me a fucking bitch. I scrambled to get out of the room but slipped backwards on the lemonade and fell to the floor, banging my head. Jennifer then dived on top of me and sunk her teeth into my right breast. It all happened in seconds. I tried to pull her off me, but the more I tried, the harder she bit into my breast. The staff ran in and tried to get Jennifer off me, but she wasn't letting go.

She held onto my hair and continued to have a death grip with her teeth onto my breast. The pain was horrific. I asked the staff to let go and leave it to me. I said, "Okay, Jennifer, you have had your fun, now let go because you're hurting me."

She looked up at me and just glared into my eyes as if considering my request. She smiled and unlocked her bite hold. I could see she enjoyed her behaviour of hurting me.

I lifted my hand to put it on my breast to stop her from biting again. I glared back at her and said in a firm voice, "Get off me."

She started to climb off me slowly, but without warning, deliberately grabbed my left hand and snapped my engagement ring finger. I heard it snap. I let out a scream as it was so painful. She jumped off me, laughed like a possessed witch and screamed, "Take that, bitch!"

Eddie and Tom grabbed her arms and laid her face down on the mattress so that I could be helped to my feet by the other staff and escorted out of the room to my safety. Eddie and Tom let go of Jennifer and left her in the room as she shouted and laughed after me. She was like a woman possessed, she looked like she had truly, enjoyed her unprovoked attack on me.

The staff took me to the ward clinic room to examine my injuries. We could see that my engagement ring finger was bruised and broken. They placed gauze between my fingers and taped it together for support until the ward doctor could look at it later. Sarah, whom I had trained with, helped me undo my uniform to look at my injured boob. Oh, my God, it was black and blue, with visible teeth marks. I was lucky she didn't draw blood. Why did she think it acceptable behaviour, when all I had done was to be sympathetic and kind to her? My whole body began to shake with shock, and I began to cry with anger at myself for allowing this to happen, even though I stuck to the agreed protocol, I felt I had let myself and the nursing team down.

The ward doctor assessed me and asked if I wanted to go to casualty to confirm the finger's breakage and check my breast.

However, I chose not to as I still wanted to go looking at engagement rings despite feeling sick and exhausted at the day's trauma. Not that I could try them on my engagement finger now, thanks to the lovely vindictive Jennifer.

After filling in the paperwork regarding the incident, the staff arranged for a taxi home on the hospital account. The house was thankfully empty. I ran upstairs and dived onto my bed and cried. There was no doubt in my mind that Jennifer had done this deliberately to spoil this special day, but I wasn't going to let her win. I was going shopping for my engagement ring, broken finger or not.

Steve arrived to pick me up at 3 pm, completely unaware of the incident with Jennifer. When I told him, what had happened and showed him my injuries, he was in total disbelief. I don't know who was more in shock, him, or me. He didn't realise that patients could be so aggressive. He wanted to call the shopping off, but I wasn't going to let that happen. "I'm going," I said, "and that's that. I'm not letting her win and spoil my special day."

Eventually, he gave in and took me to a jeweller in town.

We arrived at the shop at 4 pm; I was like a kid in a sweetie shop. There was so much choice, many designs, too much sparkle. The pain vanished for a while due to my excitement.

"Well, off you go," Steve said after giving me a budget range I could spend on the ring. I first tried on a cluster of diamonds in the shape of a flower, a trilogy of small diamonds, then a few diamond solitaires, square and round. I eventually chose the round solitaire, but I had to try it on my right hand because my left hand was still bandaged and swollen.

After telling the shop assistant briefly what had happened to my finger, he took pity on me and kindly said, "You could bring the ring back if it didn't fit once your hand was better, and we would adjust the size free of charge."

Now all Steve had to do was pay for the gorgeous ring, and tell his mum and dad we were getting engaged, which he still hadn't done. We decided to make the ring's giving, the official engagement, on Christmas eve at midnight. So, this would give my finger time to heal and get the ring adjusted if required. My GP instructed me to take two weeks off sick from work to enable my finger to heal.

On arrival on the ward two weeks later, I observed that Jennifer was missing from her room. At handover, I asked where she was. Surely, Jennifer hadn't gone home. They told me that she had been admitted to a specialised secure psychiatric wing at a prison, fifty miles away, as her behaviour had become too extreme and unsettling for other patients on the ward and she had assaulted another nurse. Got to admit, I was so relieved Jennifer wasn't on the ward anymore. Truthfully, she scared the shit out of me. I had two weeks of sleepless nights worrying about what she might do to me, once I was back at work. While I drunk my coffee, I wondered what would happen to her in the future, and was terrified at the thought I might bump into her in the street someday. Thankfully, I didn't.

CONGRATULATIONS STAFF NURSE

*O*n the morning, my nursing results were due. I couldn't eat my breakfast of boiled eggs and soldiers (toast, for those who aren't British), my belly felt like a washing machine on spin. I just sat looking at the front door waiting for the letter to fall through the letterbox. Usually by 8.30 am the postman had delivered the letters, but today of all days, at 9 am he hadn't arrived. I went outside into the street in my dressing gown and looked up and down the street. I could see him chatting to a lady outside the shop. I flew back into the house in anticipation and sat on the stairs, willing the letters to drop on the mat. Five minutes later, the letterbox opened, and three letters fell to the floor. There it was – a brown envelope with my typed name in bold letters. I ran upstairs and sat on the bed.

I sat a few moments gathering my emotions together. I slowly lifted the letter out of the envelope. I read the first few sentences, then shouted, "YES! YES! YES! I've passed." I jumped on the bed as if it were a trampoline. I shouted, "I'm a staff nurse!" It gave me great pride to say that out loud. I honestly couldn't believe it. My childhood dream had, at last, come true. I was a qualified nurse.

I was due on duty at the hospital at 1.30 pm, so I had time to ring my mum, dad, and sisters to tell them the good news. We didn't have a phone in the house; mobiles were

non-existent then, so I had to go to the red phone box on the street corner, still in my dressing gown. My family were all immensely excited for me and so proud.

I showered and got changed into my uniform, and wondered when I could hand in my pale blue and white checked uniform and get my staff nurses blue uniforms from the stores. An hour later, the doorbell rang. It was a man from the local flower shop holding three massive bouquets. I looked at each card; one was from mum and dad, the other two from my sister's, Sondra, and Tina. They were stunningly beautiful. I realised I had a problem because I didn't have enough vases to put them all in. Thank goodness for my lovely neighbour, Gloria, who came to the rescue with two more vases.

I arrived on the ward with a massive smile on my face. Eddie picked me up and spun me around and said, "I can tell by the smile on your face that you've passed. I was never in any doubt. Congratulations!"

We sat in the office ready for the ward handover to begin when the phone rang. It was the director of nursing, asking for me. *Oh, shit,* I thought, *what have I done, for him to be phoning me on the ward?* I took the phone and felt my body stand to attention out of respect for his position and said, "Good afternoon, how can I help you?"

"I heard today you got your results and you qualified. Congratulations, Staff nurse." Oh, it felt so good to hear the words 'staff nurse' again. He then said, "Seeing as you're now qualified, we need a staff nurse to take charge of Ward 15 because of sickness. I would like you to take charge of the shift. Is that okay with you?"

OMG! My mouth dropped open in surprise.

"Of course, I would love to take charge of Ward 15. Thank

you for the opportunity. Thank you so much. I'm on my way now." I put the phone down and looked at Eddie and told him what he had asked of me.

Eddie was thrilled for me and said, "There won't have been many newly qualified nurses asked to do that today; he must be impressed and trusts you, so go on, off you go, and do your stuff. You know you can do it, and ring me if you need advice, okay?"

I gave him the thumbs-up; I loved and trusted Eddie. He was my rock.

I ran down the corridor and up the red steps to Ward 15. I walked through the door, and my mind instantly went straight back to my first day on this ward three years ago, but this time I wasn't terrified. I was excited to be the nurse in charge. I walked into the office and introduced myself as the staff nurse, and guess who was there? The battle-axe, Joan. She stood up and said snidely, "You're a third-year student nurse, or that's what your uniform states."

I stood and looked her straight in the eyes and said, "I'm waiting for my staff nurse uniform, it's on order. The Director of nursing has just asked me to come and take charge of Ward 15 this afternoon. If you have a problem with that, then I suggest you ring him about it." Internally I said, *Put that in your pipe and smoke it, battle-axe.*

She sat back in her seat and said nothing else, though I could see she was upset that I stood up for myself. It was if Joan hated change or taking orders. She liked to think she was in charge — being the SEN of Ward 15 — because she had worked there for over ten years. But they wanted a staff nurse because of the administration of the controlled drugs.

If only Joan mellowed a bit at change, she would be great as she was a good nurse and was deeply knowledgeable about the patients and the hospital. You don't nurse for twenty-five years and not gain great experience. But she had an attitude that needed tackling, and I knew I would have to nip it in the bud. After the handover and allocation of patients to staff, I asked Joan to stay behind for a moment.

You could see she was uncomfortable at my request. Her body language said it all; nose in the air, mouth and lips pursed, arms folded across her chest and legs crossed too, but the top leg was swinging back and forth out of irritation.

I said, "Joan, it's great to see you and have the opportunity to work with you again, and I thank you for the help you gave me when I was a student nurse here, but — and this is a big but — I need you to work with me, not against me today. I need you to be my right-hand woman, okay?"

She sighed and rolled her eyes, then nodded and shook my hand reluctantly, but she knew deep down I was right. I sighed in relief and said to myself, *Thank God that's over and done with.* I thought for a young, twenty-one-year-old, I handled it well without being patronising to her.

MOST OF THE patients I still knew, and surprisingly, a few seemed to remember me, which was nice. The routine seemed the same, and I soon got back into the routine of the ward. It was like I had never been away. It was a fact that there was something special about Ward 15. I'd always have lovely memories of my time there.

I couldn't believe Dotty was still on the ward, but sadly, she had deteriorated and was now bedridden and having terminal care due to having inoperable breast cancer. I took hold of her hand and said gently, "Hello Dotty." She opened her eyes and smiled. She looked like she recognised me and squeezed my hand. I sat with her for a few minutes, and she fell back asleep. I was despondent to see her like this, as I expected her to be her bubbly bustling self, making poo chocolates for all the nurses.

Surprisingly, Joan and I worked well together during the shift. She helped me give the patients medication to those I didn't know and even made me a cuppa as I wrote up some nursing notes.

At 6 pm, the phone rang. The nursing officer asked if I would mind working on Ward 15 for at least two more weeks, as one of the staff nurses had sprained her ankle. I said, "Yes, of course, as long as it was okay with Eddie from the other ward, as he had rostered me in for shifts."

He said, "I have spoken with him, and it was okay with him too."

So that was me, on Ward 15 for a further two weeks. I couldn't have been happier. I just had to keep Joan on my side.

ONE EVENING SHIFT, while we helped the patients get ready for bed, Joan closed the curtains in the small dormitory. She screamed and flapped her hands in the air. She ran down the corridor into the office and shut the door behind her, still screaming as she hid behind the desk.

"What the hell's wrong with you, Joan?" I asked.

"There's a bat, a big bloody bat. It was in the curtain. When I closed it, the bat flew out and around the dormitory. It seemed to be dive-bombing me."

Bless her, she'd had the fright of her life, but I found it funny.

"Come on then. You're in charge, Mel, do something," she said.

Well, what could I do? This situation wasn't a nursing duty I had ever had to deal with before.

Joan looked so funny hiding behind the desk, with her hands protecting her head. By now, we were both hysterically laughing as we didn't know who to ring to sort it out. Joan suggested sarcastically calling for Batman and Robin. The best idea I could come up with was to ring the service department. When I phoned to tell them about the bat, they laughed and put the phone down on me, thinking I was joking or a crank call. I rang back and said, "Seriously, guys, there is a bat in the dormitory. We can't get the patients into their beds because it's flying everywhere. It's enormous. According to Joan, it's the size of a Pterodactyl."

Eventually, they believed me and phoned the pesticide guy. A tall, well-built, handsome man, with clean overalls, arrived on the ward carrying a large bag. He said with a smile, "I hear you're all a bit batty on here."

I said, "Yes, very funny," and showed him the way to the dormitory. I kept well back as I was not too fond of the thought of a bat flying at me.

He took out of his bag a large, fine white net and placed it over the window. He told me to turn all the lights off and stand immobile, as the bat would sense where the breeze was coming from, and fly towards the window, then into the net.

I could hear the bat flying around just above my head. It was horrible, the draft of its wings just inches away! It gave me goosebumps!

He shouted, "Got it!"

That made me jump out of my skin and bolt to the light switch to turn the lights back on. In the white net was a bat. I had never seen a bat before, never mind up close. I was surprised at how cute it was. It was the size of a rat but with large leather looking wings and beady little eyes.

The pest control guy took it to the door and released it into the darkness. He then said, "Well, that's a cup of tea and a biscuit you owe me because I'm starving. I was about to eat my dinner when I got the call out."

The staff put the rest of the patients to bed, and I made him a cup of tea and gave him two chocolate digestives and two Jaffa cake biscuits. We always had nice biscuits on the ward because relatives always bought them for the patients to share with us.

~

I WAS BACK on duty the next morning at 6 am. The night staff said it had been a strange night and convinced that the bat had come back as they'd heard strange noises. All the patients had a good night, except Dotty. She was deteriorating fast, and was now unconscious and probably wouldn't last the day. The on-call doctor had been contacted and would be on the ward soon. We were all incredibly sad about little Dotty, as she was not only a wonderful character of Ward 15 but of the whole hospital. I allocated a nurse to be with her as I didn't believe anybody should die alone. We come into this world with love and people around us, so we should never leave this world without love and people around us too.

The on-call doctor arrived to assess Dotty's medical condition. He listened to her chest and shook his head. Her heart was failing, and her chest was rattling; it's called the death rattle, and we knew it wouldn't be long before she died. I asked Joan to sit with her as she had known her longer and knew her the best out of all of us, plus Dotty had a soft spot for Joan and vice versa. It's strange when someone is dying; there always seems to be an aura around the patient that can give you goosebumps and a particular smell that I can't describe. I could already sense it in the room. Death was upon us.

After fifteen minutes, Dotty took her last breath, and the room became silent. Joan was upset and asked to go on her break so she could pull herself together. She asked, "Would it be okay when I come back from my break if I could lay Dotty out, ready to take her to the mortuary, as I think that Dotty would have wanted that?"

"Of course," I agreed instantly and said, "I will help you if you'd like?"

Joan nodded and thanked me.

We laid Dotty out, telling her she looked beautiful and what a pleasure it was to have known her. When attending a post-mortem as part of my training, a professor told me that the hearing is the last thing to leave a patient, so you should always talk and reassure them at death. Research with people who had come back from death had given concrete evidence that they could hear everything around them.

We placed a flower out of the ward garden into Dotty's hands and kissed her cheek to say goodbye. Dotty had no rela-tives, so nobody to inform of her death, which seems so sad. Mental illness was a taboo subject; families disowned relatives because of it, as they didn't want people to know their mad rela-tive was in the 'madhouse' as they eloquently put it.

We knew that Dotty's funeral would be well attended by staff as she was loved by us all, and no doubt we would have a drink in the social club later to celebrate her life and send her on her way.

I began to warm a little towards Joan after going to the social club after Dotty's death. She told me she lived alone after her husband had died of a sudden heart attack twenty years ago. She had no other family and was a very private person, so her work friends were her family; this made some of her behaviour understandable, as nursing had become her life. She even apolo-gised for being a bit off with me when I started on the ward as the staff nurse. She said, "In my experience, most newly quali-fied nurses didn't know their arse from their elbows and didn't have a clue how to run a Ward efficiently. However, in your case, you proved different."

I said, "Ahhh, thanks, Joan. I take that as a massive compli-ment, and I couldn't have been able to do it without you, you're my right-hand woman." We sort of bonded a little, which I hoped would get better as time went on because Joan always kept people at arm's length.

~

WHEN I CAME on duty the following afternoon, the staff were noticeably quiet and subdued, and a couple of them were crying.

"What on earth has happened?" I asked as I sat behind the desk.

I didn't expect the answer I received from Judith, the other staff nurse on duty, "Joan didn't turn up to work this morning."

Which was very unlike Joan, I thought, as she had never had a day off sick in her life. They had phoned her but received no answer at home, so they thought that perhaps her car had broken down and she intended to walk into work. But after an hour of no sign of Joan, they asked her friend Graham, who was a porter, if he had seen her this morning as they lived next door to each other. He'd immediately said, "I will take my break now, so I can call and see if she's okay," as it was so out of character.

Graham arrived at Joan's house to find Joan dead on the front porch, wearing her uniform and holding her car keys. She had been there a while as she was stone cold. He rang the police to report what he had found. They'd arrived a few minutes later to assess the scene. There was no evidence of foul play, so after assessing the situation, they said they would take Joan for a post-mortem. They then asked Graham to go to the police station later to make a formal statement.

Graham came back to the ward about an hour later to inform the staff of this tragic news. Apparently, he was in terrible shock, and inconsolably cried when he said how he had found her dead on her porch. He had only just left the ward to go home moments before I arrived.

The staff were visibly upset and in total disbelief. How on

earth were we going to deal with this sad news? I didn't know, but I knew that all the patients still needed nursing, and I needed to take charge of this horrible situation. So, I asked, "Was there anything unusual on the ward with the patients I need to know?"

The staff nurse said, "No. All was as usual. Nothing really to report, and all the patients were satisfactory."

I informed the morning staff to go home early because they were in dreadful shock. The afternoon staff were willing to get on with the shift, even though they too were in shock and incredibly upset. I'm afraid that's what nurses must do, put their feelings behind them to get on with the job in hand. Eventually, it does catch up with you when you shelve your feelings somewhere in the brain; that shelf breaks, causing us to let it all out at once. Usually at home, on our own, drinking lots of wine, eating chocolate. Releasing tears, many, many tears, until we fall asleep. It's like a release valve for nurse's emotions.

Two weeks later, we found out that Joan had a massive stroke and had probably died instantly. How sad; she had died alone. If only she had managed to get to work that day, she could have died among friends who loved and cared for her.

MY LOVE FOR HETTY

*A*fter four weeks on Ward 15, I became the staff nurse on a long stay ward. I would have preferred to go back to Eddie, but they had filled the staff nurse position while I had helped on Ward 15. Disappointing, but a job was a job, as there were only a few positions available each year. I knew many patients, as over three years at the hospital, I bumped into them on the wards or in the grounds daily. They were, as usual, always scrounging for cigarettes. I was still rolling a twenty a day supply for them, despite me still not smoking, well, saying that I did like the odd menthol MORE cigarette if out drinking with friends. I thought I looked cool but could never get the hang of inhaling; it was all for show.

HETTY WAS a lady in her early sixties. I had never seen her before despite her being in hospital since she was fifteen years of age. She was an unusual character, who kept herself to herself. She would never give you eye contact, and I didn't see her smile or communicate with anyone herself, but she would politely answer when spoken to and followed instruction. She seemed a sad, lonely soul. She often sat in the same chair in the corner of the dayroom, watching but never joining any activities, like quizzes or singing. But her favourite pass time was she loved to draw.

Her drawings were very unusual. They were vibrantly coloured swirls all wrapped inside each other, but within the swirls, faces, and within these faces were more faces. It was bespoke and fascinatingly brilliant at the same time. She would sit with her legs crossed, but her lead leg continued around the calf then back to the ankle, like tied in a knot. Her face would grimace, and her body gyrate in a circular movement. How she didn't fall off her chair, I will never know.

During my shifts, I would always try to find fifteen minutes to sit and drink coffee with Hetty, taking great interest in her drawings. I wanted to get to know her more, her reason for admittance and her history. Over a few weeks, Hetty began to enjoy my time with her. I even got a little eye contact and a smile some days. Long-term patient notes were minimal on the ward, but old notes were stored in the bowels of the hospital. I asked if I could collect them as I was intrigued by how, and why they admitted a lovely lady like Hetty to the hospital in the Asylum/mental institution days, as none of the staff could answer that question either.

I had to be escorted by a porter to the archives. We went through a glass tunnel and then under the hospital. Rows and rows of dusty brown files met my eyes, the smell of mustiness overpowering. Covered in dust and cobwebs, these files had undeniably remained undisturbed for many years. Thankfully, they were in alphabetical order. It took me a while to find Hetty's file; I blew the dust off and walked back to the ward with it. I opened her notes and began to read. My God, I was so shocked; just one file for forty-odd years of hospitalisation.

How could someone's life be recorded so little? I continued to read to find her history, statements and assessments.

Hetty was born in 1915 to a religious family, her father being a clergyman for the Christian faith and her mother a teacher at a local junior school. She had a brother two years older than her and a sister that had died as a baby.

It seems her life as a child was without problem. She was a naive little girl, but she brought shame onto the family at fourteen as they suspected Hetty was pregnant. The notes confirmed that her mother had observed Hetty's stomach swelling over a few months and suspected the pregnancy. She asked who Hetty's boyfriend was. Who had been in her bed? Who had got her pregnant? Unfortunately, Hetty didn't understand, because she told her mother she didn't have a boyfriend and didn't know how you got pregnant. Her mum had asked her to tell who had been in her bed with her. But she said something innocently that destroyed her life forever. She said that the only person in her bed with her was her father. In the middle of the night, he'd laid on top of her. He said it was to rid her of evil because she'd sinned.

When her mother told her father what Hetty had said, it seems all hell broke loose. He completely denied the accusation and said she was telling lies and was possessed by the devil, and that it must be the devil's child she was carrying and that she was evil. He beat Hetty so severely with a belt to try and get the evil out of her, she ended up in a hospital, unconscious.

In the hospital, the father had stated that Hetty must be crazy and influenced by the devil and required immediate admittance to the asylum for her safety. Sadly, they took his word because he was a clergyman and poor Hetty was admitted that very day, never to come out again. Somehow, even after the horrific beating of which her father also denied, Hetty still was pregnant and gave birth in the asylum a few months later. They took the baby immediately away, never to be seen or spoken of again. The notes didn't even state if it was a boy or girl.

They left Hetty in hospital from then on. No member of her family contacted her again after her admission. She was abandoned at the age of fifteen, frightened and alone. There were two letters of communication to the hospital in her notes. One to say that her father had died, and the other to say her mother had died a few years later. It also said that added into her hospital account was some money from the estate. There was no correspondence from her brother.

The notes stated she had received heavy sedation due to her depressed behaviour. She had also received ECT several times during the years in hospital, and that was about it; apart from a few words each year to say she needed to still be in the hospital because she was believed unfit to be released into the outside world. Poor Hetty; punished because of her father's lies. No wonder she isolated herself and didn't give eye contact, she must have learned never to trust anyone again.

I closed her notes and was devastated and ashamed about how society had been only fifty years before and how it ruined someone's life because of their innocence. I just sat for a few moments and reflected, in tears, on what I had just read. My God, the world was so cruel; this poor innocent girl, now an old lady, had been stripped of a typical life through no fault of her own. How had she survived this trauma? I really couldn't imagine. My heart was bursting with pain, and I knew me and my empathetic heart was going to let Hetty feel some happiness and worth in her life before it was too late.

Usually, at tea break, I would sit with Hetty and chat with her about her drawings. I asked her why she drew such unusual drawings. Her answer said it all, "It's what I see in my mind, confusion and angry people."

It made sense to me. Hetty's mind, over the years, must have been turbulent and this was her only outlet. I loved her drawings even though they were always similar. They were always so different and multicoloured. You could look at them for hours and still see more and more hidden faces within faces. I think if she had been an artist today, she would have made a fortune as a famous bespoke artist.

The more I got to know Hetty, the more I was shocked at what little life she had truly lived. She had never been on a bus or train and indeed never a plane. She had never had a job or a friend to call her own. She'd never been to the pub or out for a meal. Never been to the cinema or had an ice-cream or gone to the beach. She had never chosen her clothes, as always since admission, had worn hospital wear. Never bought anything from a shop or handled money and had never had a boyfriend or even a kiss. My God, how sad was that? Bless her; she'd had no life at all. She just existed as a number in a hospital, as if she were worthless.

I asked if I could work a little more with Hetty, and volunteered to come in once a month so that Hetty could see a bit more life in today's society. The charge nurse agreed. So long as it didn't interfere with the rest of my work on the ward.

Hetty began to trust me, and her face lit up with a smile, and she gave me a wave whenever I walked on the ward. She was afraid at the thought of leaving the ward, but one day I managed to persuade her to come with me to the hospital shop to get sweets for all the patients. I told her I needed her help to carry them all back to the ward and assured her that she would be safe with me. We walked outside the ward and down the corridor towards the hospital shop. Hetty looked terrified, looking behind her every few seconds. Hetty had an unusual walk; she walked on her tiptoes. I reassured her and took her arm in mine. We were linked, which seemed to help her anxiety a little. We got the ward order of sweets, put them into two carrier bags, and slowly walked back to the ward. Hetty was pleased to get back to the ward and undoubtedly excited at the thought of toffees, especially chocolate eclairs, as they were her favourites.

We used to mix the whole variety of sweets into a big bowl, and the patients would choose ten sweets of their choice. It was the quietest afternoon each week as all the patients sat and enjoyed their treats. Of course, some exchanged sweets for cigarettes; after all, that was the hospital's currency.

After a few weeks of getting to know Hetty better, I asked if she would like to go on a bus into town and back again with me, as you had to introduce learning to be in the community, and everyday life slowly, a bit like treatment for OCD. Hetty was anxious at the thought, and said, "We don't have to get off the bus, do we?"

"Of course not," I said, "it's just about travelling on a bus for the first time and enjoying the experience of the outside world, and I will be with you all the time. I promise."

Hetty thought about it over her coffee then agreed she would like to try. So, I arranged with the ward staff that the following day, which was my day off, I would come in just 10 am until 1 pm to take Hetty for her first bus ride and have her back for her lunch.

When I arrived on the ward at 9.30 am, Hetty was already sitting waiting for me. Her face deep in thought, while grimacing and her body gyrating. She saw me and did her usual smile and wave. I waved back and mouthed, "Five minutes, okay?" She nodded, but I could see she was incredibly anxious. I signed for her money out of her petty cash. From their benefits, each patient received an allocation of a few quid a week for anything they wanted. Such as cigarettes and sweets, but in this case, her bus fare to town.

It was a cold day, so I ensured that Hetty wrapped up warmly with her coat, scarf, gloves, and hat. We walked off the ward, down the winding path of the hospital to the bus stop. Hetty couldn't remember the last time she had been outside, off the ward. She was so out of breath because she wasn't used to walking far, so we had to slow down. We missed the first bus, but they were every fifteen minutes apart so that the next one would be there in the next few minutes.

Hetty was so shocked at the outside world, especially the cars and lorries, which passed us on the main road every few seconds. She was amazed that most people had a car in their household, because in her day if you saw a car once a day you were lucky. Only the elite could ever afford one. The cream double-decker bus arrived a few minutes later. I thought her false teeth were going to fall out of her mouth; it was so wide open in wonder. She couldn't believe how big the bus was. I encouraged her to get on the bus. I gave her the ten pence for her fare to give to the driver. She managed it confidently.

"Do you want to sit upstairs or down?" I asked Hetty, and unbelievably, she chose upstairs, which was difficult as she still walked on her tiptoes. We sat on the front seats to get the best view, ready for her first journey on a bus. Hetty smiled and appeared excited. She also surprisingly asked lots of questions. I had never heard her talk so much.

"What are those buildings?" She pointed at some flats.

"They are small dwellings built on top of each other for different families to live in."

Hetty thought about that for a moment, nodded, then asked, "How long would we be on the bus?"

"At least thirty minutes," I said, "as the driver has to stop many times to pick up other people to go into town."

She seemed to take it all in her stride. I was enormously proud of her. She was very shocked at how many people there were on the streets and the number of shops and heavy traffic. I thought about the late twenties' early thirties; it must have been quite a different world.

When we eventually arrived in town, the bus had to wait twenty minutes to turn round as another driver had to board the bus. There was a little coffee kiosk in the bus station, so I asked Hetty if she wanted to get a drink or stay on the bus. She surprised me yet again and stated she wanted a coffee, so we got off the bus. She was mesmerised at the bus station because there were twenty buses or more coming and going. Hetty couldn't believe how busy life was nowadays. She sat open-mouthed as she watched the world go by.

We got back on the bus and travelled the thirty-minute journey back to the hospital. After ten minutes into the journey, Hetty had fallen asleep with her head on my shoulder. Bless her she was exhausted. I woke her up at the stop before we got off. Hetty was surprised she had fallen asleep, as often she had trouble sleeping. Our walk up the drive for Hetty was challenging. She struggled as she was tired, and it wasn't easy walking uphill on her tiptoes. A porter passed in his truck and we thumbed a lift back to the ward.

I reported to our nursing office how successful the outing had been, and told Hetty that we would try to discuss and organise something for the following week. She looked exhausted but incredibly excited at the thought of another outing. I felt, as a psychiatric nurse, that I had achieved so much in a few hours. To me, it was what psychiatric nursing should be all about.

The hospitals were just beginning to try and rehabilitate institutionalised patients, and I was proudly on the crest of that wave. I couldn't help every patient, but I sure as hell was going to make a difference in Hetty's life.

Over the following weeks, Hetty seemed to come out of her shell, and even joined in the singing, especially on a Sunday when we would sing hymns as we watched a Sunday service on TV. She remembered them from being at church with her family as a young girl. However, Hetty's walking difficulties hampered her mobility, so we arranged for her to have physio-therapy to place her feet flat on the floor when walking, instead of walking on her toes. After an assessment, they discovered that her feet were in working order, and it was more of a habit she had developed over the years. Her foot ligaments were tight, but after a few weeks of physio and stretching of the ligaments and muscles, she began to walk normally.

AFTER SEVERAL TRIPS on the bus, and trips to local cafes, I thought maybe now was the time to progress with Hetty's rehabilitation. It was her birthday in a few weeks, so I thought the next week we could go shopping for a new outfit, then the following week, on her birthday, we could go out for a meal in a nice restaurant.

Hetty was very eager to go shopping for an outfit. She had never been clothes shopping before, or even chose what she wore. We travelled on the bus to the town centre. As we got off the bus, there was a big department store on the left-hand side called Rackham's. We had passed it a few times, but until now we hadn't been inside.

Hetty was amazed at the store's size and the variety of clothes, shoes, handbags, and cosmetics. She flitted from one area to another, looking, staring, and touching. Eventually, after an hour of looking, we chose a few outfits together, and we decided to try them on in the changing rooms. Hetty was so talkative with excitement that I had to keep telling her to be a little quieter and calmer, which she did for a few minutes. Then excitement took over again. She was honestly like a little girl in a toy shop.

Eventually, she chose a jade green dress with a fawn embroidered neckline and edging of the sleeves, a jade green cardigan, and matching fawn shoes and handbag, which complimented her dress's small pattern. As I looked at her reflection in the mirror, I realised that she looked a proper bobby dazzler in her new outfit, as a Yorkshire person would say. I looked at her face and smile and couldn't believe that in a few months, Hetty had gone from an introverted, unconfident person to this vision of strength and happiness. She had achieved so much. I was so happy and proud of her.

On the bus travelling to the hospital, Hetty opened and shut the bags with her dress and cardigan in many times, admired them and smiled. I don't think she could believe they were hers. When we got back to the ward, she couldn't wait to show the staff her new clothes and even tried them on again. Then walked up and down the ward like a model on a catwalk.

ON THE MORNING of Hetty's birthday, it was my day off, but I had organised that I would collect her at 11 am to take her to get her hair styled first at the local hairdressers, then on to a restaurant just out of town. I asked that the restaurant place us in a quieter area, so we didn't cause problems if Hetty got overexcited and talkative again.

Hetty came out of the dormitory looking very glam in her new clothes, but it was evident that she needed the hairdressers as her hair was combed back off her face, and looked lifeless. The staff had done a collection for a few birthday gifts for Hetty. I had wrapped them in a small red glittery box. Hetty opened it to find a packet of chocolate Eclairs, a red lipstick, a small bottle of perfume and some new felt pens for her drawings. She had never worn lipstick before, and I had to show her how to apply it, and she dabbed far too much perfume on herself, but who cared, it was her birthday. They gave her special attention at the hairdressers as I had requested, giving her a head massage and tea and biscuits. Her new curly hairstyle complemented her new outfit and red lipstick. She looked so glamorous, a million miles away from the lady I knew six months before.

On arrival at the restaurant, I became very anxious. Had I pushed Hetty too far? Would she cope with so many people around her? There was only one way to find out. We entered the restaurant and was shown to our seats in the far corner.

I told Hetty she could have anything she fancied on the menu as my treat for her birthday. She studied the menu but didn't understand half of it. "What's cordon bleu?" She blinked at the unknown terms, "What's a Barnsley chop, Scampi and Steak Diane?"

I realised how much of life in the present day Hetty had no idea about. I explained the menu, and eventually, she chose chicken with mash and vegetables, something she was used to and felt safe for her. I chose one of my favourite meals, scampi, and chips. The charge nurse told Hetty before we left the ward that she should try champagne. After all, it was her special birthday. So, when I asked her what she wanted to drink, she loudly said, "Champagne!"

I thought, Oh God, this meal was going to cost me a fortune. Happily, they served it by the glass. The waiter poured the champagne into the glass, and Hetty had never seen so many bubbles. When she took a sip, they tickled her nose and made her retreat from the glass and giggle. I had orange juice, as even though not officially on duty, I was still in charge of Hetty's welfare.

We ate our meal and chatted about the restaurant, how it was beautifully decorated, with large print wallpaper, plants, and flowers, and watched the birds on the ground outside feeding, and the squirrels jumping from tree to tree.

Hetty had a sweet tooth, so I jokingly said, "You won't want a dessert, will you Hetty?" and pretended to close the menu. Her look at me said it all. I thought she was going to cry because she didn't identify it as a joke. I said quickly, "I'm joking about the dessert, my love. Of course, you can have one. You can even have two if you want," as I felt very guilty.

Predictably, Hetty ordered chocolate sponge and custard, her favourite. I ordered a banana split, which she thought looked very strange. Her glass of champagne didn't last long as she gulped it down like orange squash, but because she hadn't had alcohol before, it made her a little giddy and a little loud. I tried to calm her down, which only lasted for a few minutes at a time. Then out of the blue, a bombshell question hit the room as she asked loudly, "What is masturbation?"

The businessmen next to me nearly choked on their lunch, and the restaurant went still and silent as if waiting for me to answer. Before I could form an answer, she asked, "Do you masturbate too?"

Bang! A double shock. I wanted the ground to swallow me up. My face flushed with embarrassment, and I became tongue-tied and flustered, it was like my life was suddenly in slow motion, and the whole world was watching and waiting for my answer. I could see all these faces staring at me. Eventually, I said in hushed tones, "This is an inappropriate subject to talk about at the dinner table. I will discuss it later with you."

Everybody stared at me, and the group of businessmen broke into laughter. One of them shouted, "Whey, hey! Answer the lady, love. We're dying to know your answer."

Dying of embarrassment, I asked for the bill, paid it as quickly as I could even though my hands didn't seem to work correctly, and dropped the money on the floor. We left the restaurant, still with everyone staring at us, and me looking like a red tomato. Hetty looked bewildered at my actions. She became noticeably quiet, and her old demeanour returned as she thought she had done something wrong.

In the taxi back to the ward, I asked Hetty why she asked me the question about masturbation. She said innocently, "I just wanted to know."

I suppose I should be honoured that she trusted me enough to ask such a question. I told her what it meant, and she became quiet for a few minutes as if digesting my answer, and then asked, "Was it a sin to masturbate? Would God be angry with me?"

I reached for her hand and said, "No, it's not a sin, but it's a very private thing and not a subject for discussion in public."

Hetty seemed happy at my answer and happily chatted about her wonderful day. It was indeed a day I would never forget, and I guess the businessmen dined out on that story for weeks if not years. We arrived back on the ward, and Hetty was so excited to tell the staff of her birthday treat. I had never heard her talk so much. It was lovely to see her happy and engaging with people. I was proud I had gone the extra mile to help her find a bit of normality and happiness in the current world.

UNWELCOME BLAST FROM THE PAST

Steve and I set a date for our wedding in May 1981. We had just over a year to save for the wedding and put a deposit on a house. I worked two to four extra shifts a month and put all the money in the wedding fund. Steve had started a new job as an electrical engineer and lecturer at a local college and paid his lecturing wage into the fund too. Within six months, we had enough deposit for a house. We looked at least ten houses but decided on a house only ten minutes away from both the hospital and college. It was a three-bedroomed semide-tached house built in the 1930s, with big bay windows, it cost just over £12,000.00. It was a neglected house and needed so much doing to it to make it liveable. It needed repointing and painting outside, had no double glazing, no heating, no kitchen, had the original old bathroom, and only floorboards through-out, no carpets at all. Fortunately, Steve was a handyman and could turn his hand to anything.

I moved from the hospital house into the wreck of our house. This saved money as I didn't now pay rent and mortgage, which helped financially toward the restoration of the house.

All we possessed was a three-piece suite, which I was paying off monthly at a local store, a small fan heater, a double bed, and a big crate box that we put a tablecloth on to eat our meals. In those days you didn't use credit, you saved and bought every item bit by bit and saw your house develop over the years. Of course, my mum had collected a bottom draw for me since the age of eighteen. She gave us a kettle and toaster, mugs, bedding, towels, and tea towels. Steve's mum worked for Sheffield Steel and bought us a posh cutlery set. I saved and bought an item at a time of the eternal beau crockery set, which was THE crockery set of the time.

The first thing we bought afterwards was a kitchen from MFI. It had dark brown wood effect units and a hob and oven. Steve built it from scratch, but it frustrated him, as often, some of the bolts and door mechanisms were missing, and we had to go back to the store. We bought brown-tile effect Lino and painted the walls tangerine. Horrid now, when you think about it, but it was the height of fashion at the time.

Next was the lounge, and Steve built a beautiful stone fireplace and units either side for storage. We had a brown and cream wooden armed three-piece suite, and brown and cream carpets to match. Sadly, we still couldn't afford any heating, so the blow heater went from room to room, and we snuggled under a blanket. After decorating these two rooms, we decided to concentrate on the wedding fund. The house would have to stay the same until after we married. It was tough to save because the mortgages were at a remarkably high rate; ours was 16 per cent, which nearly used all my wage for the month. Fortunately, the nurses got a substantial pay rise, which meant we could start saving for central heating. Our wedding present from Steve's mum and dad were the units for the bedroom from MFI, which were white and mirrored, and our bedding and curtains were pale blue and white chintzy flowers. Slowly but surely, we were getting our marital home in order.

A NIGHT STAFF nurse position came up at a psychiatric wing of the local general hospital. It was a bespoke unit, because it was an assessment ward but had a mother and baby unit attached to it for four mothers suffering from severe puerperal depression or psychosis after their babies' birth. I thought what a wonderful experience this would be, and could have more days off with Steve as the work pattern was only four longer shifts on and three days off. I felt guilty for applying for this position as I loved the long stay ward, and adored Hetty and didn't want to leave her, but now she was becoming more independent, she didn't need me as much, and other members of the nursing team took her and other patients out weekly.

Hetty even walked around the grounds to the patient cafe alone. But I would miss her all the same. She was one of my favourite patients whom I was honoured to nurse. I told Hetty I was thinking of going to work on another ward.

She said, "I hope you will continue to visit me sometimes so that we can have coffee together?"

"Of course," I said, "I would, but maybe only a few times a month as I have to sleep in the day."

She looked sad, and I felt guilty, but she hugged me and said, "Okay."

I continued to visit Hetty about twice a month and always on her birthday and Christmas. Hetty gave me one of her drawings, which I treasured, and it took pride of place in a wooden frame in my kitchen, so I could see it when eating my meals.

I WAS QUITE anxious about starting my new job, as it was at a different hospital, with a different environment, and staff, so I took a deep breath and walked up the stairs to the office. The night staff greeted me. Mary was an SEN, and Betty was a nursing assistant, both in their fifties. They were both friendly with a fun personality. They were a bit of a double act, like Morecambe and Wise. I was to be in charge on my first shift, and these two ladies reassured me when Mary said, "Don't worry, Mel, we've got your back; just pay us £20 each and we tell you anything you need to know."

Betty chirped in, "And tell you even more if you make us a cup of tea."

They then shoulder bumped me.

I listened to the handover and took as many notes as I could. On these twenty bedded wards there were only fourteen patients in residence. One included a mother and baby in a single room. I collected the drugs trolly and asked Mary to help me as I didn't know any patients, and they didn't wear wrist bands to identify themselves. So as each patient came for their night medication, I made a mental note who was who.

Anna was a skinny young lady being treated and recovering from Anorexia. Carol was a middle-aged Irish lady with red hair who suffered from severe depression and was a hypochondriac. Cherry was a young lady who suffered from a reactive depression after the death of her father. Roxy was a young lady with a personality disorder and behaviour problems. Sharon was a young lady who suffered from puerperal depression with her baby Tom of ten days old, so the list went on; this was why I loved psychiatric nursing. All the patients presented their illness differently; it affected their thought process and mind.

After the medication round, I looked around the ward to find out where the fire escapes and fire equipment's were positioned. I also observed where all the patients slept in bays of six people. I checked where all the side rooms were, and which ones were occupied. The location of the night station was on the elbow of the ward. It looked down to the bays and left to the side rooms. It was a great observation point.

All the patients were capable of putting themselves to bed, and by midnight they were all tucked up and sleeping, except for one, Roxy. She decided she wanted to sit with me in the night station. Mary had warned me she liked new blood to annoy, and I was to set the boundaries with her, or she would take advantage and misbehave all night.

Roxy started chatting to me and asked, "Where do you live? Why were you sent here? Are you married? Do you have children?" The questioning continued.

I explained to Roxy that I was willing to chat with her for only fifteen minutes. Still, she would have to talk in a whisper as I had to work and didn't want her disturbing the other patients. I preferred for her to go and lay on her bed, even if she couldn't sleep as that was the best place to either, eventually fall asleep or just rest her body.

We chatted for fifteen minutes, and I answered most of her questions without giving too much detail of myself, as I felt she was collecting information to use later. I had no sooner helped Roxy to her bed and sat back at the night station when she shouted for me.

"Oh nurse, new Staff nurse, can you come here, please?"

I walked to her bay and asked what she wanted.

"I want a drink because I'm thirsty, it's the medication."

Hmm, this made me wary as I had fallen for this before when nursing Jennifer. However, she wasn't Jennifer, so I told her I would get her one this time.

"However, in future," I said, "you should get one before going to bed and also take one with you if you got thirsty in the night because I don't want the rest of the patients disturbing. Sleep is a great healer for all patients."

She smiled a sickly-sweet smile and said, "Okay, sorry nurse."

I got her a drink of milk she'd requested from the kitchen. I brought it back and passed it to her. Deliberately, or accidentally on purpose, she let it slip out of her hand and over the bed, knowing that we would now have to change the bed, and for her be the centre of attention again.

"Whoops-a-daisy," she said with a grin on her face.

I didn't let her see any reaction and said, "I will get some clean linen, and you can help me change it, but in silence so as not to disturb the other two patients in the bay."

I stripped the bed. Fortunately, the pillows were dry, and I took the sheets and blanket to the linen room. When I arrived back to the bed with the clean linen, Roxy had disappeared, but I could hear her down by the nurse's station. She was complaining that I spilt the milk on her and what a clumsy idiot I was. It was a good job that it wasn't hot tea, or it might have scalded her. Of course, I didn't rise to her antics, but I thought to myself, *Here we go again, another Jennifer.*

I made her bed, went back to the night station and asked her to go back to bed, which she reluctantly did. Mary said to me, "We're going to be in for one of those nightshifts with her tonight. She's going to test you to the limit, Mel, and try and manipulate you. So be aware because she stores everything you do and say, and will try and use it against you especially if she doesn't get her way."

I was well and truly warned and armed with this information. I made myself and the staff a coffee and settled down to read some notes, so I knew as much as I could about the patients. I decided it best to start with Roxy, seeing as I would have to learn how to handle her, and her behaviour, very quickly.

Roxy had been diagnosed with a personality disorder at the age of eighteen. She had attempted suicide and self-harmed many times, but nothing ever serious. Roxy also had set fire to her mum's house and had been in minor scrapes with the police for drug and alcohol use. She liked being the centre of attention and showed no remorse for her unpredictable and manipulative behaviour. Often, she enhanced and confabulated events to get people in trouble with any authority.

In the past, she had responded well to setting boundaries with behaviour, but not always, it depended on if she liked the nurse or not. She had a total of twenty-two admissions in three years, mainly due to self-harm or suicidal tendencies. She was also prone to allergies from certain foods and non-natural products containing additives. At times, she had deliberately taken or used them to get medical attention because it caused hives or swellings requiring treatment. This admission was due to her taking ten paracetamols and cutting her wrists, but not deep enough to cause a significant bleed or require sutures.

I looked up from the notes and stared at Mary and Betty and said, "Oh God, I'm in for a challenging ride. I think she is going to eat me alive. I nursed someone like this before, and it ended badly for me with a broken finger and bruised boob."

Mary said, "You had better get your battle gear on, girl, and show her you're not a pushover. We have seen it many times; how she loves to misbehave with new staff. Make sure you're not ever alone with her, so you have a witness with everything you say and do because she will try and get you into trouble if she can't get her way."

At 2 am, baby Tom woke for a feed and because his mum was so depressed and could hardly move or take notice of her baby, the nursing staff did the feed in the night so that she got her much-needed sleep.

Betty said, "I think it's your turn, Mel, go and meet little Tom; he's adorable."

I didn't need asking twice because I loved babies. I crept into

Sharon's side bedroom; she was sleeping deeply. Tom stirred and made a whimpering noise and nuzzled at his fist. Betty had made his feed, so I changed his nappy and brought him outside to the nurse's station to feed. He was a hungry baby, not wanting to have a break between mouthfuls, but of course, I did wind him halfway through, which he was not best pleased about. Tom started to cry but did give an enormous burp, so I quickly gave him back his bottle, which he continued to suck until empty. Thankfully, he had fallen asleep, so I burped him again and put him back in his cot without a stir. They were right. He was adorable.

Mary and Betty looked at each other and gave a knowing smile.

"What?" I asked them. "What's the smile for?"

Betty said, "You're next."

"I'm next for what?" I didn't understand.

Betty explained it was apparent, and they could feel it in their waters, that I was broody, and I would be pregnant soon, as they could see that I was a natural with babies.

I laughed and pulled a face at them and said, "You're talking rubbish," but it did make me think that perhaps it was time to think about it. After all, I had been married over a year now, and I did want to start a family. It was a case of discussing when with Steve.

I had just settled down to read more notes when Roxy came down the corridor. She wanted another drink and a cigarette because of being woken by the baby crying.

"Go sit in the day area, and I will get Betty to bring you a cup of tea. You could have a cigarette there, away from the sleeping area." I didn't want to encourage her to sit at the night station all the time. I asked Betty to stay with her until she had finished, as I didn't trust her with the tea or the cigarette in case, she scalded herself or set the room on fire.

The night had passed quickly, and it was now 6 am, just the

notes to write and the day staff would be here at 7 am for handover.

Roxy went back to bed, and Betty washed the mug.

Suddenly, the fire alarm rang. I searched the ward, but there was no evidence of any fire. However, I could see the activated alarm. I collected the handheld patient and staff list for the night and evacuated the ward into the emergency waiting area. I contacted the nursing office to say it looked like a false alarm, but the fire brigade was on their way and still had to come and search for themselves.

It was chaos, getting all the patients outside and doing a roll call with my patient list. They were all present and correct. Roxy was dancing about the corridor and laughing and grinning from ear to ear like a Cheshire cat. I knew it was her who had hit the fire alarm, probably on her way back to bed; it was written all over her face.

"Did you set the alarm off, Roxy?" I asked her.

"Yes, I did," she proudly replied. "I thought my cigarette wasn't out in the ashtray properly, so I thought I had better be safe than sorry and set off the alarm so the fire brigade could check."

It was all a game to her. She was enjoying every moment of excitement, especially the sight of the firemen walking towards us all. Truthfully, I enjoyed the sight of the firemen too.

Two fire engines had arrived, and four firemen searched the ward for fire and gave it the all-clear. Eventually, most of the patients went back to bed. Tom cried for another feed, and a few other patients were in shock. They wanted a cup of tea and a cigarette.

The day staff arrived, and I had to hand over to the morning staff, write the nursing notes, and write a nursing officer report regarding the non-fire. What an eventful, hectic first shift it had been.

I didn't get home until 9 am, thanks to Roxy and her

shenanigans. I was physically and mentally exhausted as I had been awake the total of 24 hours. My bed was calling me. My head throbbed. When my head hit the pillow, I was out like a light.

∾

THE NEXT NIGHT SHIFT, a male SEN joined us called Jay, who also had worked on the ward for a few years, so knew the patients and routine well. At the beginning of the drug round, a horrid blast from the past walked onto the ward. I froze as I saw the tutor that had failed me at my first student nurse assessment, the one who tried to get in my pants. I was shocked and felt uneasy at his presence. What the hell was he doing here on nights?

He asked, "Could I have a word with you in the office?"

I obliged and followed him.

He sat behind the desk where I usually sat as nurse-in-charge. He asked me to sit. I didn't like this feeling or his tone. What was he up to? Why was he here? He stated in a very smug voice, "I'm not a tutor now at the school of nursing, but a night nursing officer for these two units."

My God, my heart sank, I thought I had got rid of this smart arse a few years ago, and now I had to suffer this man again. At that moment, I honestly wished I had stayed on the long stay ward because if I had known he was the nursing officer, I wouldn't have applied for the position. After the initial shock, I pulled my surprised face together and asked, "What do I owe the honour of you visiting me tonight?"

He gleefully replied, "The incident of the fire alarm last night. I want to go through your report with you." He began to read it to me out loud as if I were a child. He continued, "You should have prevented this incident from happening and been

194

more observant of the patients because someone could get injured."

Ahhh! Bless him; he still hated me. It was apparent, and he was going to try and intimidate and humiliate me a second time. I wasn't going to let him phase me, so I just said, "Okay, I will try harder next time." I made no fuss or further explanation. He tried to make a further point of the incident, but I just kept quiet and smiled and nodded. I wasn't going to give him the satisfaction of lording it over me. He thought he could get the better of me, but sadly not. I wasn't afraid of him anymore, and that was his only weapon to attack me. FEAR. He left the ward a bit disgruntled that he hadn't upset me, but I knew in my heart that this feud wasn't over, which worried me a lot. I questioned whether I wanted to continue working on the ward, but time would tell.

AFTER THE PATIENTS were in bed, and we were sitting in the night station, the only patient up and about was Roxy. She was trying to flirt with Jay, but he was like Teflon man. He just deflected every advance; this displeased her a lot. We gave each other a knowing look because we were in no doubt, she would start being mischievous as the day staff had allowed her to sleep on her bed most of the day. Which meant she was now raring to cause problems.

I thought to myself, *How can you prevent this from escalating into another drama?* I could try reverse psychology, that might throw her emotionally off-balance. I said, "Roxy, are you off to bed now?"

She said, "NO!" with her usual stroppy attitude.

"Oh good," I said, "come and join me for a cup of tea before you go to bed and tell me about your day."

Her face was a picture, for once I had her hopping on the

back foot as she wasn't used to someone having the upper hand and taking control.

We chatted for a while, and I thanked her for quietly talking and not waking the other patients. You could tell she was very suspicious of me and didn't know how to handle my reverse psychology. She decided to take herself off to bed within twenty minutes. What a positive result, or so I thought.

Baby Tom woke for his feed right on time 2 am. His mum stirred a little, so I asked her if she wanted to feed him herself. However, she declined and said, "I'm too tired," and turned over and put the bed covers over her head.

I changed Baby Tom, he had a right pair of lungs on him now and was sucking his fists and screaming frantically. I put the bottle into his mouth and he began to suck the hell out of the bottle. He had such strength and was reluctant, halfway through again, to let go and screamed until he burped and could get the milk back in his mouth. After he finished and burped again, he was still wide awake, though content, and looking around the ward. What a little darling he was. I walked up and down the ward's outer corridor and sung *hush little baby, don't you cry*. Eventually, he fell asleep in my arms. I could've put him back in his cot, but I just wanted to snuggle with him all night. I just loved the smell of babies.

At 4 am, Jay did the observation round. All the patients were asleep, so out came the knitting for Mary and Betty, and Jay his book, but I got stuck into some more patient notes.

As I began to read, a hell of a commotion and screams came from the second sleeping bay. Of course, I instantly thought it was Roxy. However, when I pulled the outer curtain to see inside the bay, Carol was crying and trying to squeeze her head out of the window, but it only opened about six inches to prevent patients from trying to jump. When she saw me, she ran towards me, straight in for a cuddle. I cuddled her back and said, "Come on, love, let's go and have a chat in the day area and have a cuppa."

She nodded and followed me to the kitchen while I made two mugs of tea and walked her to the day area. Carol sat sobbing but didn't speak for at least five minutes. I said, "You get your emotions out, love. It's okay. You can tell me what's bothering you when you're ready."

Jay came and asked, "Is it okay for us to carry on with the rest of the duties for the other patients?"

I gave the go-ahead.

After about ten minutes, Carol stopped crying and started to open up about how she was feeling. She said she knew that everyone thought she was a hypochondriac, but it wasn't true. Carol said, "I know I have cancer of the stomach, but nobody believes me. It is so painful to my heart and mind that everyone thinks that I'm just a nutter. I'm so depressed." She began to cry again, "Nobody takes me seriously; my husband and family think I'm a nutter, my GP must think I'm a nutter, too, because he sent me here."

I asked Carol, "What are the symptoms you have, which concern you that you might have stomach cancer?"

She said, "I feel nauseous after eating and have a strange pain in my bloated stomach all the time, especially after I have eaten." She wiped her nose on a tissue I gave her, then said, "I feel tired and weary most of the time, and have lost about a stone in weight in just a few months without even trying to diet." She began to cry again and shouted, "Why doesn't anyone believe me; I know I have cancer!" She was very frustrated.

I held on to Carol's hand to comfort her and asked, "Have you had any tests arranged to see if you have cancer?"

"No," she replied. "Because nobody takes me seriously or believes me. This week on the ward, the medical staff were evaluating my mental health, not any physical health."

I said, "Okay Carol, so why don't you ask the ward doctor

tomorrow morning if you could have tests to confirm whether or not you have stomach cancer?"

Carol was pleased with my idea but was concerned that her husband wouldn't like her doing that because he always said she made a fuss about nothing.

"It's up to you," I told her, "but maybe finding out if you have cancer would help you either concentrate on your depression or fight the battle of cancer."

After drinking her tea and chatting about her family, she went back to bed. She felt a bit more positive at her plan for the next day.

Before I knew it, it was time to recheck the patients, write the nursing notes and get ready for the hand over to the morning staff.

MY BED WAS CALLING me again, would I ever get used to nights?

At home by 7.45 am, I had a glass of milk and snuggled into Steve for fifteen minutes before he got up for work. Our phone rang. Who the hell could this be, calling us so early? I answered it. It was the staff nurse I had handed over duties to. She asked, "Do you still have the drug trolly keys?"

Shit, I thought. I didn't remember handing them over to her. I looked in my uniform pocket, and there they were. So, Steve had to get up and take me on the ten-minute journey back to the ward. Once again, it was 9 am before I got back to my bed.

A few weeks went by, and I was beginning to get used to the ward and patients. Sadly, Carol's results confirmed she did, in fact, have stomach cancer, and was transferred to an oncology ward for treatment. Plus, we had some new patients, including a new mother and baby, Donna, and baby Charlotte, which she liked to call Lottie. She had puerperal psychosis. Donna believed the baby was her reincarnated grandma who had died only three months before her baby was born, and her real baby Lottie had either died at birth or had been hidden somewhere by her grandma. She was incredibly angry with Lottie, so she always had to be supervised as one-to-one. In case she injured the baby or herself.

Little Lottie was a sweet, tiny baby and weighed only six pounds at birth five days before. She was feeding about every three hours, which took a lot of time with the staff to supervise Donna, as she was still breastfeeding because she thought it would bring her daughter back. Fortunately, she had not been prescribed medication that would prevent her from breastfeeding. During the night shifts, Donna expressed her milk for the two feeds — 1 am, and 4 am, but she would feed Lottie the 10 pm, and the 7 am feed. She called her baby Grandma Lottie when she spoke to her and said, "I know you're hiding my baby; you must tell me where she is. Is she still alive?" When Lottie didn't answer, she'd become angry and would pass the baby to a nurse and storm out the room.

I'm not sure that new babies should be on a psychiatric unit with other psychiatric patients, because of the possibility of vulnerability, neglect or injury, but understand that it's best to keep mother and baby together to ensure that the bond is still there for both of them. I'd prefer just a small unit precisely for this type of illness. Still, because of the rarity of the severity of this illness, there are very few cases requiring hospitalisation. Therefore, it wouldn't be financially feasible. Our ward did its best for mother and baby. Plus of course, it was lovely for the nurses to get cuddles from the babies too.

One-night, Roxy was up and refusing to go to bed, so I told her to sit with me for a while because she was disturbing the other patients. She was very talkative and loud. I told her I was too busy to talk to her for long because I needed to catch up on nursing notes but didn't mind her joining me for five minutes if she spoke quietly. My hands used to get very dry and rough from washing them in Hibiscrub, an antiseptic wash, so I brought in my new Dior hand cream that Steve had bought me. It smelt gorgeous and made my hands soft and smooth. I applied some cream onto my hands, and Roxy eyed it up and asked if she could use it.

"No," I said for two reasons. One, it was my hand cream, and I didn't want to share it with anyone as it was too expensive and a present from Steve, and two, Roxy had allergies to additives and unnatural products, and I didn't want to cause her any problems because it was perfumed.

Well, you would have thought I had said no to her ever-eating chocolate again, the way she kicked off. She jumped up and overturned her chair, shouted at me and said, "How selfish of you."

I explained again in a calm manner that it was best only to use products prescribed by the doctor because of her allergies, as my hand cream had perfume in it. She ran off the ward and knocked everything in sight onto the floor like chairs, mugs, and pictures off the wall. I ran after her, but I had to stop for a few seconds to hand the ward keys over and tell the other staff what happened; she had gone when I got outside. Oh God, this meant that I would have to phone the police to find her as a vulnerable adult. I waited outside for a further five minutes and called her name. A porter passed by in his buggy. He told me he had seen her sitting on a bench near the entrance to the hospital. I walked over to her and sat beside her. It was 1 am on a freezing, winter morning. Neither of us had a coat or jumper and were both visibly shivering. I said, "Come on, Roxy, we're going to catch our death of cold out here, surely the hand cream is not worth dying for?"

She shrugged her shoulders, but within seconds agreed to come back with me to the ward, for some hot chocolate I had promised. I would have preferred a hot toddy made with brandy because my teeth were chattering so much, and my goosebumps now had goosebumps. I was so cold.

Back on the ward, Roxy drank her hot chocolate and stated at great lengths how cruel I was for not letting her use my hand cream. It was like conversing with a two-year-old as I tried to get her to understand. I just kept reinforcing that it was for the best, and it was because I cared about her, as I would hate her to have a bad reaction, and that was my final decision. But she wasn't listening. She went on and on in the hope I would change my mind. I stood firm and said, "No. Right, Roxy, it is 2.30 am. I have things to do, and I think it's past your bedtime."

Surprisingly and reluctantly, she went to bed, and we didn't hear a thing from her all night. I wrote in her notes about the incident and handed it over to the morning staff. I also made sure I double-checked I had handed over the drugs trolly keys.

The next night shift, I was greeted at the entrance to the ward by the nursing officer. His face was like thunder. "You had better come to my office," he said and walked off, expecting me to follow him into his office. "Sit," he said like I was like a puppy at Crufts in the obedience section. "Well, Staff nurse, you sure like to cause trouble."

What the hell was he talking about, or was it the fact the Roxy had a hissy fit because she couldn't use my hand cream? I was right. Roxy had made a formal complaint, which he had decided to deal with personally. No surprise there. Roxy had stated that her hands were dehydrated and she had asked to use my hand cream. I was horrid to her, allegedly, and stated I would never let her use anything of mine because I didn't like her, yet I let other patients use it.

I was shocked at her version of events and said, "No, that wasn't how it happened."

Unfortunately, he didn't want to listen to my side of the story. He just wanted to belittle me and have the last word. So, I kept quiet and listened.

"Next time," he said, "let Roxy use the hand cream instead of deliberately upsetting her."

Indignant I said, "It's my private property, for my use only, and she shouldn't use it because—"

He interrupted, "Just do it, so as not to cause any more problems on the ward."

I was about to tell him of her allergies, but he was too busy delivering his ritual humiliation. I left the office, fuming that Roxy had lied, and he had taken her side. He hadn't done any research into her past behaviour of deliberately getting people into trouble with false allegations, or that she had allergies. She went and flirted with him, and he was taken in by it, plus because it was me, she'd reported, he must have thought it was revenge on a plate for rebuffing his advances all those years before.

Mary and Betty were worried about me as they could see that I was visibly upset. I told them what had happened, and they, too, were angry at Roxy's behaviour of blatant lies, though even more angry at his attitude towards me. They couldn't understand why he was like it with me, as they had known him for a year, and they had never witnessed him like it before. Well, that was until I told them about the history between us. Then it became crystal clear why he was behaving in that manner towards me.

I walked out of the ward office to the night station to sit and have my coffee and a few deep breaths, as Jay was doing the drug round, and Betty and Mary were helping patients to bed. Then to make my night perfect, up flounced Roxy. She smirked and laughed, then stated that the nursing officer had told her she could use my hand cream whenever she liked.

I just replied, "Did he, now?" and continued drinking my coffee.

Roxy then had the cheek to pick up my handbag and take the

hand cream out of my bag. She laughed and twirled around, taunting me with it.

Honestly, I don't know how I kept my temper, because it was not the first time tonight that I was bloody fuming. I just sat and watched Roxy, she thought I would react, but I surprisingly didn't. She opened the cream and pushed out a large blob of cream on her hands and threw the lid and tube onto the desk. She proceeded to rub the cream into her hands, doing a little dance as if to taunt me.

I retrieved my cream and put it back into my handbag and continued drinking my coffee. I could see that Roxy was expecting me to go crazy at her behaviour, so she taunted some more. She said, "How soft and sexy my hands feel."

I still just sipped my drink and didn't respond to her antics. She then looked a bit embarrassed and awkward about her behaviour because I didn't respond, and decided to flounce off as quickly as she'd come up the corridor back to her bed.

I went back to the office and phoned Steve at home. I broke down and cried, telling him what had happened. "I've had enough of her and the nursing officer," I concluded. "I want to hand my notice in."

"Keep calm," Steve said, "and don't let Roxy or the nursing officer get to you."

After five minutes of talking to him, I felt better, and all my frustration and anger had gone. I wasn't going to let them get to me, no matter what they did to annoy me.

The rest of the shift was reasonably uneventful until Roxy got up for the loo and said after she had washed her hands that they were dry again, and with a smirk on her face, took the hand cream off the desk, without permission, and used it again.

I just let her because I knew she wanted to get me in more trouble by reacting. However, I swear you could see the smoke billowing from my ears from anger and frustration. It was taking all my nursing skills to keep calm.

Roxy went back to bed, and thankfully it was nearly time for me to go home. When I got outside the ward, Betty and Mary gave me a big hug and said, "My God, Mel, you handled her brilliantly, don't forget we have your back."

I arrived home and snuggled into Steve's arms and cried my eyes out. It had been a hell of a night; I didn't sleep well, and I couldn't get the events of that night out of my head. I was dreading going to work the next shift because my enthusiasm for nursing and making a difference in patients' lives had been well and truly knocked out of me. I usually tried to go the extra mile to ensure patients felt secure and genuinely cared for. I felt sick and lightheaded, but I still went to work the next night.

I entered the unit and was pleased that Mr High and mighty wasn't there to greet me or tell me off at the door, so that was a bonus. I arrived on the ward, where they informed me that Roxy had an allergic reaction on her hands from my hand cream. Her hands had swollen with small blisters, and she'd had to be seen by the doctor.

Roxy couldn't wait to show me what my hand cream had done, as if it were my fault!

Nevertheless, I said, "Oh, how dreadful for you, Roxy. They look painful," I shook my head sorrowfully. "I bet you had wished you had listened to me now, and not used MY hand cream. If you had, they wouldn't be in this mess, would they?"

Surprisingly, she agreed with me and said, "Sorry, you were right," and started to cry.

I could see she was remorseful and in a lot of distress, so I sat with her and put my arm around her to comfort her. She had been prescribed antihistamine tablets and antibiotic cream to prevent infection as some of the small blisters had popped. She also had analgesics for the pain as, at this stage, she couldn't wear a dressing over her hands because it would have caused too much pain when changing it.

I did feel sorry for her because she usually craved attention, drama, and excitement. But now she had a lot of unwanted attention from the nurses, as she couldn't eat by herself or hold a mug so, needed help with feeding. She needed help to go to the toilet and wipe herself, and couldn't wash or dress because her hands were so swollen and blistered. Every aspect of her life had been affected because of one foolish act. I doubt she learned a lesson, though.

Roxy felt sorry for herself and retired to bed much earlier than usual, probably because the antihistamine and analgesic tablets made her sleepy.

Jay and Mary were on duty with me. We were all shocked at the extent of Roxy's allergy and checked on her hourly throughout the night in case of further shock.

The ward seemed incredibly quiet tonight, except when both babies woke simultaneously, so Mary and I fed and changed them, and I gave them a little cuddle. I had big boobs, and I was always hot to the touch, and the babies liked to get snuggled over my chest and shoulders, with their little legs tucked under them. I had one on each side. Tom and Lottie instantly fell fast asleep. It was like my warm boobs drugged them. It was just what I needed too after the last twenty-four hours drama, a little snuggle with two little cuties.

Mary said, "Mel, just look at them. They absolutely love your boobs."

Jay looked up from his book, and dryly said, "I'm pretty fond of Mel's boobs myself."

I burst out laughing, but it made my boobs wobble up and down, wobbling the baby's heads. The more we laughed, the more the babies wobbled. I put them back in their cots quickly before I gave them brain damage. On my return to the night nurses' station, I heard the corridor door open. The man I disliked the most in the world, the arrogant, nursing officer, entered. He seemed quite chatty and full of himself.

He pulled up a chair and said, "Is there any coffee going, Mel?"

"Yes," I said, "there is, but you will have to put into the coffee fund ten pence per mug like the rest of us and make a drink for all four of us."

When I sat down with the coffee, he asked, "How were all the patients tonight?"

"All were okay," I said. "Except for Roxy, of course."

He looked puzzled as he didn't know what had happened since yesterday. I know I shouldn't have, but I took great delight in telling him that I followed his instruction and let Roxy use my hand cream. He smugly said, "Oh, good. I'm glad you took my advice!"

I then continued, "Mmmm, bad advice, I'm afraid, because the poor love has had a severe allergic reaction, which has caused her hands to swell and blister."

His smug smile on his face dropped.

I went on to tell him that I had recorded in Roxy's nursing notes his advice because I was apprehensive, seeing as she was prone to an allergic reaction to certain non-natural products. I also explained that she now needed help with all personal care and feeding until her hands got better. I don't know what made me say the next sentence because it was a blatant lie, but I enjoyed telling him anyway, "Roxy had been looking for you earlier in the evening because of your advice to me, which caused the allergic reaction." I swear he looked pale and sweaty.

He jumped up from his seat, left his un-drunk coffee and made his excuse of being busy and left the ward.

Jay, a man of very few words, looked at me and said, "I think that's one-nil to you, Mel."

I WAS in the middle of having my well-earned three days off but had been feeling sick, and my period was late, so I bought a pregnancy testing kit. Steve and I were going to go on duty for the Red Cross, and he had gone to pick up the ambulance then pick me up from home to go to an event. I peed on the strip and nervously waited. During the few minutes I waited, I remember thinking, *Oh, my God. I could become a mummy in the next few minutes; this next five minutes could change my life forever.* Time was up, and I dare not open my eyes, but slowly I did. Sheer joy filled my heart as I saw the two blue lines indicating pregnant. I screamed and ran around the dining table doing a little jig; Steve arrived twenty minutes later and was shocked at the result. He hugged me and said, "Don't tell anyone just yet, just in case."

It made me cross and deflated because I wanted to shout from the rooftops, I'M HAVING A BABY. But when did I ever take any notice of him anyway? I told everyone except his mum because Steve wanted to tell her the following week, on her sixtieth birthday.

We bought a pretty birthday card and wrote, 'Have a wonderful 60th birthday love from Steven, Melanie and the bump!!!!!!' She opened her card and read it, and looked puzzled at first. We were both smiling at her, so she reread it, and the penny finally dropped. She jumped up off the settee and said, "You're pregnant!" and gave us a huge hug and did a little jig too.

I couldn't wait to get back to work to tell Betty and Mary. After all, it was their waterworks that wished me to be pregnant in the first place. I walked on duty and gave them both a cheeky smile and a wink. Mary looked at Betty, and simultaneously they said, "She's pregnant!"

I grinned even more and said very proudly, holding my belly, "Yes, I am."

They hugged me so much I thought they would squeeze my

baby out of me there and then. Then the instructions came from them both.

"No lifting or getting near anyone if they're aggressive," said Mary.

"If you feel sick or tired, then rest; we will cover for you," Betty chimed in.

"Come on, girls," I protested. "I'm only about six weeks pregnant, so I'm sure I can manage without you two clucking and protecting me just yet."

Betty lightly clipped my ear and said, "You will do as you're told, mummy-to-be, because we're in charge now."

It seemed I couldn't argue with that.

Over the months, I suffered from terrible morning sickness, or should I say martini sickness, as it was any time, any place, anywhere. I felt nauseous at some degree or another at least twenty hours out of my day, and was sick several times a day or night. It seems I wasn't a natural at being pregnant. I would turn up to work feeling dreadful, and sometimes it was impossible to turn up for work at all. I kept thinking it would pass, as most women get this during pregnancy in the first few months, but I was getting worse, with added problems of feeling faint and migraines. I thought it was just me, as I had never heard of anyone else having it as bad as me. The midwife said it was probably just anxiety making me feel so ill. I thought perhaps I was being a bit dramatic and hoped it would pass too. It was only recently that I learned that it's a rare condition, of which the Duchess of Cambridge was diagnosed with the same problem as I, called Hyperemesis gravidarum (HG).

AT FIVE MONTHS PREGNANT, I arrived on my night shift, not feeling too nauseous but was starting with a headache. Unfortunately, by the time I had listened to the handover and chatted to patients, the headache became worse. The ward lights were unbearable, and I could hardly keep my eyes open because of photosensitivity, a horrid migraine was advancing very quickly. Jay and Betty were on duty with me and told me to ring the nursing officer to ask to go home because I was in no fit state to work, and I was getting worse by the minute. I didn't want to, but I knew I had to. I rang him and began to tell him I was feeling very unwell.

He said, "Wait there, I will come to see you on the ward."

I waited in a side room with the lights off and a vomit bowl, and flannel over my head. Five minutes later, he arrived. I heard him ask Jay, "Where is she?" and bustle his way down the corridor to me. He walked in, put the light on and said, "What are you sitting in the dark for?"

How inconsiderate. I put the flannel over my eyes and asked, "Please can you turn the light back off, as I have photosensitivity due to a migraine?"

He then said, "You're only pregnant, woman! There is no need to play it for all its worth."

I was so shocked by his unempathetic manner and the sheer cruelty and uncaring behaviour. After all, he was a nurse, and I seem to remember him lecturing us when I was a student nurse that empathy was the main ingredient of being a good nurse. What was wrong with this man? Surely, the incident of rebuffing his advances as a student still didn't cause problems for him now. It was obvious it was so personal towards me. I then vomited into my bowl and held my head in great pain, as each time I retched, I thought my head would explode. He stood outside until I had finished. "I need to go home now," I said. "Could you organise a taxi for me because I didn't bring money onto the ward?"

His answer was unbelievable, "I will have to try and get a nurse now to cover your bloody shift. That is my main priority, not a taxi for you, so if you want a taxi you will have to sort it out yourself, but I'm telling you now, the staff cannot leave the ward to help you."

He put his head in the air and stomped off the ward. I just sat there feeling vulnerable and shocked at this man's appalling attitude.

Betty rang for a taxi and gave me the money for a taxi too, but because there were only the two of them left on the ward, they could not help me get down the outside corridor and down to the main entrance. I kissed them goodbye and held onto the wall rails to steady myself and slowly through half-opened eyes, walked towards the entrance where the taxi was waiting.

The taxi man got out of the taxi, helped me into the car, and drove slowly to my house. He was extremely kind and concerned about my condition and told me if I needed to stop at any point then to tell him.

I had to knock on our house door as I couldn't see to get the key in the door. Steve answered the door. He was so bewildered at the state of me as I cried. Steve got me a drink of water and put me to bed with my bowl and a clean flannel on my forehead, as whenever I felt sick, the magic, ice-cold flannel always made me feel better. I explained what had happened and how I had been treated by the nursing officer. He was outraged at how the nursing officer had treated me and wanted to get in the car and go and speak to him there and then, or should I say he wanted to go and knock his block off. I told him not to bother because he wasn't worth the drama and he would cowardly deny it anyway, plus I was feeling too ill and frightened to be left alone because the migraine felt like my head would explode into a million pieces. I couldn't take any medications because I was pregnant, so I just drank water and hoped it would pass very soon.

Next morning Steve said, "You're not going back to work; you're going to the GP and going off sick until after the baby is born. I'm not having that bastard upset you anymore, or you might end up losing our baby. How could he be so cruel to a vulnerable, extremely sick, pregnant woman?"

When I visited the GP, I told her how I struggled with severe nausea, fainting and migraines. She immediately became sympathetic and said, "I agree with your husband; you need rest and love for the next few months before the birth of your baby." She then signed me off sick for a month. "Come and see me every week so I can keep an eye on you," she continued. "Plus, if you feel any worse, contact me."

My blood pressure was, unsurprisingly, high.

HE STOLE MY HEART

*A*t just over forty weeks pregnant, I was the size of a house. I carried my baby all at the front. When I sat down, my belly sat on my knees. I had a fifty-inch waist! When I walked, I had to cradle my belly to give it support, as it was difficult. I visited my midwife at the hospital for my weekly tests to find out I had protein in my urine and raised blood pressure. She could see how difficult it was for me to walk and how uncomfortable I was, so she decided it best to admit me into the maternity hospital in case I developed pre-eclampsia.

Once admitted to the ward, I could now rest and put my feet up. At home, I couldn't rest, as I was still looking to clean everything in sight. Thankfully, we had sorted the nursery, and I had my baby clothes all washed and folded in the draws. I had been nesting for the past month. I was ready and waiting for my baby to be born.

My first morning in the hospital, I awoke, and a male student nurse called Mark greeted me. He took my blood pressure and helped me off the bed. Once laid down, I was like a turtle on its back and unable to sit or get up from a lying position. He ran a hot bath with my favourite Fenjel oil. I sat having time to myself for the first time in ages. I laid back and closed my eyes and gently stroked my enormous belly and hummed the song, *Sometimes When We Touch* by Dan Hill.

My baby must have felt me stroking my belly and began to move. It was amazing to watch my glistening belly move from right to left, and up and down. Unexpectedly, I felt a kick on my right side and saw the outline of the baby's foot. I could see the whole footprint embedded next to my skin. I could trace with my finger all its five little toes one by one. It was such a beautiful mummy and baby moment. It was if it knew I was there and singing just for baby. I became very emotional, and tears ran down my cheek. The more I touched its foot, the more it pushed its foot into my hand. Nature could be fantastic at times; this was a beautiful memory I'll take to my grave.

MY DUE DATE, 6th September, came and went, and I still stayed in the hospital. I was still gaining weight, and my belly was now the size of a tanker ship, super enormous, in fact, beyond belief. Everyone asked if I was expecting twins or even triplets. I waddled about the ward and held this great lump of baby, and got breathless at the slightest journey.

I talked to the baby, and said, "Come on little Boo-boo, come and see me today. I'm getting tired and can't wait to meet you." Baby sometimes responded and gave me another kick. The consultant told me that if the baby hadn't tried to be born naturally, then on the 25th of September, they would give me drugs to induce the labour.

Steve asked the midwife if he could take me out for lunch, as it was my twenty-fifth birthday on the 26th of September, so he would like to take me out just for two hours before the induction. The midwife agreed, and Steve took me to the restaurant hotel where we had our wedding reception. How romantic it was that Steve had put a lot of thought into surprising me. But sadly, it wasn't romantic, because I was so uncomfortable, and couldn't eat much and moaned a lot about wanting just to get back to the hospital for a rest. However, I did manage to polish off a glass of champagne before we left.

Steve took me back to the ward within the two hours, he helped me into bed, and within minutes I was sleeping like a baby.

At 8 pm, the baby started to move excessively in my belly, arms and legs pushed my belly in all directions. All night the baby wriggled; I suspected it was getting into position for the big push.

At 6 am, the baby was still and sleeping, thank God. I could then get some well-deserved rest at last, as I had been awake all night.

Mark, the student nurse, came in to see me at 7 am, to take my blood pressure and to see if the baby was now in position. He asked, "Would you mind if I did an internal examination under supervision, as I need to cross it off my training manual?" He shuffled his feet uncomfortably then said, "I thought you would understand because of you being a nurse and how training was essential."

I thought, *Well, it's not like I'm going to see him after this spell in the hospital*, so I agreed to the internal examination.

Mark looked under the sheet and examined me, and said I was about two centimetres dilated, the midwife checked too and agreed.

I just wanted this baby out now. I was feeling battered and bruised and very tired of being pregnant. I was at 40 weeks and nineteen days. Mark suggested I have a nice bath again with my Fenjel oil and said, "Who knows, it might start the labour." So off I waddled after him into the bathroom for my bath. As he held me steady, I lifted my left leg in the bath. I felt a sharp pain, and my waters broke with a woosh. His face was a pure picture of panic, "Oh hell," he said and went to find the midwife. He left me stranded half in and half out the bath.

Mark returned with the midwife who told me to carry on having the bath, and they would arrange for me to go to the birthing suite after my bath. I was frightened as hell, but happy at long last baby was on its way, because I was beginning to think it would come out a toddler it was so late. Mark asked, "Could I be at the birth to help? I haven't watched a birth, and need that part of my training signed off too."

I said, "Okay, the more, the merrier. Perhaps I could sell tickets and make money out of this experience. What do you think, Mark?"

The cheeky bugger said, "Yes, why not. Shall I ring a few friends to join us?"

THEY TOOK me to the birthing suite on a trolley, and wanted to know if I wanted to ring my husband to come in for the birth. I was just about to ring Steve when a nurse said, "I have your husband here, on the phone."

How spooky was that? I thought. The nurse left so I could talk in private. "I had a horrible night," I moaned. "The baby behaved like an alien in my belly and has turned and now in position. Not only that, but my waters also broke, and they are going to induce me." I took a breath and said, "My fanny is throbbing, and I feel I need to pee all the time. I just wish it were all over," and burst into tears because I was frightened and tired.

He said, "Come on, Mary, you will be okay. I will get there as soon as I can, but I have a few things to do before I come to the hospital."

Well, that really pissed me off. I lost it. "What the hell are you talking about? How dare you call me Mary, you know I never use my first name, and what the fuck is more important than being with me at the birth of our baby?"

Steve's reply was not what I expected, he said, "What the hell are you talking about Mary? It's your name. I always call you Mary, have they given you some drugs making you confused?" By now, I was beginning to lose my temper with him. He often tormented me, thinking he was funny, but this wasn't the time or place to do it today. Steve was taking the joke too far. He then said, "Okay, love, keep calm. I will feed the cat and be there as soon as I can."

"What Fucking cat? We don't have a cat."

Steve said, "I think you're confused, love. I'm worried about you."

Time stood still for a moment, then I asked, "Who is this?"

He said, "It's Steven, Steven Barker, your husband."

Shit! I was talking to the wrong man. My Steve was Steven Baker, not Steven Barker. I didn't realise it wasn't even his voice in all this confusion. We both realised the misunderstanding when I said, "I'm Mary Melanie Baker, not your wife."

We then laughed and apologised to each other.

The midwife had only got the wrong husband when she handed the phone to me. How ironic; his wife was called Mary, and my first name was Mary, a name I had never used.

I then rang my Steve and told him to come to the hospital because they would be starting induction in the next hour.

Steve arrived as they hooked the drug up to induce my labour. I was quite excited but terrified at the same time. However, I knew that millions of women went through this process daily. I thought, *With pain relief, surely it can't be that bad, and even if it was, it's only the last few minutes until you hold your baby.* How naive was I?

Mark, the student nurse, introduced himself to Steve and asked if it were okay with him if he could stay for the birth. Of course, Steve agreed.

At first, nothing seemed to happen, the labour didn't seem to progress much, so they increased the medication, and very slightly I felt some discomfort in my back. I fell asleep for a few hours as I was already exhausted from the night before. Steve and Mark got on like a house on fire. They supported the same football team and chatted about every game known to man.

Two hours later, Mark woke me and asked once again to take my blood pressure and do an internal examination to see how I was progressing. Blood pressure was on the high level of normal, and in three hours, I had only dilated to three centimetres. God, it was going to be a long day. For some reason, they wouldn't let me eat, but I could have sips of water or suck on a sponge which tasted horrid.

By now it was 2 pm. Steve went to get a little lunch and left me with Mark. He was a lovely young man, nearly twenty years of age, just starting his second-year training to be a general nurse; this was his three-month placement on maternity.

Mark was enjoying it so far but was more interested in my psychiatric nursing, and what it involved, as the following year, Mark would have his psychiatric placement. He was surprised that I had knowledge of most medical illnesses and was embarrassed that he hadn't realised that psychiatric patients had medical ailments.

The consultant came in to see me at 5 pm and said, "I think you have a lazy baby in there, Mrs Baker, who is quite happy to stay inside, so I'm turning up the drip and increasing the dose to see if we can jolly things along." He gave me another internal examination and seemed much heavier handed as if encouraging the baby to find the route out, it was quite painful. However, after twenty minutes, the contractions started. They also offered me an epidural to help with the pain. It was bearable but beginning to make me wince. Thankfully, only every fifteen or so minutes.

Mark should have gone home off duty at 4 pm but wanted to

be with me at the birth, hopefully in the next few hours so that he could observe and help. He decided to work a double shift and take the day off the following day. That was okay with me, as we were beginning to get to know each other, and I liked having the same nurse with me for support, alongside my Steve.

At 8 pm, I was still only five centimetres, and the contractions were coming every ten minutes but not really any more robustly. The midwife spoke with the consultant, and they decided to put me up to full strength in the hope that would do the trick. I was tired and weary, and so bloody hungry. I fantasised about the largest bacon sandwich ever, covered in brown sauce in a huge bread roll. Unfortunately, they still said no food; in case I needed a section. I could only have sips of water or suck on that tiny disgusting sponge.

By 10 pm I was seven centimetres, and the contractions had increased to every five minutes. God, it was horrific now, I was in so much pain. At 11.30 pm Mark was tired, he had been on duty since 7 am and was sad he couldn't stay any longer. I was sad to lose him too. However, at the rate I was going, it would be next week before I gave birth. I had been in labour at one stage or another for nearly seventeen hours. I sadly said goodbye to Mark. At midnight, Steve burst into song and sung, *Happy Birthday to You*. I had forgotten it was my birthday. It looked like my baby was going to be born on my twenty fifth birthday. What an honour.

I was so emotional I burst into tears yet again.

At 2 am, I was still at seven centimetres, and contractions were every minute and lasted for forty-five seconds. The epidural was topped up but didn't numb my groin area. My legs I couldn't feel at all. The pain was way above what I thought it would be.

I had gas and air for every contraction, but the fifteen seconds in between meant I had hardly time to catch a breath before the next wave of pain came.

The consultant decided that the baby might be in danger, and a section was now the only answer. I was terrified as I had never had an anaesthetic before. The nursing staff and doctors went to the theatre next door to prepare.

I held Steve's hand and said, "I don't want a section. I just want our baby out." The next contraction came, I sucked on the gas and air and pushed as hard as possible. When the nurses returned a few minutes later, I was now crowning, and all hell broke loose in the birthing suite. They lifted my left leg onto Steve's shoulder and said, "Push on the next contraction." It came, and I pushed, and they gave me an episiotomy. I screamed, but the next contraction was here, and I had to push again.

They placed my hands on the baby's head; it felt like a wet soggy sponge.

Steve said, "My God, I can see a full head of black hair."

The nurse explained that the baby would be out at the next push, so I had to give it everything I had. The contraction came. I gave it everything I could, and seconds later, at 2.50 am, a baby with a cone-shaped head came out of me.

Steve burst into tears and said, "It's a boy!" and kissed me.

They placed my baby boy on my breast, and he nuzzled instantly. Thankfully, his head went into normal shape within seconds, and these two beautiful eyes stared up at me, while his tiny hand wrapped around my little finger.

They cut the cord and took my baby boy to weigh him. Good God, he weighed ten pounds exactly, no wonder he had difficulty getting out a small hole, and no wonder it smarted a bit. They wrapped him in a blanket and passed him to Steve. At that moment, we were a family, a mum, a dad, and a baby boy. I have a photograph of that very moment, of which I treasure.

The nurse said, "What do you want to call your baby?"

We had decided on either Lewis or Adrian. The midwife

looked at me and said, "I hope it's not Lewis because they might call him loo brush at school."

So, our beautiful baby boy was called Adrian.

People told me a mother's love is unique, but I wasn't prepared for him at a second old, stealing my heart. I was in total love. To this day, I have the same love and love to smell his Adrian uniqueness.

FROZEN REVENGE OF THE BASTARD

*A*fter six days as an in-patient, they discharged me from the hospital. Steve picked me up to take me to his mum and dads. I have never seen him drive so slowly. It was like we were transporting a fine piece of precious porcelain, not a baby. We didn't go home because we had to collect our springer spaniel, Ben, from Steve's parents. We also thought it best to introduce the dog to Adrian on neutral territory.

Ben had been very protective of me when I was pregnant, and he laid beside me throughout my pregnancy. When I felt sick or in pain, he would put his head on my belly and never left my side. Ben followed me everywhere. If Adrian, inside my belly, kicked he would jump up and run to get Steve to tell him to come quick, he was so sweet.

When we walked into the lounge of Steve's parents, I could see Ben was so excited to see me. I had been in hospital for nearly a month. He wagged his tail so much I thought it would send him airborne. I crouched down beside him and held Adrian in my arms so he could smell him. In his excitement, he nipped Adrian's leg while smelling and nibbling.

Adrian screamed, and Steve grabbed hold of Ben, afraid that Ben had bitten him.

I said, "It's not because he's rejecting Adrian; it's because he's enthusiastic at wanting to get to know him."

I decided to place Adrian on the fluffy rug on the lounge floor and bravely let Ben smell him. His little tail wagged like a helicopter blade, his nose smelt every part of Adrian as he nuzzled and investigated gently with his teeth and tongue. After a minute of investigation, he laid beside Adrian and snuggled in, put his head on Adrian's belly and fell asleep. That was it. They bonded.

I WOULD RETURN to work after six week's maternity leave, so I had a further five weeks to enjoy Adrian at home without distraction. Steve took a few days off work, too, so we could bond as a family. I hadn't realised how exciting a new baby was, not only for us but for everyone else. The phone and doorbell always rang, and friends and family came and went.

Our lounge resembled a florist and baby shop.

One afternoon, I sat, breastfeeding Adrian. The back door flew open and in walked Howard, our next-door neighbour. He came straight towards me and didn't give me time to cover up my breast. He stood, bent over me with his hands on his hips, and watched Adrian devour his milk. I was shocked at his intrusion.

Howard said, "Oh my God, nature is bloody marvellous don't you think? How a mother has the equipment to feed her baby, and a baby instinctively knows what to do. It's marvellous, bloody well marvellous."

I began to laugh and said, "Howard, are you enjoying the view?"

He looked down at my breast, and said, "Yes, it's beautiful

what nature creates," then realised he had intruded, and I had my boob out. "Oh, shit! Sorry Mel, it never occurred to me, that you might be uncomfortable when breastfeeding," and turned his back to me with a blush.

"Don't worry, Howard. You've seen it all now. Want a cuppa?"

He sat in the chair, genuinely mesmerised at nature.

I felt comfortable, as I could see he wasn't a pervert catching a crafty glimpse of a boob, just a guy in awe of nature.

The next day, we needed to go to the supermarket to do a big shop, as Steve had lived off sandwiches and takeaways while I was in the hospital. We also had a new American style fridge freezer with drinks dispenser for the kitchen delivered, which needed filling.

It was a present to myself because I had health insurance that paid out twenty Pounds per night when I was in the hospital, which came to the grand total of five hundred Pounds for the twenty-five days I was in the hospital. I hated being in hospital all that time, but this made all the suffering worth it, what a bonus!

However, the biggest reason was I wanted to show my new baby off to the world in his new purple corduroy pram.

We didn't get far down any of the aisles in the supermarket as everyone stopped us to stare at a new baby. They all asked the same questions. Is it a boy or a girl? How old is he? How much did he weigh? It seemed that this was the standard meet and greet of a new-born baby.

As we approached the freezer aisle, I noticed in front of me a person who I dreaded to see: the nursing officer, the nasty unempathetic bastard. I hadn't seen him since the night I left the ward with a migraine. I stood dead still in fright as he was only a few yards in front of me, rummaging in a large chest freezer. He was small in stature and had to go on his tiptoes to reach to the back of it.

I nudged Steve and said, "Look, it's the Bastard, let's go home. I don't want him to see me or even look at our baby because he will pretend to be happy for us and nice in front of you. I don't want to give him the satisfaction of trying to be superior."

Steve exactly knew who he was and saw red. Before I could stop him, Steve walked up behind him as he reached in the back of the chest freezer again, and lifted his legs, tipped him into the freezer and put the lid on his head. Outside the freezer, his little legs wriggled like two hand puppets. He struggled to get out and shouted for help.

Steve bent over and shouted sarcastically in his ear at full volume, "That's for being a total bastard to my wife, you big bully! Enjoy the rest of your shopping."

I was shocked at what Steve did, but found it so incredibly funny, and nearly peed myself laughing.

A fellow shopper helped the Bastard out of the freezer. He looked across at us, shocked, as he didn't know who Steve was, or why it had happened until he saw me. He then recognised Steve. The Bastard knew what a lucky escape he had, as he could see that Steve was twice as big as him. I think by rights, Steve should have done far worse to him, and believe me he genuinely wanted to, but Steve wasn't an aggressive man.

The Bastard brushed himself down and left his full shopping trolley in the middle of the aisle. He looked very red-faced, either with temper or embarrassment or both, and walked out of the supermarket without giving me a second glance.

I said, "Thanks Steve, you have now made it impossible for me to return to that unit ever again."

Steve replied, "No love, he made it impossible for you to go back to that ward ever again because of his disgraceful bullying behaviour towards you."

Whoever's fault it was they had done me a favour because I

was dreading going back, and there were plenty of staff nurse positions available within the hospital trust for me to choose.

The following day, I contacted the nursing director and told him I wanted to expand my knowledge, move to a different ward, and reduce my hours to three nights per week because I had just given birth to a baby. He congratulated me and said, "Leave it with me, blondie, and I will get back to you." He had always called me blondie from the first week he met me as a new student nurse unless he was speaking to me regarding official business.

I didn't tell him the real reasons I wanted to move, because in those days, they would class you as an outcast or troublemaker and nobody would want to work with you, and it could affect promotional prospects for the future. It was a case of shut up and move on and hopefully never work with that horrid man again.

The nursing director phoned me back within a few hours and offered me a position for three nights shifts a week on a mixed-sex geriatric assessment ward at the Northern General. This ward was not in the new psychiatric building that I had worked in, but a building in the hospital that was an old workhouse in Victorian times. I accepted verbally and awaited the confirmation letter.

SUPERNATURAL ENCOUNTERS

$\mathcal{M}$y first shift after Adrian was born was very emotional. I kissed him night-night and walked out the front door, crying. I got to my car overwhelmed with emotion and felt I couldn't go to work and leave my baby, so I ran back in through the back door. I cuddled him and tried to leave again but did the same thing and came back and cuddled him again. I was heartbroken and told Steve, "I can't leave him. I just can't do it; I don't want to work anymore."

Steve stood from his chair and said, "I understand love, it must be hard as a new Mummy, but if you don't go back to work, love, we can't afford the mortgage, and we will lose the house and become homeless."

I realised he was right, but I honestly didn't want to leave Adrian. He was my little Boo-boo, who I loved so much. I never even had an hour away from him since birth. Even when I suffered from viral meningitis and was sent to the hospital when Adrian was only ten days old, I refused to leave the house to be admitted to the hospital without him by my side. After the third attempt at leaving, I got in the car and drove to the hospital in floods of tears.

As soon as I arrived on the ward, I rang home to see if Adrian was okay. Steve didn't answer the phone at first, nor the second time I phoned him. I became even more anxious and thought something horrid had happened to Adrian. I rang a third time, and Steve answered the phone, all flustered.

I heard Adrian screaming in the background. "What's the matter with him? What's wrong?" I asked in a panic.

Steve said, "It's you, you're the problem, bloody phoning us in the middle of his feed. I've had to lay him in the cot to answer the phone, now stop worrying and stop phoning. He's okay, we will see you in the morning." Steve put the phone down.

I felt such a fool and told myself, *Try not to worry, he's in safe hands, just get on with your job.*

I introduced myself to the night staff; two nursing assistants called Jo and Carol. They seemed friendly and told me to just follow the routine with them as they washed and got all twenty-four patients into nightwear and in their beds. This task wasn't easy, as the patients were on the lower floor in the daytime and had to get in the lift, five patients at a time with one staff member, to the upper floor at night where the bedrooms were situated.

One staff member stayed with the other patient's downstairs, and the third member of staff ran up and down the stairs to greet the lift and help the patients wash and get ready for bed. I volunteered to do the running up and down the stairs as I had a bit of baby weight to shift, and I was the youngest out of the three of us.

My God, by the end of the hour, I was shattered, and my legs were aching like hell. I wish they had invented Fit-bit watches back then. I swear it would have vibrated off my arm and told me to sit down for a rest.

We collected all the patient's false teeth and soaked and cleaned them, then placed their denture pots on the top of their locker.

By midnight all the patients were asleep, and we could have our first cup of tea of the night. The night nurses station separated the male and female sleeping areas; this meant we could see all patients right and left of us.

Carol was a lady in her early thirties, married with two little girls. Jo was a lady in her early forties with teenage children. They both had worked as nursing assistants for five years and were keen to learn all about my new baby. As usual, like most women, they became very broody, just by looking at the endless photos I had of him in my handbag.

IT WAS QUITE A SPOOKY WARD, noises, and bumps throughout the night, and I could see why they insisted on keeping a small lamp alight on the corridor where we sat, as well as the night lights. I didn't like the set-up of the ward. The nursing office on the ground floor housed the files and drugs trolly, which meant I was up and down the stairs all night, to administer drugs or write notes.

I hated going downstairs alone. It seemed very scary. I could see the reflection of trees blowing through the windows. I had a strange feeling. It was as if someone was watching me. I guess it kept me fit as I did everything in record time, so I could get back upstairs where the other nurses worked quickly.

After my first month, I arranged to have a meeting with the charge nurse at 9 pm to ask for some changes for the night nurses. I wanted a mobile notes trolly to put the nursing notes in as we carried them up and down the stairs a few at a time to write in them during the night, as I wasn't going to sit downstairs alone because it scared the shit out of me. The charge nurse fully understood as he had done a few nightshifts himself to assess the night staff only a few weeks before.

He stated, "I had the same problem and was even more scared of the dark than you."

He ordered a trolley that we could easily transport up and down the floors in the lift.

I requested that the linen room be moved to a room upstairs. "After all," I said, "that's where the beds are."

He agreed to sort my valid requests for my next shift.

One of the main reasons I had asked to see him was about what happened at 3 am every night. The lift seemed to have a mind of its own. At 3 am, it would click into action, travel to the ground floor from the first floor then make its way back to the first floor, and yet it appeared to have no one operating it. I wanted maintenance to assess if there was a mechanical problem. I didn't want to listen to the night staff telling me their stories about a friendly ghost.

The charge nurse said, "The same thing had happened when I worked a few nights but thought maybe someone was messing with my head to scare me."

I honestly hoped that that was the case, that someone was playing a prank on us, as the thought of a ghost freaked me out, even though I didn't believe in ghosts.

When I next arrived for my shift, I received the engineer's report, who stated that the lift engineers couldn't find any obvious problem. However, they had serviced it anyway, so hopefully, the lift would behave itself tonight.

A young, third-year student nurse called Sarah joined us on the ward. She was a bubbly, confident student nurse, and didn't need supervision to provide personal care, as she had passed her patient care assessment.

After drinking a cup of coffee, I asked Sarah to collect the patients' false teeth for cleaning. She was to bring them to the bathroom. She returned about ten minutes later, with all the twenty-four pairs of patients' teeth. I nearly died on the spot when I saw all the teeth on a tray in a big bowl. She had only gone and taken them out of their denture pots and put them in a big bowl, so it was easier for carrying.

"What have you done, Sarah?" I asked her.

Confidently she said, "I've collected the teeth, as you asked so that we can clean them."

I could see she had no idea what she had done wrong. I said, "Yes, I asked you to bring the teeth for cleaning, but normally, you bring them in their individual denture pots."

She replied, "Well, I thought it was quicker and easier to carry in the big bowl."

I replied, "So you think it was quicker and easier, do you, Sarah?"

"Yes," she said, still feeling confident. I was sadly about to knock that smile right off her lovely face.

"Sarah, I don't know how to say this, but how do you know which patients' teeth are which? Are they marked with their names?"

Her smile faded, and her expression changed to shock and fear as the penny dropped, "Oh, shit!" Tears brimmed in her eyes.

I started to laugh and said, "Well, we are in for a hell of a night after we have cleaned them all."

"What do you mean?"

"We're going to have to try them in all the patients' mouths until we find the right pair for the right patient."

She put the bowl of teeth on the side and sat with her head in her hands. "I'm so sorry, how could I be so stupid?"

Eventually, she did see the funny side and started to belly laugh.

I couldn't believe that all the patients wore false teeth. Usually, there were a few that still have some teeth of their own. Unfortunately, not tonight, we had a lot to do.

After cleaning them all, we put some of the teeth on top of each other. It was as if they naturally paired, so we put those to one side. We put large sets of teeth together for the men, as we logically thought that men had larger mouths. While smaller teeth for the women. We tried to colour-match them too.

We discovered there was a problem. Somehow, we had twenty-five sets of teeth, and only had twenty-four patients, so someone must have brought two sets of teeth into the hospital with them. We had one lucky pair of teeth which had A. Brown printed on the top and bottom set, so we spared Mr Albert Brown the humiliation of trying teeth.

We hysterically laughed as we didn't want to start the job of asking the confused, and demented patients to try some teeth. It was like trying to do a thousand-piece jigsaw blindfolded.

We started at the men's dormitory and told them we had brought them a drink. We gave them a sip of water, then looked in their mouth and tried a pair of teeth that we thought would fit in them. Some of the patients cooperated, but others gummed my fingers to death because they were confused and unhappy at our intrusion.

After an hour of trying teeth for the fourteen men, we still had four sets left. And four men without teeth. No matter how hard we tried to make the teeth fit, they just didn't.

Next, we tried the women, so we applied the same method, but because the women seemed to have smaller mouths, it was more challenging to get them in and out. An hour or so later we had all the women with teeth, what a result!

We went back to try the men with five sets of teeth left for four men. No matter how hard we tried, they didn't fit. So, someone must still have incorrect teeth. It was beginning to become a nightmare. We decided to wait until the 6 am toilet call for the patients to try them all again.

Eventually, after switching and swapping, backwards and forwards from male to female dormitories, they all had teeth, and we still had a spare set, but who they belong to God only knew. The funniest thing of all was that two patients looked like

Ed, the talking white horse with a permanent smile. The teeth fit into their mouths okay but were not their teeth, as the length was too long.

We had done the best we could in the time we had. It took us more than three hours of the night, cleaning, switching, and swapping teeth.

We handed over to the day staff and told them of our dilemma in the teeth department. Sarah flushed bright red, and the day staff laughed out loud at our teeth experience, and they said they would try again later in the daylight to get a better fit. We all agreed that a tooth stencilling kit was required to prevent this from ever happening again. An innocent mistake took hours to sort out and caused belly ache from laughing so much.

I made sure that if I asked someone to collect the teeth for cleaning in the future, I would explain how to collect them individually in the patient's denture pot. I also always told the story of the night of the student nurse and the terrifying teeth.

I LOVED THIS WARD, as some of the patients were great characters.

Bertie was an old chap in his eighties who suffered from dementia. He still had most of his personality, and some long-term memory, which was full of fun and always sported a twinkle in his eye, especially for the ladies. Bertie was a proper cheeky-chappy, but his short-term memory was sadly missing, and couldn't remember new instructions or information or direction longer than a minute.

He thought he was still a captain in the army, and it was currently wartime. Bertie would march up and down the corridors, salute the nurses and ask what the new orders were and had they arrived yet? We used his short-term memory loss to ours and his advantage so he wouldn't become anxious or agitated. If he got angry, he said, "I'm Captain Brown, why isn't anybody giving me the orders I've been sent to collect?"

We replied, "Come and take a seat in the lounge captain, and we will get them for you. But not until you've had a delicious cup of tea and biscuit."

He would be excited at the thought of a biscuit and take his time to choose which biscuit he wanted. He would drink his tea and have forgotten about the conversation before.

Bertie's wife died a few years before his dementia diagnosis, but he thought she was still alive and would ask if we had seen Doris several times a day and night. If told that she had died, he would become heartbroken. It was as if he heard it for the first time, so the staff decided to say she had popped to the shops and he could deal with that answer without getting upset until next time he asked.

His younger sister, Edna, visited him every evening from 6 pm until 9 pm to help with his anxiety, because when he was tired, he became more confused. Sometimes he would think that Edna was his mum because she looked like her. He would cuddle her as a son hugs his mum. Sometimes it was easier for Edna to pretend she was his mum to help calm him. Bertie would sit and hold her hand, behaving quite childlike, but she didn't seem to mind because she hated to see him distressed.

However, when cheeky Bertie was on form, with a twinkle in his eye, he would be a joy to be with. He would spin you around as if on a dance floor, doing the foxtrot and waltz. Bertie usually walked with a bit of a shuffle and didn't pick his feet up correctly. Though, when dancing, he was so light-footed and instantly became Lionel Blair. He also had a beautiful voice and would often start a singsong with the other patients joining in. One of his unusual hobbies was knitting. He told me his mother had taught him how to knit when he was a little boy, and he had continued it ever since. His ability to follow patterns now lost, but a knit-one, pearl-one he could still do with his eyes shut, so we encouraged him to make squares, which the occupational therapist could make into blankets and cushions.

One night there was a storm; lightning flashed, and thunder boomed. It made a hell of a noise. I heard Bertie shout in the male bedroom, "Get down! Get down! Everybody get down and take cover!"

I went to see why he was shouting. I found Bertie under the bed.

He grabbed my leg and whispered, "Get down, lass, the Germans are coming, so take cover."

Bless him; the thunder and lightning had reminded him of war.

I said, "The Germans were captured further up the road. The soldiers who captured them sent me to inform you, so there was nothing for you to worry about, and it's safe for you to get back to bed."

Relieved, he said, "Thank you," and climbed into it.

As a psychiatric nurse, I had to think of all different answers to many different situations, which made my job remarkably interesting and varied every shift.

Eventually, all the patients were settled by 2.30 am, and Carol, Jo, Sarah, and I, settled in the night station with a cuppa and our sandwiches. We chatted away in quiet voices so as not to disturb them.

Unexpectedly, precisely at 3 am, the lift clicked on and travelled to the lower floor. This event hadn't happened for a few weeks since its service, so we were frightened to the core. We just froze and looked at each other. We could hear the lift door open then close and click, then the lift travelled back to the first floor slowly and stopped. By this time, we were all standing on our feet, heart-poundingly terrified. We grabbed hold of each other's hands as the lift doors opened. We screamed as the doors fully opened and found it empty.

Sarah shouted, "Shit, I really don't like this lift," and hid behind me.

Jo said, "Do you now believe me? It's our friendly ghost back again."

I didn't know what to believe. All I knew was I needed a brandy to calm the nerves, and a full bottle for poor Sarah, as she physically shook with fear. I did what all trained staff nurses did when in this situation, I trained for three whole years to do this very task. I turned on all the corridor lights.

Jo started to laugh and said, "Well, that will stop the ghosts revisiting us, Mel. I bet they're shaking in their boots right now because of that professional ghostbusting — turning on of the lights."

We all burst into laughter out of pure fear. There was infinitely something spooky about this ward. It just had a feeling that gave you the shivers. Having four staff tonight made us feel a little safer because we could work in two's when attending to the patients. I wasn't a believer in ghosts, but I sure as hell was beginning to think it was a possibility.

Most nights, the lift did the same thing at 3 am. We used to look at the wall clock and brace ourselves. Then we would hear the click of the lift going to the ground floor. I would shoot up out of my chair to turn the corridor lights on, ready for the lift to come back up.

One night, the doors opened and a night porter was in the lift, delivering laundry bags I had ordered the night before. We screamed and nearly died on the spot. The porter screamed even louder because we frightened him with our screams. How the patients slept through this racket, I will never know. Poor David the porter was, ironically, as white as a ghost from his fright, we had to ply him with tea and biscuits to calm his nerves. He said, "I've only worked nights for six months as a porter, and this building always scares me." He shuddered, then said, "Another porter has seen a young girl in Victorian type clothes crying by the front door of the ward one night."

Before the conversation got out of control, talking about ghosts again, I quickly changed the topic of conversation to the shocking weather we'd had over the past few days.

My last shift of the week was very eventful. Sarah and I were checking the patients in the female beds at 4 am. We found that little Mary had died in her sleep. She was two days off her ninetieth birthday, and I knew that the family had organised a big birthday party for her, the staff, patients, and relatives. How was I going to break this news to them? The ward doctor came to certify the death but refused to make the dreaded phone call to her daughter. "You do it, Mel, you're so much better at it than me," he said, showing great sympathy by giving me a wink and a tap of the bottom.

"How cheeky," I said. "Get off my ward." Followed by a wink and a tap on his firm bottom too. As I don't think anyone else had done it back to him before, he looked shocked, but we smiled at each other. He was saved by the bell when his pager went off for him to go to another ward.

Sarah had never, in her three years of nursing, seen a dead body. I asked her if she would mind helping me, as she needed to learn how to deal with this situation. Apprehensively she said, "Okay," but I could see in her facial expression the same look of fear I had the first time on my first day on my first ward. I sat with Sarah and told her about my bad experience and explained everything we were going to do beforehand and what to expect.

She seemed reassured but still terrified at the thought of what she was about to do. I talked through what items were required on the trolley, then slowly walked to little Mary's bedside and pulled the curtains around her. We washed and dressed her in a shroud, put her teeth in and gave each other a knowing smirk, hoping she had the right teeth in her mouth.

We brushed her hair. Then found a rose from a bunch of flowers that a relative bought for the nurses. She looked perfect.

I then asked Sarah to come and observe how to tell a relative when someone had died. We sat in the office, and I opened Mary's notes to find her next of kin, her daughter Doreen. Usually, I would wait until morning, but Doreen had explicitly asked if anything happened to her mum then to call as soon as possible, even if it was the middle of the night. I took a deep breath and dialled the number; it rang four times then was answered by a croaky, sleepy voice.

"Good morning, I'm sorry to ring you in the middle of the night, but could I speak with Doreen, please? It's the staff nurse from the Northern General hospital."

"Yes, it's Doreen speaking."

"I'm afraid I have some sad news regarding your mum." I took another deep breath, "I'm sorry to tell you that your mum has just died peacefully in her sleep tonight."

After a stunned silence, all I heard was Doreen begin to cry as she relayed the message to her husband.

"If you would like to come and see your mum," I continued, "to say goodbye, that will be okay with me."

Doreen sniffed back her tears. "I will be there in about an hour."

"Okay, I will wait for you at the door."

"Thank you so much for letting me know. Goodbye."

"Bye for now," I said, then put the phone down, feeling incredibly sad. I found Sarah sobbing in the corner of the office. It had all been a bit much for her. I remember that feeling well from my first, and even second time, I had to deal with a dead person. I hugged Sarah and said, "Right, now I need you to pull yourself together and be strong, and set a tray up for the relatives in case they require a drink."

Sarah wiped her eyes, took herself off to the kitchen for another secret cry, and set up the tray.

Doreen and her husband arrived as they had said, an hour later, she was relatively calm, but I could see she had been crying. I took them upstairs to a single room where we had wheeled Mary on her bed so that they could see her in private. I asked, "Do you want to be left alone, or do you want me to stay with you?"

They asked me to stay because they were a bit afraid of what they might see.

Mary looked beautiful in death, and as soon as Doreen saw her, she flew to the bed and laid her head across her chest and cried. After a few minutes, she sat up and stroked her mum's face and held her hand. Doreen exclaimed, "She's still warm and soft to touch." Doreen then wiped her eyes, "What a lovely, kind mum she was."

Doreen's husband then added, "We were proud to be her daughter and son in law."

They came out of the room and felt a little more relaxed, and welcomed a cup of tea in the visitors' room. Doreen asked, "Could we still celebrate my mum's ninetieth birthday with the patients because we have become fond of them when visiting Mum? Not to mention we've paid for the food and waitresses in advance."

"Speak with the charge nurse during the day, as it would be his decision," I said.

Of course, he said yes, and arranged for afternoon tea, two days later. It was my day off, so I decided to go to the party and bring baby Adrian, who was now five months old but was the size of a one-year-old.

I entered the ward. Bunting dressed the room. A waitress, dressed in an old-fashioned maid outfit, but not the sexy one bought in naughty shops, offered me a drink of non-alcoholic fizz from her tray. They had turned the ward into the experience of tea at the Ritz, what a beautiful idea. When I walked into the lounge of the ward, it was like stepping back in time. There was a gramophone in the corner playing old-time music, there were six waitresses in fancy dress, who walked around with trays of salmon and cucumber, and egg mayonnaise sandwiches, pork pies and sausage rolls.

On a table in the corner sat a beautiful two-tiered cake in pink and white, with roses cascading down the front. Either side of the cake were two vases of pink and white roses and two beautiful photos of Mary in silver frames. Doreen came to meet me and hugged me. She thanked me for being so kind to her the other night when her mum died, and introduced me to her daughter, Mary, named after her grandma. She too had her baby with her, a little girl six weeks older than Adrian but half the size. They locked eyes and chatted in baby noises. It was so sweet to watch how they interacted with each other.

After the sandwiches, sausage rolls and pork pies, but before the cake, we cranked the music up on the gramophone and got a few patients up, dancing, transporting them back into the 1920s, 1930s and 1940s. They sang and danced, clapped and smiled, such joy to see the patients enjoying life again from another era.

Doreen stood up, made a speech about her wonderful mum, thanked the staff for giving her mum fantastic care, and wished us all good health and happiness. I don't think there was a dry eye.

Adrian was passed around the ward like a pass-the-parcel to patients, staff, and relatives, all giving him attention and cuddles. As long as I won the end prize of my Boo-boo to take home, I didn't mind at all.

THE FOLLOWING EVENING, I returned to work. My usual colleagues, Jo, Carol, and Sarah were with me. It was a full moon, so we knew we would be in for a difficult night. It's true that when it's a full moon, it affects people's mood and behaviour, or so it seemed to in a psychiatric unit. Some patients could become irritable and unsettled, and some could have a full-blown psychotic meltdown: having confusion, hallucinations, and delusions. That's where the word lunatic comes from — Luna means moon. The word 'lunatic' refers to a kind of insanity supposedly dependent on the moon phases.

The night began with two of the patients arguing over who's biscuit it was on the table between them; they were nearly at the bare-knuckle fighting stage when we split them up. We gave them each a new biscuit and made them reluctantly shake hands. The audible noise level seemed higher than usual from people groaning and making every-day noises, which irritated both the other patients and us. Some patients were so irritable they shouted out loud "Hey," for no reason at all. It indeed began to feel like an old-fashioned lunatic asylum.

Eventually, by midnight, we had assisted all the patients to bed. We were exhausted. Nearly every patient was resistant or uncooperative to one degree or another. It was hard to undress and get them into their night attire, or they wouldn't take their medication or kept getting in and out of bed; this took all our skills and patience to ensure they were eventually safely tucked up in bed. It certainly was unusual behaviour, it had to be the moon interfering somehow, but don't ask me how.

At 3 am, the lift clunked into action and travelled to the lower floor, doors opened then closed, and it travelled up to our floor, where we waited for the doors to open. As usual, there was nobody there. However, it felt extra haunting, despite me putting the lights on.

Carol suddenly gasped and said, "Look." She pointed at the big comfy chair at the side of us. It looked like someone sat on it and the air from the cushion puffed out, making a gentle noise, and there was a dint in the seating cushion. We all looked at each other in total panic and couldn't speak for a few seconds.

So, I broke the ice and said, "Good morning, ghost, have you come to join in the gossip with us?" As quickly as the cushion had deflated, it inflated and puffed back to normal. "I think I must have upset the ghost." We started to laugh nervously, but none of us could explain what we witnessed.

A few patients were up and down during the night: no specific reason, only confused or irritable. The usual trick of offering them a hot chocolate generally settled them. We all couldn't wait to get home off-duty as it had been an unforgettable night.

Thank goodness it was eventually 6 am, all I had to do now was write the nursing notes with the student nurse, and do the handover to the morning staff. We all heard a noise in the male bedded area and could see a small gentleman in a blue nightshirt. I jumped up to go and see if he were okay. Carol said, "It's okay, Mel, I will go."

I said, "It's okay. Why don't we go together?" as I suspected it was Bertie looking for the loo, and if he had been incontinent of urine, which he often did, it would need two of us to change him and strip his bed. As we walked up to him and linked our arms in his to take him to the bathroom, he totally disappeared. Gone! Like a puff of smoke devoured him. We stood in horrified disbelief. I looked around and could see all the male patients tucked up in bed.

I looked at Carol wide-eyed. She burst into tears and said, "Fuck this! I'm off home, really, Mel, I'm terrified." She ran out of the bay, picked her coat and bag up and said, "I'm off home, I can't do this ghost shit anymore; my nerves can't take it."

I tried to reassure and comfort her, but she was adamant she was leaving. She ran to the main door, got into her car, and sped off.

Jo and Sarah said, "What the hell just happened?"

How the hell was I going to explain to them, when I could hardly explain or believe it myself? I asked, "Did you see the patient that was out of bed before Carol and I went to help him?"

Simultaneously, they answered, "Yes, is he okay, what happened?"

I tentatively answered, "We walked up to him and linked his arms, and he just vanished from sight, disappeared. Piff-paff-puff, gone." Their mouths fell open. I was not sure if it was the shock that it might have been a ghost, or the fact that they thought I might have lost my marbles. But they soon shut their mouths when I said, "Don't forget, you saw him, too." I didn't believe in ghosts but, I wasn't sure now because I know what I witnessed. It wasn't a hallucination, because other people witnessed it, so there was only one explanation. It was a GHOST.

Carol was scared half to death and handed in her notice that day, never to nurse again. Honestly, it tempted me to do the same, but the love of my job won over my head of fear. I just had to put the ghost down to experience, part of my fantastic job, and a hell of a conversation stopper.

THE UNEXPECTED STUDENT NURSE

I remained working nights for a few years while Adrian was a baby, but once he started nursery at the age of two, it enabled me to go back on day duties. Steve changed his job to an engineer for the north of England, for a company specialising in hot melt glue applications. His new job meant sometimes he would be away overnight, so I needed to be home with Adrian. There was a choice of two wards, but I chose one of my old favourites, the lovely Ward 15. I couldn't have been happier.

The ward sister, June, had a little girl the same age as Adrian, and she was at the same nursery, making it easier for us to take it in turns dropping off and picking up if either of us got delayed on the ward.

I attended a course on back care, where we were shown different devices to help with manoeuvring patients: a hoist, slide sheet, and slide board. The use of this equipment would make nursing staff's working life much easier and more straightforward. The ward ordered the equipment immediately. Before lifting equipment, we had to manually lift a patient with our arms around their body and lift and take their full weight to manoeuvre them onto the toilet, bed, chair, or bath, a bit like a weightlifter with weights, but sadly no belt for supporting our backs.

At the end of a shift, sometimes your back would ache from the wear and tear of lifting many times. For example, we would need to lift a non-weight bearing patient twenty times a shift, so six allocated patients would be one hundred and twenty lifting actions per shift. Not surprisingly, we suffered from back pain.

The hoist came without training instructions, so June and I decided to play with it to work out how it operated. June sat on a chair, and I wheeled this monstrous sized hoist to the side of her, this was not an easy task at first as it was like pushing a large shopping trolley with a wonky wheel. I scooped her up in the seat, strapped her in so she didn't fall, and wheeled her down the corridor so I could get used to the handling of it. I hit every door and obstacle I could find, as it was difficult to navigate its big feet with wheels.

I placed the seat over an empty bath and lowered her into the bath using the battery-operated button. It took a lot longer than man-handling a patient from a wheelchair to the bath. But it was progress. It ensured we kept our backs as safe as possible.

After a few weeks, it became normal using the hoist in our everyday work. The only drawback was that some patients were terrified of it because of their confusion and vulnerability.

One morning I ran the bath for Doris, an eighty-year-old lady with dementia and Parkinson's. I undressed her and managed to get her on to the hoist, but she just screamed and screamed. You could tell she was frightened of it, but she needed a bath due to her being doubly incontinent. Before I lowered her into the water, I checked the temperature to make sure the water wasn't too hot and lowered her slowly into the water, reassuring her that she was okay. Once she was in the water, she thankfully calmed down, and I continued to wash her hair and body. I got three towels, one small one to wrap her hair, two large towels to dry her and one to place around her, so she kept warm when I lifted her out of the water. I emptied the water from the bath, and lifted Doris as slowly as possible out of the bath, reassuring her that she was okay and safe. All of a sudden, she started screaming, blood-curdling screams that echoed around the tiled bathroom. I stopped the hoist's movement, but she still screamed a scream I had never witnessed before from her.

June heard the screams and ran down the corridor to the bathroom to see what was wrong. Doris was only a few inches out of the water, so we decided it must be just the movement of the hoist. Plus, her feeling out of control and confused; this must be terrifying for an old lady with dementia. No matter how we tried to calm her, we couldn't stop her screaming, so we decided to get the task done and get her dried and dressed before she got too cold. I pressed the button to lift her again, and her screaming got louder, it was like we were murdering her.

Then we saw it, she had a total womb prolapse, like a small baby's head, dangling between her legs. I got a clean towel and took the weight of the prolapse, it felt heavy, and I could see we wouldn't be able to get her off the hoist as it had fallen below the hole in the seat.

June wrapped her in a blanket and phoned for the ward doctor, the ambulance, and fire service because she would need cutting out of the seat and taken to the general hospital to have surgery.

The doctor arrived on the ward and took one look at the prolapse, and nearly fainted. I swear he went different shades from white and green. He had to sit on the bed outside the bathroom with his head between his legs, taking deep breaths. Some use he was going to be in this emergency. I continued taking the prolapse weight as we didn't think it wise to lower her back in the bath in case, we inflicted more pain or damage to Doris.

An ambulance and fire crew arrived together as their stations were only a few minutes from the hospital. The doctor managed to pull himself together and drew up some sedation for Doris because she was still in great distress and screaming. One of the ambulance crew took over from me because bending for at least fifteen minutes holding the prolapse was beginning to hurt my back due to the angle of me being bent sideways over the bath.

Doris began to calm a little after her injection. However, her screaming soon started again as two of the firemen began sawing the seat off the hoist. The saw made a hell-of-a noise that echoed around the bathroom. Four firemen held another blanket under Doris so they could take her body weight. They managed to cut her free quite quickly and laid her on her side on the stretcher, still with the seat wrapped around the prolapse. They placed her into the ambulance, and blue lighted her to the Northern general hospital.

We were exhausted. Thankfully, one of the cleaning staff made us all a cup of coffee so we could have a ten-minute break to gather our thoughts before we started work again.

The ward phone rang, it was the doctor from casualty at the Northern General stating that sadly Doris didn't make it, she had died in the ambulance from shock on the way to the hospital. Now, all we had to do was to inform Doris's family about the tragedy. We had tried to phone earlier, to inform them of her condition and admission to hospital. They failed to answer their phone. So, this wasn't going to be an easy task, to tell them that poor Doris had not only been taken to hospital but had died from her condition. Thankfully for me, June made the call to the relatives.

~

As a staff nurse, I was responsible for helping train student nurses allocated to the ward. I decided to become a mentor for degree students and attended a week's training course to attain my certificate. It was to learn all about their paperwork, assignments, and levels of training required. Part of this training involved providing training notes and designing a slideshow in a specific subject of my choice. I chose pressure area care and presented notes on the skin, its layers, structure, and its purpose; the cause of pressure sores; the degrees of pressure sores and finally, how to treat pressure sores.

I had lectured for the Red Cross on first aid and nursing, so I was used to setting up a presentation and delivering it to maybe twenty people. Therefore, it wasn't as scary as it might have been. At the end of the week, I passed my exam and was presented with my certificate, ready to start training with degree students as their official mentor. Attaining this certificate would also give me a better chance of promotion; in becoming a ward sister in the future.

Mark and Kay, the two new student nurses, joined Ward 15 at 9 am on a Monday for their twelve-week allocation to psychiatric nursing. I greeted them and made us all a cuppa before browsing through the training expectations and how we would achieve their learning objectives. The morning flew by, and it was lunchtime before I knew it. I sent them for their lunch to arrive back at 1.00 pm for the hand over to the afternoon staff.

During the handover, I couldn't stop looking at Mark; there was a familiarity about him, but I couldn't put my finger on how I thought I knew him. He kept looking at me, then embarrassingly looking away, so I smiled and asked him, "Do I know you from somewhere, Mark?"

He blushed and shyly put his head down and replied, "Yes."

I was puzzled. Where had I seen Mark before? I wracked my brain, thinking, *Where the hell did, I know him from?* Then it hit me like a bolt of lightning. My God, it was Mark. Mark who worked at the maternity hospital when I was in the hospital, pregnant. Mark, who had performed an internal vaginal examination, not once but twice. Mark, who had seen me naked when helping me in the bath, and checked my stitches on my bits after the birth. OMG. I hadn't recognised him at first because he had grown a full beard. Holy shit! I never expected to see him again.

We both became awkward and looked away, flushed with embarrassment.

Debbie, the SEN, noticed this awkwardness between us and said, "What's gone on with you two? There's definitely a connection between you both." Everyone in the office glared at us. Debbie continued with a puzzled look, "You both look very shifty. Are you having an affair?"

We both looked down at the floor, not giving each other eye contact. I didn't know what to say. Debbie said, "Oh, my God! I'm right, you've been at it like rabbits! You naughty little people, tell us more. You kept that quiet, Mel."

All the staff laughed, and we became even more uncomfortable and embarrassed. I decided I had to tell them the truth before we died of embarrassment.

"Okay, okay, I will tell you, if that's okay with Mark?" I looked at him, and he nodded, though continued to look at the floor. "I want to introduce you all to Mark. He was my student nurse at the maternity ward when I gave birth to my son, Adrian. He practised all his nursing skills, inside and out of me during the labour. I think he knows me exceptionally well; in fact, I don't think there is any part of me he hasn't seen naked." The staff erupted into spontaneous laughter again. I got up and said, "Well, that was an awkward baptism to the ward for you, Mark," and put my arms out as he stood and gave me a big hug.

He said, "It's lovely to see you again, Mel, shame it's with your clothes on this time." I burst into nervous laughter and punched his shoulder. He then asked, "How is Goliath?" That was his nickname for Adrian because he was a big baby. Mark had loved to bath Adrian because the other babies were much smaller, and he felt he would break them in two when handling them. I loved him bathing Adrian too, as it gave me half an hour to myself to sleep.

I replied with a grin, "Growing bigger."

We continued with the handover. The staff said nothing more; I think they were a bit disappointed that it wasn't juicy gossip.

A BIRTHDAY TOAST

*F*or some reason, whenever we made some toast on the ward for the patients, the fire alarm would sense the minutest whiff of smoke and set the alarm ringing. I would check the ward for fire, even though I knew it was the toaster. I had to report to the nursing office that all was clear. But the fire service still had to come and do a physical sweep of the ward and investigate.

My favourite part of this regular occurrence with the toaster was the firemen, strapping gorgeous firemen in their uniforms and helmets. It sent my heart racing; I can tell you. I'm sure I subconsciously swayed patients daily to choose toast for breakfast, just so the fire alarm would activate. As you can imagine, we got to know the firemen very well as they attended the ward most days. They were always professional but full of mischief and fun. On my birthday, one of the nurses was making toast for breakfast and set the alarm off. I checked the ward as usual and reported no active fire on the ward to the nursing officer. I waited by the side door to let the firemen on the ward. They checked the ward and agreed that the ward was fire-free.

Six of them unusually followed me back into the office.

"Can I help you?" I asked.

They stood to attention, hands crossed behind their backs, sporting stupid grins. They cleared their throats, and counted "3,2,1," before bursting into the song, *Happy birthday*. What a wonderful treat just for me. I thanked them, feeling a little embarrassed, but secretly enjoyed every minute. I led the firemen to the door to get back into the fire truck.

Unexpectedly, Tom, the sexiest fireman with the bluest of eyes, and arms that rippled with muscle came towards me. He grabbed me and hurled me right over his shoulder in a fireman's lift. I squealed with delight, holding onto the hem of my uniform as I didn't want to give a flash of my stockings and suspenders. I hoped he would put me down on the ground fairly soon, as I hated being out of control. Unfortunately, no, he and his fellow firemen had different plans.

Tom stood on the cage of the hydraulic platform of the fire engine. It slowly started to move upwards to the roof of the building opposite Ward 15. I can tell you I screamed so loud I think they heard me twenty miles away. I'm not a person who enjoyed heights and felt very shaky, and I pleaded for him to put me down. Eventually, he gently placed me on the rooftop. He gave me a peck on the cheek and said, "Happy birthday, love," all the firemen cheered below.

My God, it was exhilarating for sexy Tom to kiss me, though scary as hell the fact that it was on the top of a building at least thirty foot in the air. After a few moments, he walked me back onto the platform, and they lowered me to the ground. I wanted to get on my hands and knees and kiss the ground, as I was so happy to have my trembling feet back on it eventually.

Every firefighter gave me a kiss and cuddle and thanked me for being a good sport. I didn't think I had any choice in the matter. Was it worth it? A thousand per cent, yes.

To this day, I love firefighters and have the naughtiest fantasies about them rescuing me as a damsel in distress, or watching them perform their duties, shirtless with braces on their wet toned, muscled bodies, wearing their helmets and holding their hoses… Okay, okay, I will shut up and jump out of my fantasy for a moment.

When I returned onto the ward, the staff presented me with a little cake and candles and burst into song. The little devils had deliberately set me up, knowing that I loved firefighters, and the firemen were only too happy to oblige as they classed it as a training exercise.

After blowing the candles out, I said with a grin, "I can't thank you all enough for my little birthday adventure. I warn you all now. I will be expecting to have toast and firemen every morning for my breakfast."

NEW BEGINNINGS DOWN SOUTH

*S*teve was offered a promotion to a senior engineer. But there was a problem. It meant we had to move down to Oxford. As I didn't want to leave family and friends, I wasn't sure, but we needed a new chapter in our lives because we had been through some traumatic years. Steve and I split up and got divorced. But we knew deep down we still loved each other; we were soul mates. Even though we had divorced, Steve visited me regularly and wanted to come back to me many times and had told me he had made the biggest mistake of his life.

When we had arrived at court for our divorce and custody of Adrian, the judge asked whether we wanted to think about it before he proceeded with the divorce, because we both were tearful and holding hands. Nevertheless, I chose to go through with the divorce mainly because Steve caused so much heartache after having an affair, and I was angry.

I decided to give our relationship another try because, we took Adrian to see Santa.

Adrian sat on Santa's knee, and Santa asked him if he was a good boy. Proudly, Adrian shouted, "YES!" Santa then asked what he wanted for Christmas. Adrian broke our hearts by answering, "I just want my mummy and daddy to get back together and for Daddy to come home."

I burst into tears, and Steve welled up and cuddled me. Santa looked at us, and we nodded our heads simultaneously, so he told Adrian it could come true, especially if he continued to be a good boy. So, we decided to give our relationship another try, because you can't fight love, and we wanted to be a family again.

With Steve's promotion opportunity, I said I would think about it but would need to know where we would live and what opportunities there would be for my career.

Steve's company paid for us to visit Oxfordshire and put us in a beautiful small, thatched hotel called the Peacock. It had several stunning peacocks walking around the ground fanning their tail feathers as if to give us a special greeting. They were much bigger than I thought close up, I felt intimidated by them as they nearly sat on my breakfast table. I gave them my toast and shooed them away and left breakfast as quickly as I could.

Steve drove me around the area where we might choose to live. It was such a contrast from a busy city suburb. There were miles of beautiful green countryside, with autumn-coloured trees glistening in the sun. The main market town of Thame was simply breath-taking. I loved it. Actually, I loved it so much that I decided to ring a few hospitals in the area over lunch to see if they had positions available for a staff nurse.

The first hospital I rang, the receptionist said, "Just a moment. I will put you through to someone."

I waited on the phone only a few minutes, and a nursing officer said they were interviewing that afternoon. He informed me they had an applicant cancel their interview and asked if I could come at 4 pm. Gosh, I was shocked; it was destiny. So, I agreed and quickly drove to Steve's office and typed up a CV and was there, waiting at the hospital at 4 pm.

They explained that the position was to work on a small

bespoke pre-senile unit. The interviewer interviewed me for about fifteen minutes and asked all about my experiences and qualifications. They seemed impressed that I was a degree student mentor, as their team didn't have anyone with those qualifications. At the end of the interview, they asked me to wait in the hall for ten minutes while discussing my interview. I paced up and down, quite anxious as to what their decision would be. I thought I had presented myself well, but still doubted that I might not be the person they were looking for, because some of the psychiatric illnesses they spoke about I had never nursed before.

The nursing officer came out and shook my hand, offering me the job there and then. I was thrilled. So that was it, the decision made; Oxfordshire here we come.

EARLY JANUARY 1991, we sold up, packed up and drove the one hundred and fifty miles down to Thame, Oxfordshire on a wet, rainy Friday afternoon.

Steve's company arranged a semidetached rental house to live in for the first six months until we could find and purchase a house in the area. Steve was starting his new job on Monday morning, but I was starting the following Monday, giving me time to sort the house out and get Adrian settled at school. Over the weekend, our main aim was to ensure Adrian was okay because it was his first time away from all he knew. We found the school and showed it to him from outside the gate, then we found the local park and sweetie shop, and introduced him to the childminder who would drop off and pick him up from school each day until we could pick him up after work. He seemed to take it all in his stride at the young age of seven.

Monday morning, Steve set off to take Adrian to the childminder. He looked so smart in his new uniform of a red jumper, black trousers, white shirt, and a red and silver tie. He looked so grown up, but incredibly nervous. I stayed at home unpacking boxes and cleaning.

At about 9.30 am, I began to feel very unwell. I felt dizzy and sweaty, with palpitations, so I decided to lay on the bed for ten minutes as I thought it must be anxiety and exhaustion from the move and all that entailed.

Abruptly, I had a severe sharp pain in my right lower side. The pain took my breath away. It was like being stabbed. I tried to get off the bed but couldn't stand because the pain was so debilitating. I crawled on my hands and knees along the landing and slowly slid down the stairs a step at a time, still with this horrendous sharp pain.

I managed to crawl to the back door and opened it. I could see the next-door neighbour about to get in her car, in her driveway, so I shouted, "HELP! Please help me."

She ran to me and saw I was writhing in pain and sweating profusely. She said, "Can you crawl to the car? I will take you to the doctors who are only a few hundred yards away."

I managed to crawl the few feet and hauled myself into the car. She drove like a formula one driver, so speedy, to the doctors. It took all of a minute.

Once again, the only way I could move was on my hands and knees, so I crawled on the pavement, while she went inside the doctors to ask for help. A nurse came out to me with a wheel-chair, helped me into it, and took me straight through to see the doctor, who was waiting for me.

I explained that I had just moved to the village two days before and it was on my list to register with them sometime this week.

Doctor Jones examined me. He found that my lower right side was incredibly tender to touch, and I showed signs of an internal bleed. The doctor was concerned as I writhed in pain on the bed in agony. He phoned for an ambulance to take me to hospital. Within minutes, I could hear the sirens of the ambulance as it made its way to the surgery. The doctor told me to ring my husband because of my condition's severity, but he wouldn't commit to giving me a diagnosis.

Steve was in the middle of his induction when I finally got through to him in the office. He was so shocked when I told him what had happened to me, because he had only just left me at home only an hour or so before, fit and well. He told me to be brave, and he would meet me at the hospital as soon as he could explain his dilemma to his new boss. It was not an excellent start to his new job.

As I lay in the ambulance, I thought, *How could this be happening to me?* It was supposed to be a new start, and here I was, cocking it up as usual. Mrs Calamity should be my middle name.

They took me immediately for a scan of the abdomen at the hospital as they suspected ectopic pregnancy; this is where you conceive a baby, but it attaches itself to the fallopian tube instead of the womb. The baby would grow and eventually rupture the fallopian tube as it grew and caused a significant bleed, and the baby would die.

The scan confirmed their suspicions. I was quickly put in a theatre gown, attached to a blood transfusion because I was haemorrhaging internally, and taken to theatre to have an emergency operation. In theatre, I could sense the seriousness and urgency as they quickly put me under the anaesthetic. The surgeon found that I was approximately nine weeks pregnant, and the fallopian tube had ruptured entirely, causing severe blood loss. They were administering blood as fast as I was bleeding; they had to remove the severely ruptured fallopian tube and baby. They stemmed the bleeding and stitched me up, ready to send to recovery.

Allegedly, panic broke out when I stopped breathing, and my heart slowed, about to stop.

Now, this is where the strangest thing happened to me. I had an out-of-body experience, where I was looking down on myself on the trolly in the theatre.

The nurse on my right side pushed down the cot side, to enable her to start to resuscitate me with a bag and mask. The pain in my elbow was horrific as she had trapped my elbow in the cot side. I was shouting from up above, "You've trapped my arm!" but they couldn't hear me.

Yet my inner self had this strange calmness despite the chaos below me. This calmness was a peace that I had never experienced in life. It was like floating on a soft cloud, with no anxiety or fear.

I watched as the nurses and doctors tried to save my life. There was no bright light calling me, but a slow feeling of drifting away. It was a beautiful and peaceful sensation.

As they continued working on me below, I wasn't afraid, just gently drifting away. Then, bang! A flash of light and I dropped like a stone back into my body. I still shouted in my head, "My arm! You've trapped my bloody arm." Unfortunately, no one heard me.

Eventually, I woke up in the recovery room to a nurse saying, "Hello, Mary, welcome back. You've had us worried."

I thought she was talking to someone else at first and didn't respond, despite her shaking me. Then I realised that she was talking to me; she was using my first name, which I had told them when admitted to the hospital that I never used. I had always been called Melanie or Mel. I opened my eyes. The nurse smiled at me and told me I was about to go back to the ward. I fell asleep again, but through the drowsiness, I felt a lot of pain.

I woke about an hour later, feeling sick. I tried to sit up, but the abdominal pain was shocking. I didn't have time to shout for help. I started to retch and vomit water. OMG, the pain continued horrendously. Trying not to burst the stitches open and vomit simultaneously, I held the operation site. Eventually, this feeling passed after they had given me an injection to stop the vomiting. The nurse told me that the surgeon would be along to speak to me soon.

The surgeon arrived at my bedside and pulled the curtains around the bed and introduced himself to me. He said, "I want to talk to you about your surgery and what happened in the theatre."

I told him, "I already know what had happened in the theatre," then mentioned my strange out-of-body experience. He was amazed at my answer.

He asked, "Could I take some notes because I'm doing a study on this phenomenon."

I nodded then explained how I floated out of my body to the ceiling and looked down on myself. "I could see I had stopped breathing. The monitor was beeping, and my heart rate was all over the place and slowing drastically. I could see the panic in the room, and the nurse on my right side. She trapped my elbow in the cot side, then placed the bag and oxygen mask over my face to start resuscitation." I took a shaky breath, remembering the pain. "You were on my left-hand side, administering drugs into my canular." He was shocked at the detail of my account. I continued, "There was an unusual calmness within me, which I had never experienced in life. I didn't witness any bright lights calling me, but had a feeling of floating, lighter than air, drifting away."

The doctor was astonished at how descriptive and accurate this experience was. He said, "That's amazing. You described it correctly as to where everyone was in the theatre, and what had happened to you. However, I was unaware of the trapping of the elbow."

"My elbow still hurts," so, he examined me to find it black and blue from bruising and apologised.

"You're a fortunate lady," he said, "because the rupture of the fallopian tube was so destructive. It had caused a significant bleed, and you were minutes from death when we opened your abdomen. We had to work very quickly to stem the bleeding and remove the tube. Unfortunately, we couldn't save the fallopian tube, though guessed you were about nine weeks pregnant."

With all the packing, Christmas and moving to a new house, I couldn't remember if I had a period or not, so I was unaware I was pregnant.

The surgeon thanked me for my detailed account and stated I would be in the hospital for a week to recover. After he left me, I burst into tears at the tragic loss of my poor baby, a baby I would never meet, and the trauma of that day.

Steve arrived. He looked shocked and tearful. He carried a huge bouquet of flowers, and Adrian cried at seeing his mum in hospital. We all cuddled together on the bed and wept. It had all been a bit much for all of us—what a start to our new life.

I STAYED in the hospital for a week and returned to the rented house.

How I wished I were still up north with my friends and family around me, because I didn't know anyone. I felt isolated and lonely, mostly when Steve went back to work and Adrian back to school. After saying goodbye to them both, I would sit with a cup of coffee and watch Morning TV; this was okay until Philip Schofield and Fern Britton had their laughing fits. It was infectious. It caused me to howl, crying with laughter while holding my wound, hoping it wouldn't split open.

Being at home did give me time to look and shortlist houses in the local newspapers. I couldn't believe how much more expensive houses were down south. Mine up north sold for £43,000 and similar houses in Oxfordshire were £110,000. We would be lucky to be able to buy a tent. We calculated our money and could only afford to buy a house up to £90,000, but it would swallow up all our savings and most of my wage; this was just another disappointing start to our move.

Unfortunately, I couldn't start work because I had to have a minimum of twelve week's recovery after my operation, as it was full surgery and not keyhole. I rang the ward sister and explained what had happened and that I couldn't start my position until the beginning of April. However, once I was driving after six weeks, I would come to the ward to get to know the patients and staff for a few days. Then observe the routine and orientate myself to the hospital. "I'm happy with that," she said. "Keep in touch."

It was so challenging just sitting at home because my surgeon told me not to drive or lift anything, not even a kettle, or empty removal boxes. When six weeks were up, I started to walk a little each day; just to the shops for bread, or a cheeky coffee and cake.

One morning, I was just about to enter the bread shop, when a large Range Rover came speeding around the corner on two wheels, traveling far too fast. It lost control, skidded, and aimed straight for me and the bakery.

Somehow, I managed to leap out the way like a SAS commander dodging a bullet, by rolling to the floor away from the bakery. It hurt my operation site, but I managed to scramble back up off the ground unharmed.

The Range Rover hit the front of the shop and entered, head-on, through into the shop, glass and debris smashed everywhere. I heard the shop attendant scream as she ran to the back of the shop, in an attempt to escape injury. I realised it was my next-door neighbour Joan.

I ran into the shop through the hole, as now there was no door visible. Thankfully, Joan was only a little shaken.

Draped over the steering wheel, the lady who drove the Range Rover slumped with a bloody nose. She groaned. I leapt into action like super nurse. I asked Joan to ring for the police and ambulance. I squeezed into the car's passenger seat, and asked the injured lady if she hurt anywhere, she didn't answer, but looked at me, rolled her eyes and groaned. I repeated, "Are you hurting anywhere?" She just closed her eyes. I was afraid the lady in the car may be concussed from the impact of the car.

I tried to take her pulse, but she retracted her arm away from me and shouted in a posh voice, "Get off me, you buffoon."

Joan recognised the lady in the car and said, "Are you okay, Camilla? Do you hurt anywhere?"

She answered, "No, I'm bloody well, not okay. Help me get rid of this northern imbecile, get her away from me."

I was taken aback and said, "What did you just say?" Thinking I must have misheard her.

She repeated to Joan again, "For fuck sake, get rid of this northern imbecile," and pointed at me, looking down her nose, like I was a piece of shit on her shoe.

I was more than angry at her deploring attitude. I said, "Hey, Mrs High and Mighty there's no need to be rude."

She looked up at me and said, "You still standing here?" wrinkling her nose as if I disgusted her.

I replied, "If you were seriously injured today, you would have been very relieved that this northern imbecile is a qualified nurse. I could have even saved your life, but seeing as your only injury is your foul mouth and ignorant discriminative manners, I will leave you to it." I climbed out of the car, across the broken window glass and left the bakery to walk home.

I sobbed on my way home. I thought of how someone could be so rude and horrid when I was only trying to help them. I wanted to go back home, back up north where people were friendlier. It was beginning to feel like this move was against me, and I wasn't sure if we had made the right decision.

FEAR AND FARTS

*T*he twelve weeks recovery was near to an end. We still couldn't find a house we liked to be our home. I decided to drive around and look at houses up for sale I had seen in the local newspaper. I looked every day for two weeks until I fell in love with a house on a corner. It was a four bedded detached with Georgian style windows, but it needed a lot of love. The garden was very overgrown, and it needed new windows and a lot of TLC. It had been empty a while as the bank had repossessed it, but it was £10,000 more than we could afford.

I tried putting our maximum offer into the estate agent. The bank declined it. I used to sit outside the house and just look at it. In my mind, I knew it was our house, and I just had that feeling inside me that we would get it eventually.

After two weeks of pestering the estate agent, I got a phone call to say they would accept our offer. I was ecstatic. I couldn't believe it. But by the afternoon, we got another phone call to say someone put an offer in at the same time for £500 more, so we upped ours by £100 more. They then upped by £200, then us by £300. We waited a few hours and got the call to ask us to put a secret bid in by 4 pm, and the one who bid the most would get the house.

I was devastated because I wanted this house, but we didn't have any more money. It was a case of asking Steve's dad to lend us the money, which he kindly did, enabling us to enter our secret bid.

At 5 pm, we received the phone call to say they accepted our last bid. The increase had cost us our new furniture money, but at least we had a house. I was furious at whoever was bidding against us, but also wondered if it was the bank playing games to get more money out of us. I later learned that it was my new friend and neighbour, Anita and her three boys, who were bidding against us. They eventually bought a house opposite our new house.

I STARTED work at the end of April at the small hospital. Which also was an old asylum from 1853. It was remarkably similar looking to the hospital I trained at, but on a much smaller scale. It felt like coming home.

On my first day, I was so sad to be informed that the hospital was closing in four weeks' time. The unit I intended working in would move to a new purpose-built unit at another hospital a few miles up the road. For the four weeks, apart from nursing the patients, we packed in boxes anything that we didn't need, like pictures and ornaments. The day before the move, they asked us to take some equipment to the new ward, which gave us an excuse to have a good old nosey around our new unit. It would allow me to drive to the new hospital as I had no idea where it was, despite it only being a few miles away. We filled my car with a few boxes and started the journey. Jean, the SEN, sat in the front and gave me directions. I pulled up at this roundabout and was in a total panic because there were three

roundabouts in one, cars seemed to be coming from all directions. I just wanted to jump out the car and let Jean drive, but
the car behind me was beeping its horn, and a man was giving
me rude hand gestures. I set off but got confused and went
round and round, as it seemed I couldn't get off the three circled
roundabouts. Eventually, I did get off it, but not without a few
swear words, screams, and tears on my behalf, which Jean found
very amusing.

Once settled in the new wing, it did seem nice, bright, and
airy with big windows the full length of the lounge overlooking
the garden; this was a total contrast to the other hospital. It had
been a bit dark and dingy. The patients were all under the age of
sixty-five. They all had different illnesses, like pre-senile
dementia, and brain damage from trauma, but the most unusual
illness on this unit was Huntington's chorea, which I had never
nursed before. So, I was eager to learn more about it and how
the patients needed nursing—caused by a faulty gene inherited
and passed on through generations with a fifty per cent chance
of contracting the disease from a parent.

It displayed severe symptoms of involuntary jerky movements of the limbs and body, clumsiness and stumbling, a
specific gait/walk, changes in personality and mood, difficulty
swallowing, and at later stages, difficulty with breathing. The
onset of this tragic illness is generally between twenty and fifty
years of age. We had three patients with this disease, and they
were related and lived in the same area. It was heart-breaking to
see how this hereditary illness displayed itself.

SHIRLEY WAS in her mid-fifties and had started with Huntington's in her early forties. She was very depressed and tended to
isolate herself, even from her two relatives living on the ward
with her. I would try to engage with her daily during personal

care but she remained insular. You could see she wanted to attend to her needs and hated that she needed help from a nurse. Her speech was severely affected, and when she did speak her mouth would over salivate, which caused her to feel embarrassed as she dribbled uncontrollably down her chin. She always had to hold a handkerchief in her hand to mop her mouth. Her movements were very jerky, and her walk was all over the place, with a shuffle, then a stop to try and get her balance, then another shuffle and a stop until she eventually sat in her comfy chair. I would warn her daily that if she tried to walk, without our assistance, she might stumble and fall onto the floor, causing many injuries, like cuts and bruises to her face and head. She didn't join in much but did like to read, and if we had fun and games on the ward, she would watch and smile and enjoy it in her unique way.

Martin was in his forties and had a larger-than-life character despite him having Huntington's. His speech was slightly affected, but it didn't bother him. He would be joking and messing about most days. He had a loving wife and children that visited him every day, bringing him chocolate and soft sweets. He was always hungry because of his constant jerky involuntary movements, which burned thousands of calories extra per day. If you walked past him, he would throw something at you to get your attention. I said every time he did that, "Now you're going to regret that Martin because next time I bath you, I'm not sure if I will dunk you or tickle you. You're just going to have to wait to see."

He would squeal in laughter and give me some cheeky one-liner in return. But he knew I would keep my word and the next time he was in the bath he would laugh so much in anticipation of me doing something, like splashing him with water or tickling his toes when washing his feet. He loved the banter, fun, and laughter.

Daren was in his mid-thirties, and also suffered from Huntington's. When I first met him, he was nervous and quiet. His involuntary movements were constant, sitting, standing, or sleeping. But as I got to know him, he developed a cheeky attitude like Martin. They became a double act, tormenting us nurses.

When the meals came on the ward for them, it was always partly liquidised food so they could eat and swallow without choking. But it was always the same food: Minced chicken, minced beef, or minced lamb, with mash, mixed veg and gravy, followed by yoghurt or ice-cream. Treat-wise it had to be soft sweets or chocolate in tiny pieces to suck.

One afternoon, I sat with them both, having a coffee, while they had tea and dunked their biscuits into their cup to eat them without choking. We got onto the subject of food and how sick they were of having the same foods every week. So, we made a list of foods they liked, to see if we could change things slightly. They loved Chinese and Indian food but hadn't had the pleasure for years. So, Jean and I put a few quid together and bought an Indian chicken curry and rice meal. We used the ward liquidiser and softened it a little, but left it with some texture. Jean and I put a pillowcase over our arms and pretended we were waiters, serving in a restaurant.

"Good evening, sirs," I said, "we have brought you an extraordinary meal tonight of chicken curry and rice, from the finest curry house in the south of England."

Martin and Daren burst into laughter, thinking it was a joke, then they got a whiff of the curry we wafted in their direction. They went crazy with excitement. Jean helped feed Martin, and I fed Daren. I said to Daren, "If you choke on this, I will be in deep trouble, so please take your time." He was so looking forward to it his arms and legs involuntary movements increased, nearly knocking the plate of food out of my hand. The first small mouthful he savoured and said nothing, his second mouthful his eyes lit up, you could see he was enjoying it. I asked, "Is it okay, and not too spicy?" he gave me the thumbs up and a smile.

Martin and Daren had never been so quiet; it was bliss. They enjoyed one of their favourite tastes from the past. They finished every mouthful and sat back in their chairs, rubbing their now fat bellies, displaying fulfilment expressions on their faces, like they were high on drugs. We high fived them and gave them a drink of apple juice to rinse it down, apologising it wasn't beer or cider.

This ward was home for younger people unable to be nursed at home, so we tried to make it homely and have as much fun as possible. We would listen to all types of music, have a dance and singalong, to the charts, play a quiz, or just do stupid things.

I remember one morning; we were serving breakfast, and I had forgotten to boil the eggs because I had been distracted by a phone call.

Jean put them in a dish to serve as boiled eggs. The first egg she took the top off went all over the floor and her uniform. She shouted at me, "Hey, Mel, you forgot to boil the eggs!" She wasn't happy with me.

I said, "Perhaps you should cook them yourself, next time," then poked my tongue out at her. The next thing I knew, a raw egg hit me in the back of the head, some of the patients laughed, thinking it funny, in fact, egging us on (no pun intended), so I picked an egg from the kitchen and threw one at Jean.

By now, the patients were cheering.

Jean flung another egg at me, hitting me on the arm, and I flung one back, hitting her on the back. We stopped for a moment and looked at the state of the ward. It was an absolute mess. I couldn't believe a few eggs could spread so far, making this mess. So, we had to stop before we went too far, and it became dangerous for patients, in case they slipped and fell. It took a lot longer to clean than we anticipated because the eggs dried quickly and stuck to the floor and walls. We may have made the patients laugh, but it cost us our breakfast break to clean it up.

~

A PATIENT CALLED James was admitted to the unit from a particular hospital that nursed brain injuries. James had been suicidal and tried to chop his head off with a chainsaw. He very nearly succeeded, cutting approximately an inch into his neck. He collapsed and nearly bled to death. But a neighbour, a paramedic, saw him in the garden, ran out and managed to stem the bleeding with clamps and thick dressings from his paramedic bag. James required reconstruction of the neck area and was in intensive care for weeks in a coma, then a further two months rehabilitation to learn to talk and walk again. James was a big six-foot strong bloke who used to be a bricklayer on the building sites.

The surgeons thought his strong muscles in his neck prevented his injuries from being a lot worse because it was harder to cut through the muscle, even with a chainsaw. He was still suffering from depression, but to add to that he suffered from anger and agitation issues. At times he used inappropriate action or speech. We were not sure if this was his typical behaviour or due to his brain injury. We never knew when James would become agitated or angry because there were no signs of build-up; it was like a switch turned on and off.

One morning, I helped James have a bath, and prompted him to wash himself, not just lay in the water. He was chatty and in a good mood, and very flirty with me. He said inappropriately, "Nice tits nurse," while stroking his penis.

I said, "Thank you, James, but please don't say things like that, because I'm your nurse and it's not the sort of thing you should say to your nurse."

He wanted me to shave him after his bath because his hands

lacked dexterity when doing fiddly things. I lathered up his face and asked him to sit on a chair so that I could reach him. I began to shave him, which seemed to irritate him because I couldn't do it fast enough.

I said, "Shall I stop for a while?"

He said, "NO, just get on with it; stop dithering woman."

I cautiously continued, trying to be as gentle as possible.

Unfortunately, James became more irritated and shouted, "Get on with it!" which made me jump, and I accidentally nicked his skin on his cheek, causing it to bleed. He jumped up and shouted at me and called me a clumsy cow. Before I knew it, James had picked me up by the front of my uniform and plopped me in the sink.

I had dropped the razor in fright, and he picked it up, putting the razor to my cheek. I was shit scared because he had a temper and could be so unpredictable. I couldn't get down from the sink because he was in front of me, holding me there by the weight of his body. I thought he was going to slash my cheek with the razor. For a minute, my brain seemed to be in slow motion. My body was trembling from fear. Then automatically, my training kicked in. I gave James full eye contact, and I said in a calm voice, "James. I'm so sorry I accidentally cut you with the razor. You made me jump when you shouted at me. I know you're angry with me, as I probably would be if you did it to me. But let me wipe your face and get you a plaster." He stood looking at me, his eyes glazed over. I put my hand on his hand holding the blade and said, "I had better take that, so we don't have another accident." Surprisingly, he let me take it out of his hand, so I threw it across the bathroom floor as far away from us as possible. He still held me with my uniform at the front and his body weight laid against me. I was beginning to panic inside because I knew I couldn't get out of the sink without his help. "James," I pleaded, "please help me down; the sink and taps are hurting me and my uniform's soaking wet.

Can I go and get you a plaster and a cup of tea which I think we both need?"

He stepped back from me, and I managed to jump down from the sink. I said, "Thank you, James, you wait here, love, and I will get you a plaster, okay?" I turned and walked a few steps then ran for my life.

Within seconds he was chasing me out the bathroom and down the corridor.

I hit the emergency button on route to the end of the corridor to alert staff that I needed help, and continued running with James a few steps behind me.

He shouted, "I'm going to kill you."

I don't know if it was fear or the mushy peas, I had eaten the night before, but I farted, trump, trump, trump with every step I ran. I couldn't help it. My arse had decided to express my fear; I was afraid, yet embarrassed and started to laugh inappropriately. I continued to trump down to the end of the corridor. I realised there was nowhere else to go and I slid down the wall to the floor, giving out an enormous, long crescendo of a fart.

James just collapsed beside me, howling with laughter. When four staff arrived, supposedly to save me, we were both hysterically crying with laughter.

Alex, the staff nurse from the next ward, said, "What the hell's going on?"

I couldn't answer because the adrenaline from feeling terrified was making me laugh even more. But James managed to answer his question loud and clear, "She's only farted all the way down the bloody corridor."

By this point, the laughter was contagious, and everyone laughed. Alex looked at James and said, "I think I would fart if you chased me too James. In fact, I would probably shit myself because you're a big strong guy."

They helped James and myself up off the floor, and we carried on as if nothing had happened, except I was embarrassed from the farting and the big wet patch on my bum from the sink. I pulled myself together and got a plaster for James' small nick on his cheek and told him, "I will shave you later if you want me to." Funnily enough, he was brave enough to say he would let me, but I would make sure next time another nurse was nearby in case I needed help.

He called me hearty-farty from that day, as he told me I was the nurse with a big heart that did the big farts. I suppose I was never going to live that incident down. I chatted to James about the incident the following day when he was calmer. I said, "You frightened me, and that wasn't a good thing if you want me to continue to be one of your nurses to look after you."

He apologised, stood up and gave me a big hug. He practically squeezed every ounce of oxygen out of my lungs. He had no idea how strong he was.

James settled into his new life on the ward as time went by, and we had very few incidences of aggression. He continued to be a big flirt and loved embarrassing me in front of everyone really, by calling me HEARTY-FARTY, followed by a wink and a grin. I loved him really, as I love people with characters that make me laugh, even if it's at my own expense.

When the unit was putting a brochure together about the bespoke nursing services it provided, they asked if I would like to be on the front cover with James. The photo they used for the front cover was a wonderful moment of James and I holding hands and chatting in the garden's sunshine. I still have a copy of the brochure today.

Jean and I were good friends and always gave our full attention and nursing care to all our patients, but we were the ward mischief-makers and entertainers. The patients loved it when we messed about, singing, doing silly dances to the music from the radio, or putting shaving foam on our faces to form a beard and eyebrows or play interactive games.

The ward had a wonderful, homely atmosphere and a close-knit community. It was sometimes challenging due to staff and patients' closeness when someone became ill or was dying.

~

DAREN BECAME ill because of a severe chest infection. His breathing was now deteriorating due to his Huntington's disease. He could not eat or drink because he had no swallowing reflex, but his involuntary movements were still prevalent, causing him exhaustion. We decided to nurse him in bed because he could not walk or transfer or sit in a comfortable chair; he couldn't even hold his head up.

The doctor gave him antibiotic medication, but his condition didn't improve. After a week, his father, himself and the medical team decided that he required end-of-life care because he couldn't fight his infection or Huntington's disease anymore. I had a great relationship with him. I don't want to be big-headed, but I was his favourite nurse, so agreed that I would attend to all his needs during my shift, and I was more than happy and proud to nurse him.

During the morning shift, I washed him in bed very slowly and gently, paying particular attention to his pressure areas, which thankfully, were all still intact. I sponged his mouth with antiseptic mouthwash on a little sponge lollipop. I combed his hair and still applied a little of his favourite aftershave, Dolce & Gabbana Pour Homme. He was mainly sleeping, which was a blessing as it reduced the number of involuntary movements to a minimum.

I would sit by his bedside and hold his hand, stroking it with my thumb, so he knew I was there. He would open his eyes from time to time and smile at me and squeeze my hand and fall back to sleep. It's an incredible privilege for a nurse to nurse someone in these last few days or hours of life because the patient trusts you and looks at you for love and comfort.

Daren's father arrived, who could see how sick his son was becoming. Sadly, he had seen it all before, when he had nursed Daren's mum with this same disease when Daren was a little boy. I left them together and made his father a cup of tea. I returned with the tea and sat for a while with them both, mainly to give his father support as he was very weepy. He said, "I have two wishes for Daren; that he would die peacefully without pain, and two, for you to be by Daren's side when he passes away, as you are his favourite nurse and he loves you very much."

I have to admit I had a tear in my eye and said, "I will try and honour Daren's wish."

I had to go and gather myself in the staff room for a few minutes, but then find the strength to carry on my duty. My shift had nearly finished. Daren was fading fast, and I didn't want to leave him. I knew he would be more than well cared for by other staff, but I wanted to be with him at the end, as he had wished.

The ward sister agreed and allowed me to stay on duty until the inevitable happened and take the following day off. When his father left and said his goodbyes, he kissed me on the cheek and said, "I leave him in yours and God's capable hands." He left the room in tears knowing that that was the last time he would see his son alive.

I made myself a drink of coffee and sat with Daren. We sat quietly for a few hours, me holding his hand and stroking his cheek, telling him what a lovely man he was, and not to be afraid. I swear he knew I was still there as he flickered his eyes if I let go of his hand.

It was dusk, and the sun was setting. A golden orange glow spread as it set through the big window into the bedroom. It was stunning and made me very emotional. It felt like someone was here to collect Daren. A few breaths later, Daren stopped breathing and died, still with his warm hand in mine. He was at last still and free from movement and looked at peace. It was the end of life at the end of a beautiful but sad day.

I sat for a few moments, said my goodbyes, kissed him on his forehead, and left the room.

Earlier in the day, I had set the trolly up to lay him out, ready for the undertaker. So, after a drink of coffee and a cry, myself and Jean attended to him respectfully and lovingly for the last time.

A few of the nurses attended Daren's funeral the following week. His father presented his eulogy. He said what a great son he was and how tragic it was that he had gone too soon, from this genetic disease at the age of thirty-five years of age. He thanked the hospital and staff for the excellent nursing care Daren had received and the fun and games we provided to make patients enjoy life while in our care. He then said, "A special thanks to Mel, for going beyond the call of duty, providing love and care towards my son in his last few hours of his life."

I don't deny it. I was proud of myself, knowing I had given my best. After all, I went into this kind of nursing to give my best and be that empathetic nurse.

EVERY MONTH, we would have a ward meeting with the nursing officer to discuss patients, training, and any other matters regarding the ward. I'm afraid to say that this unit's nursing officer was similar in attitude to the one that gave me grief all those years ago. He was a bit pompous and loved himself. The month before, he had walked onto the ward and jokingly clicked his fingers because he had missed his lunch and said to me, "Make me a sandwich and coffee."

I wasn't too happy about it because that wasn't my job, he could have got one from the canteen or machine. However, I thought, *Okay, perhaps he's had a busy day, so I will make him one as a one-off.* I could only find ham and cheese in the fridge, so that's what he got. I presented it nicely on a little tray, cut into triangles with a serviette at the side. He just took the plate out of my hand, without a please or thank you. *How rude,* I thought to myself, as it doesn't cost anything to have manners.

He then said after he had eaten it, "I've had better sandwiches from the garage." The next time he walked onto the ward, he said, "Make me a sandwich, duck, because I've not had time for any lunch. Oh, and two sugars in my coffee."

This request made me annoyed at his attitude; I stood and looked at him open-mouthed.

He just swanned off to the meeting room.

I looked at Jean and said, "Cheeky bugger! Does he think I'm his caterer now?"

Jean was a bit miffed at his lack of manners too. The next thing I knew, she had found a small tin of tuna cat food. She mixed it with mayonnaise and served it between two slices of brown bread. We were like little kids laughing at our mischievousness.

I took it to him and said, "I hope it's the PURR-fect sandwich this time, Brian."

He just stared at me and then carried on talking to the ward sister, though, still no please or a thank you.

Joan and I couldn't look at each other, or we would have burst. We carried on with the meeting, and after five minutes, he took his first bite of the sandwich. We expected him to have a hissy fit and spit it out, but he didn't and looked at the sandwich, giving it an approving smile. Jean and I couldn't believe it. He took his second and third bite and talked about the new student nurses they intended to allocate to the ward. Brian finished the sandwich and turned to me and said, "That was delicious. Mel, what was in it?"

Oh, shit, do I tell the truth and risk him throwing up and reprimanding me, or do I keep my mouth well and truly shut?

Jean gave me a shake of the head, so I said, "It's a new tuna sandwich filler by Marks & Spencer's with a dash of mayonnaise."

He replied, "I loved it. Much better than the last sandwich you made me."

As he was leaving, Jean couldn't help herself and said, "Brian, your 'tash is looking good, got some real puuuurfect whiskers going on there."

"Do you think so?" he replied and fiddled with his 'tash.

Once he left the ward, we erupted into spontaneous laughter. I smelt the sandwich mix out of curiosity, and I dipped my little finger pad into the bowl and tasted it. He was right. It was quite tasty, but I didn't think I would make myself a sandwich with the leftover cat food.

SEXUAL ASSAULT AND REVERSE PSYCHOLOGY

*J*he following week was one of the nurses' birthdays, so a few of us decided to go out for a drink and then on to a nightclub, which was a welcome break from unpacking and cleaning, as we had moved to the new house on the corner only a few weeks before. I was so up for letting my hair down. We met at a pub in town for a few drinks. Then we got a taxi to the club at about 10 pm. The taxi driver gave us his card and said, "Ring me, and I will come and collect you all."

We agreed we would call him because, sometimes, getting a taxi could take hours to arrive, especially late at night.

We danced the night away to 80s and 90s dance music, and met up with a few guys who asked us if we wanted to go back to theirs for a few more drinks, as it was on our way home, so we could share a taxi back.

At midnight, we decided to go and have a drink at the guys' house, mainly because one of the nurses fancied the farmer, but didn't want to go alone to his house. The taxi man was true to his word and arrived within fifteen minutes of our call to take us on to our next journey of the night. When we got dropped off at the barn house, I asked the taxi man if he would be still working at 2.30 am as myself and Jenny would need a taxi to get back to where we lived. He said, "No problem, see you at 2.30 am."

We sat, chatting and listening to music. The girls drank wine with the guys, and I drank diet coke because I had a chest infection and was on antibiotics.

At 2.15 am, I shouted to Jenny, "Are you ready to go now?" as she had gone upstairs with one of the guys.

She shouted downstairs, "You go without me. I'm busy," she giggled like a teenager in love.

The taxi man arrived spot on time to pick me up. He said, "Where's your friend?"

"She's decided to carry on partying," I said. "But it's way past my bedtime, and I'm working tomorrow and need my beauty sleep."

"No problem," he said as he opened the front taxi door like a proper gentleman and closed it behind me. He drove off the drive and onto the main road to begin our ten-minute journey home. It was a straight road but in the middle of the countryside, with very few streetlights and fields right and left of the road. There were no houses until nearer Thame where I lived. He asked me, "Did you have a good evening?"

"Yes, thank you," I said. "It has been a change, as I haven't been out to a club for ages, and my legs are killing me from dancing in heels." As we reached an even more secluded area, where there weren't any streetlights, he suddenly grabbed my hair. He pulled me towards him and tried to kiss me. The taxi flew across to the other side of the road. I pushed him away, and the taxi swerved back to the left. I screamed at him, "What the hell do you think you're doing?"

He said, "I know you want me; you've been flirting with me all night. Why else would you keep booking me?"

I disagreed and said, "You're a very much mistaken, mate. I'm a married woman, and I just want to go home." I folded my arms across my chest, thinking that would be the end of my ordeal. However, I could see his whole body was shaking from the adrenaline rush he was experiencing due to his sexual urges and could see his erect penis in his trousers.

He increased the taxi's speed, then grabbed my right hand and forced it between his legs so I could feel his hard penis. He rubbed my hand into him and stated, "This is what you want."

The taxi swerved across the white line again, if a car had been coming the other way we would have collided.

I screamed at him, "Let go of me!" For a second, I thought he had stopped, but he grabbed my hair, pulled me towards him again, and tried to kiss me, his mouth forceable on mine as he pushed his tongue into my mouth.

Once again, the car lurched out of control to the opposite side of the road and clipped the curb.

I screamed frantically at him, "Stop, stop this now!" and hit him everywhere I could. "I'm not interested. I don't want you; please stop!" I tried the car door and found it locked.

The taxi was still speeding. The driver seemed in a frenzy, and he was driving even more erratically all over the road, zigzagging from curb to curb. I thought he would turn the car over. He still had my hair in his hand while he tried kissing me and pushing his tongue into my mouth again. I could smell his foul breath and pungent body odour.

I continued to kick and scream. I was terrified and tried my hardest to push him off me.

He then slowed down, looked at me and coldly said, "I'm going to fuck your brains out."

He pulled over onto a dirt track and stopped the engine. I tried the door handle again, but it wouldn't open. He lunged towards me, grabbed my breasts and tried to kiss me again and again. At the same time, he put his other hand between my legs and tried to undo my trousers. I kicked and fought with every bit of strength I had, but it was futile.

Total panic hit me at the realisation he was going to rape me. He was so sexually charged, aroused and incredibly strong. My mind blanked, and I froze mentally; time stood still. I kept trying to fight him off, but he was too strong, and I was getting weaker. I realised I couldn't escape, and even if I could get out of the car, there was nowhere for me to run for help. My mind was in turmoil. I feared the worst of rape or even murder; this was a living nightmare.

THEN MY TRAINING kicked in to try reverse psychology. I had nothing to lose. It was worth a try. "Okay, okay," I said. "Stop, stop. I don't want to do it at a roadside in the middle of the countryside, have more respect for me, please. I want to go home, and we can have sex there. I will give in to you, I promise." His hands continued to roam all over me. His actions repulsed me. He stopped and looked at me as if digesting what I had just said. I was now shaking too, but not from sexual urges, but pure fright. I could hear my heart pounding in my ears. "Please," I urged him again, "please, let's go to my house."

He then said, "You're married, your husband will be at home. I'm not stupid, I know you're trying to trick me," he seemed incredibly angry.

"No, no," I said, "he's away on business; that's why I was out tonight. Because I'm home alone."

He thought about it for a moment then took the bait and said, "Okay, back to yours, it is."

He started the car and drove so fast towards my home that I clung on to the seat.

I was so relieved. It meant I could escape to my front door and knock Steve up, who was at home in bed, not on a business trip. I kept quiet, the few minutes journey to my house. We drove away from the countryside and into the well-lit housing estate. I felt relieved that at least a scream might get heard. We pulled up outside my house, and I tried to keep calm as I didn't want to alert him to my real intention. We sat for a moment, and I asked him to unlock the car door, which he did. I got out of the car slowly as I was shaking so much, I thought my legs would give way.

He radioed to the taxi firm to say he would be out of contact for a while.

I ran as fast as my legs would allow me, banged on the front door, and rang the doorbell frantically. The landing light came on as Steve got up out of bed to come down the stairs. I screamed for help, "Hurry up, Steve! Quick, hurry up, Steve, help me!" as I continuously banged on the door and rang the doorbell.

Now out the taxi, the taxi man looked at me as if he wanted to kill me. I could see he was so angry that I had tricked him. However, when Steve opened the door, it must have frightened him. He jumped back in the taxi and sped off.

As the door opened, I fell into the hallway onto my knees, hysterically screaming and crying, weak from the trauma. I just couldn't stand. Thank God I was home safe with my Steve.

Eventually, Steve managed to get me up from the floor onto a chair in the lounge. He cuddled me and held my hand; I just sobbed and shook uncontrollably. I couldn't speak to explain for at least fifteen minutes. I just continued whaling as if in pain. He knew something horrific had happened, but knew not to pressure me until I was ready to speak.

After some time, I just babbled out that the taxi man had tried to rape me. He was so shocked and angry and told me we should ring the police. But I didn't want to, I begged him not to as I didn't want to have to relive my nightmare to a stranger. I ran upstairs and ripped my clothes off my body, scrubbed my mouth and teeth with the toothbrush and toothpaste, until my gums and mouth bled. I stood under the shower and tried to scrub the horrific memory away. I got out of the shower, ran a bath and laid in bubbles up to my neck sobbing and wailing to let out all my fear. I felt so violated and dirty.

Despite being on antibiotics, Steve brought me a large Brandy which I slowly sipped as I sobbed. I stopped crying eventually as I felt numb and exhausted. Steve had to help me out of the bath and dried me as I stood still and in silence. He got me into bed and cuddled up behind me in his big protective arms. He told me, "You are safe now; it'll be okay."

I didn't sleep. I just laid with my eyes wide open, reliving every moment, over and over again in my mind until daylight. I didn't want to get out of bed and face the day or any more questioning from Steve. I just wanted to hibernate under the safety of my duvet for the rest of my life.

BRAVERY AND COURT

*A*t 10 am, I still wasn't up out of bed, which was unusual for me, but I guess it was acceptable as I had just been through an ordeal. Steve brought me a drink of coffee and a slice of toast upstairs and sat on the bed. He took my hand and said, "You must call the police about this, Melanie. It's so serious, love. He was far too confident for it to have been his first time from what you have told me, and he could do it again to another woman. I know you're scared, but I know you! You would never want another woman to go through what you have. Other women won't be psychiatrically trained. There's no doubt in my mind that if you hadn't used reverse psychology, he would have raped you. You must report this today, love, please."

I began to cry. I just wanted to blank this horrific experience out of my mind but was failing miserably. I knew deep down that Steve was right, and I needed to do the right thing and report this to the police. I couldn't live with the thought that this beast would do this again to another woman; they might not be as lucky as me to get home. I was terrified but agreed. Steve was a special constable for the police force, so he knew who to ring and made the phone call for me.

An hour later, two female plain-clothed police officers knocked on our door. I knew this was the start of a long terrifying journey to come. They introduced themselves to me and informed me they were from a special department of the police dealing with these incidents. The blonde officer said, "Tell us in your own time and words exactly what happened."

My mouth dry, my body trembled, I couldn't seem to find the first word to start the conversation. I just sat and opened and closed my mouth like a fish.

Steve sat beside me on the sofa and held my hand, and said, "It's okay, love, just take your time; nobody is here to judge you."

I felt so ashamed that this had happened to me. The first words to bumble out of my mouth were, "HE TRIED TO RAPE ME!" I burst into tears at that statement, knowing how lucky I was that he didn't manage to rape me, but had threatened it.

The police asked me to start right back at the beginning of the night, from where I first met the taxi driver and to stop whenever I needed to if it was too distressing, then to take my time and start again when I could.

At first, I didn't know where to start, but I couldn't stop once I started, I just relived every moment, every word, every touch. I don't think I drew breath. It was as if I had to get it out of me, as part of my cleansing process to heal myself. When I finished telling the police of my ordeal, they made a phone call to arrange the taxi man's arrest to question him at the station.

After a short break, the police then sat down with me and asked about every detail to write my statement. It was as horrid as the first time, reliving every detail again. I had to read through what the officer wrote, which was heart-breaking to read, as it was about me. I squirmed in my chair and sobbed. I ensured every detail was correct and that I hadn't missed anything out. In my mind, I knew it was all correct because when you're telling the truth about a traumatic incident, you don't just only remember it, you see it in 3D. You can describe the finest or most obscure detail, you can relate to sounds and smells, and actions, where it happened, and how it happened, you can describe how you felt and what you did. It was downright exhausting.

The police left the house, and I cried again, inconsolably, as I knew that this was only the start. I eventually felt drowsy, and laid on the sofa, and Steve covered me with a blanket to help me get some sleep.

I woke up with a jolt as Adrian came through the door from school, he was his usual tornado self. My God, the poor love didn't know anything about what had happened, and I wanted to keep it that way, he was far too young to understand, and I was envious at his ignorance of my situation. "Mummy, what's wrong? You've been crying," he said as he gave me one of his Adrian big hugs. I told him I had fallen and hurt myself, but I was okay now. He squeezed me again and kissed me, then said, "That will make you feel better, Mummy," and went upstairs to change out of his school uniform and to play in his room. His love and cuddle filled my heart with love. It was just what I needed to keep going.

I phoned the hospital and said that I wouldn't be in work for a week, due to being traumatised and that the police wanted to see me again if it went to court. My colleagues were shocked, as some of them had met the taxi guy on the night and said they thought he seemed to be a genuinely nice guy. "You might have to make a statement about the night," I said. They were happy to do so and hoped it would help my case.

The next morning, one of the two policewomen phoned to ask if they could come and see me at home. I was so anxious that I thought I might pass out as life seemed a bit hazy and surreal. When they arrived, they told me the taxi man had been interviewed at the police station and denied all the allegations. I hung my head in disbelief. However, they said that with the evidence from me, the taxi firm, and the other nurses, they presented it to the CPS. Who decided that the evidence passed their threshold for prosecution. "So," I asked, "what does that mean?"

The officer told me, "We will be taking him to court for sexual assault."

"Why only sexual assault," I asked, "because he had threatened and made attempts to rape me?"

"It's because he didn't manage to get your clothes removed and as there wasn't any actual exposure of himself or penetration, they class it as sexual assault," said the other officer.

I was angry as hell because I knew what he would have done if I hadn't been so creative and used reverse psychology. It was a case of his word against mine. But it meant so much to me to be believed by the police and CPS. We didn't know when we would be going to court but knew it would be in the next few months.

I TRIED to put it in the back of my mind, but I struggled. When I travelled to work, I had to drive on the same road as my attack, causing me to relive my ordeal every day. When a taxi passed me on my way to the ward, I was frightened that I would see him again. It was always in my mind, and I had nightmares where I relived the attack. Some days I would be in bits and couldn't go into work, the attack just ate away at my brain daily. I was so angry at myself for not being able to cope. I was a psychiatric nurse with nearly twenty years' experience dealing with other people's mental health problems, but I couldn't fix myself. My mental health deteriorated. I felt depressed, lost, ashamed and afraid. The police arranged a counsellor from victims support to meet with me. The word victim resonated with me; that's what the problem was. I was a victim; he had made me a victim.

The day at the magistrate's court was tough. I had to relive the ordeal and be cross-examined by the defence. The defence lawyer relentlessly tried to discredit me, by stating that I was a naughty, drunken nurse who egged the taxi driver on to get a free ride home, and wanted to pay him with sex. After all, it was me who invited him to my home to have sex. I knew he was trying to intimidate me. It was humiliating to hear what he was saying about me, but I knew the truth, so I stood up for myself and repeated what happened over and over again.

The taxi driver's family stared at me in disbelief as I told my account of that night. I was so relieved once I got off the stand.

Eventually, after deliberation, he was found guilty of sexual assault by the judge.

The relief took a weight off my mind. Hopefully, now I could get on with the rest of my life, especially with the cognitive behavioural therapy (CBT) and counselling Sue gave me.

Once I felt better and had finished my therapy, I decided to take a CBT and counselling diploma to enhance the nursing skills I already had learned. It would enable me to help others. I thought that at least some good could come out of something so devastating.

A few weeks later, I received a phone call from the police. They stated that the taxi man had appealed his conviction and we now had to go to Crown court in front of a judge and jury. Just when I got my head around the thought that it was over. I was devastated and horrified that I had to relive this ordeal all over again. Didn't this man have any feelings of guilt for putting me through this again? One of the most traumatising experiences was the fact that the local newspaper had recorded the appeal and put my name and where I lived in the paper.

I hadn't wanted people to know of my attack. I wanted to keep it private. What upset me the most was that my son, Adrian, only eight years old, came home from school and said, "My friends told me that you were sexually assaulted." He also wanted to know what it meant because it was in the newspaper.

There and then my world fell apart. I just wanted the ground to swallow me up away from this predicament. I sat with Adrian, held his hand and told him that a nasty man had attacked me, but because I was smart, I got away. I continued, "Even though this nasty man attacked me, I'm okay now. Don't worry, because the police are dealing with it, and we are all safe." Thankfully, he only understood a bit and accepted that I was okay.

I contacted the local newspaper. I complained, "How dare you publish who I am and where I live. I should remain anonymous because I was the victim. Plus, my poor innocent son knows of the attack because of it being in the newspaper." The editor honestly didn't give a shit.

"News is news; people need to know," he said. He showed no remorse and gave me no apology.

I wrote a letter to their column of how disgusted I was at their behaviour and stated that no wonder women were afraid to report these crimes if they were going to get splashed all over the paper. Still, there was no apology. However, I did get messages from women who said how brave I was, and how proud they were of me, which gave me the strength to carry on to the next stage.

WHEN I ARRIVED at Crown court, I had to pass all the colleagues from the taxi company sitting in the foyer. They tried to intimidate me by glaring and spitting at my feet. I was rushed into a private room by the police officers so that I didn't have to sit with them. It truly unnerved me and made me even more anxious than the first trial.

Once again, I had to give a full account of what happened that night. The defence tried to discredit every word I said. Eventually, he said, "Isn't it true that it was YOU who invited him to your house for sex?"

"Yes," I replied, "to stop him attacking me."

"If he were attacking you, then surely that would be the last thing you would do," the Brief said, "inviting him to your home. Indeed, it doesn't make sense. I believe you confabulate. I put it to you that you wanted him sexually and have made all this story up to cover your tracks from your husband finding out your true intentions of wanting sex."

I was so repulsed and angry at his suggestion. I replied, "I have twenty years in psychiatric nursing and have dealt with many situations with patients who have personality disorders, schizophrenia and many more psychiatric illnesses. I learned different techniques to defuse aggressive, violent behaviour. Reverse psychology is one of the techniques I have practised many times. It works to deflect the aggressor as they can still achieve what they want without aggression; they enjoy the feeling that you have succumbed to them. I had asked him to stop and fought him, which only fuelled his sexual frenzy and nearly caused us to crash the taxi." I took a deep breath to steady myself, "On this occasion, reverse psychology worked. Luckily for me, it meant I got nearer to my home and other houses, so if he continued attacking me, maybe my screams could be heard by someone, or get to the safety of my husband." By now, I was fuming, and I think he could see that. He had no further questions as I don't think he was expecting my answer.

We just had to wait for the verdict which seemed to take forever. The clerk called us back into the courtroom. I could see the taxi man standing in the dock. He made my blood boil with his smug look. The judge announced the taxi man guilty of sexual assault once more, fined him a few hundred pounds, and banned him from driving a taxi for life. Which to me seemed futile for the damage he had caused me mentally and the ordeal of going to court twice.

Unfortunately, the biggest shock of the day was that the

policewomen informed me, as we walked away from court, that they had reports and evidence that the taxi driver had done it before, but the young girls were too afraid to press charges. So, they were grateful for my bravery, because it hopefully meant he wouldn't be able to do it again.

For a moment, it felt good, being brave enough to take him to court, and I was proud of myself. But then I looked up to see the taxi man. He looked at me and arrogantly laughed. It was only a small fine and a ban from driving a taxi, after all. He was taunting me; what a cruel bastard he truly was, not one ounce of remorse. I grew livid. Steve held my arm and said, "Come on, love; it's over. Leave the animal to it. Don't let him anger you; he's not worth it."

He should have been charged with attempted rape and sexual assault, in my opinion, because he had said those were his intentions and he should have gone to prison. The punishment undoubtedly didn't fit the crime. It took me years to get over my ordeal and be able to get a taxi again.

I CONTINUED to drive to work past the assault area and bumped into the taxi man's family members in town, which caused me great distress. One day, his father approached me in town and asked, "Why did you lie about my son?" He genuinely looked devastated.

"Every word was true," I said. "I found out after my case that your beloved son had done it before to some young girls, who were too afraid to take him to court, but did tell the police of their ordeal. I'm proud that, hopefully, my bravery stopped him assaulting any woman ever again." His father looked at me in disbelief. I continued, "Why don't you ask your son about that when you get home, because it seems a hell of a coincidence if I made it up." I put my head in the air, stood tall and walked away.

I realised that going to work in this town couldn't continue as it was causing too much anxiety. I was afraid all the time in case I bumped into him. So, I applied for a nursing sister post in Oxford on a small assessment and rehabilitation unit. I was interviewed and got the job. I was so pleased as it meant a new start and promotion. I also arranged to take a diploma in counselling at Brooks University. Hopefully, I could now put some of my ordeal behind me.

INJURIES AND BEAR

The week before I started my new job, I had to attend the hospital for an orientation day and visit occupational health to have a medical and ensure all my injections were up to date. I arrived far too early as I was unsure of the length of the journey at that time of the day. I decided to visit the new unit just to have a look around and meet the staff. I rang the doorbell, and one of the nurses let me onto the ward. "I'm sorry," I apologised, "I'm too early for my appointment at occupational health, and wondered if I could wait on the ward?"

The nurse said, "Yes, sure, come on in and take a seat in the lounge." She made me a drink of coffee and just left me there while she started the drug round.

The patients were in the process of getting up for breakfast. I observed that the laundry trolley was there outside the linen room, but not being used, and dirty linen was all over the floor in the bedrooms to be eventually collected. A patient walked around in his shirt and pants and socks. He shouted, "Help me. I need a pee!"

Meanwhile, some medication was on a windowsill, left for

when a patient got up and sat in their favourite seat. A patient had urinated on the floor, and there was a big puddle that no one had attended. I was shocked at all the incorrect procedures and inferior nursing that I was witnessing. I got up to go and thanked them for my coffee. I walked to the door, and one of the nurses said, "Oh, by the way, who are you?"

I hadn't even realised that they hadn't asked who I was. I said, "I'm your new ward sister, and I'm shocked at what I have witnessed today. I'm afraid things will change when I start on this ward as I'm a stickler for rules and regulation and correct nursing procedures, so you had all better prepare yourselves for change." Their faces displayed total surprise as I walked put the door. As I walked to the occupational health department, I thought, *Well that's set the cat amongst the pigeons, I will have a hell of a reputation as a tyrant, before I've even started.*

I worked the hours of 9 am to 5 pm for my first shift so the ward manager could orientate me. When introduced to the staff, they were very friendly, but you could tell they were a little apprehensive of me. Allegedly, word had got around that I might be a bit of a battle-axe. I observed the staff caring for the patients, and I couldn't fault their dedication and nursing skills, but there were areas for improvement. I couldn't understand why they changed all the beds, placed the dirty linen on the floor at the end of the bed, then carried the linen to the laundry room to place in the mobile skip. Instead, I would have taken the laundry skip to the bed and immediately put the laundry into it, saving time walking backwards and forwards. It wasn't hygienic and could cause cross-infection and took a lot longer. They would also walk backwards and forwards to bring clean linen for each bed instead of filling a trolly up with clean linen and taking it to the bedrooms to be more accessible, obviously it was a bad habit they had got used to.

On my first morning shift, I asked them to take the skips and a ladened trolly of clean bedding into the bedroom before they started. They realised it worked well and seemed happy with my small change. I also ensured that medication was not left out for a patient at any time, as someone could take it by mistake; after all, some patients were confused and others suicidal. Plus, I ensured that a staff member was always in each patient area of the ward to observe patients and attend to their needs.

I spent my first week getting to know the patients, the reason for their admittance, and what their nursing care and rehabilitation requirements were. The general time pattern of care was six to twelve weeks in the hospital. The patient was either discharged home or to a relative, required home care, or transferred to a nursing home.

In my first week, I met Gloria, admitted with chronic anxiety and depression. She was in her sixties. I admitted her by filling in the nursing assessment and arranged for the ward doctor, Tom, to examine her medically and take blood tests. Taking blood from Gloria was a challenge as she was very anxious and had a great fear of needles. I helped by putting the pressure cuff onto her arm to encourage the veins to stand proud, making it easier to take the blood. Tom attached the needle to the syringe and said to Gloria, "It will just be a small scratch, try not to worry so much. Please try to keep calm and still, okay?" She nodded but was holding onto my arm hard, as I sat beside her, giving her reassurance. I held the two blood receptors to pass each one to the doctor once he had drawn blood. "Okay, Gloria, on the count of three, take a deep breath, and the needle will be in," he said. She nodded again but was white with fear and trembling.

Tom got to the count of two, and she screamed, "No, stop, wait a bit, I'm not ready. I don't think I can do this." So, we stopped and waited for about a minute for Gloria to gather herself. Gloria nodded her head and said, "Okay, I'm ready now."

"Look at me and not the needle, as it may help reduce your anxiety," I said, which she did.

Tom didn't count to three this time, but on the count of one, just got on with the job and placed the syringe into Gloria's vein. She yelped but remained still. This time he was successful.

Gloria's eyes filled with tears as her anxiety built up inside her as the doctor took a full syringe of blood. She began to tremble more as she watched the syringe fill with her blood, tears ran down her cheeks. He said, "Well done, Gloria, it's all done," but as he began to take the syringe out of her arm, she screamed and flailed her arms in the air as she tried to stand to her feet and flee. Unfortunately, she knocked Tom's arm and made the blood-filled syringe jab into my arm.

Time stood still for a second as the doctor looked at me, and me him. We both knew how dangerous this needle stick incident could be, but we were both aware not to alarm Gloria and continued to behave professionally. He put the blood into the receptors and wrote the request for the required blood tests. I wiped her arm with an antiseptic wipe and placed a plaster on her arm. I asked another nurse, Janet, to make Gloria a cup of tea to help calm her nerves as she had been courageous. Tom and I walked silently and calmly to the clinic room.

Once in the clinic room, I was in bits. "My God," I said. "What if she is HIV positive, or has other transferable diseases?"

Tom tried to reassure me that it was more probable that she didn't have these diseases because of her age and background. However, I would still have to take a blood test at occupational health the following day to test for HIV and Hepatitis B and C contamination. I had only been on the ward for three days, and this had bloody happened. I knew it was an accident and it wasn't anyone's fault, but I was well and truly pissed off, mainly because I knew I had up to six weeks to wait to get the results, causing six weeks of anxiety. In the meantime, I just had to carry on and hope and pray for the results to be negative.

After a few weeks of nursing and assessing Gloria, it was apparent she was lonely. When her husband had died, she continued to live in her huge five-bedroomed cottage. She felt like she wandered around the cottage from room to room, not knowing what to do and didn't have many friends or family to converse with daily. So, she now just used the kitchen, bathroom, and a bedroom. Her only son would call on her on a Saturday with his wife to get groceries for her, but didn't phone or visit any other time because they had busy lives. Her husband had been a detective in the police force and once retired, liked to keep himself to himself and relax attending to the garden and doing crosswords together. They would go on holiday to Europe three times a year. Now all this had suddenly stopped. She was stuck at home, grieving for her husband, as well as her past life. Tom, the ward doctor, prescribed antidepressants, and iron tablets as she had become anaemic due to not eating correctly. Nursing-wise, we encouraged a healthy diet and tried to find out activities she might like to do. She just seemed to love human company and enjoyed chatting, singing, and quizzing or reminiscing therapy. Her favourite was reminiscing therapy, where we would talk about a subject from years gone by and what they remembered. It reminded patients of happy memories and helped bring back confidence to speak about their personal experiences with the item.

One day, I held a group session with six patients, and I put a photo up on a big easel of an old laundry tub with a mangle. Each patient would then give their memories of that item. Gloria's memory was as a little girl, probably about four years old. She sat by an open fire at her grandma's house. She would watch Grandma separate all the clothes into piles of whites, lights, coloured, and blacks. Grandma then heated a big kettle on the fire until boiling; then filled the tub with several heavy kettleful's, and how Grandma asked her to stand over by a wall until the kettles were empty, so she didn't get scalded. Then

Grandma would ask her to put the whites in the tub and press the magic button to make the tub work. She loved to watch the water swish one way then another. Grandma always washed whites first. Then she would ask Gloria to help by holding the whites at the other end when she passed them through the mangle. Then put into a basket so they could be pegged outside on a line in the wind. Her main job was to pass her grandma the pegs out of a little pinafore her Grandma had made her. She told the group, "This would take from morning until after lunch to do the whole wash, as Grandma worked her way through all the laundry. We would have a slice of bread and butter with sugar on top, and I would curl up with the dog in the dog basket in front of the fire and fall asleep." All of the patients had similar but different memories. This reminiscent therapy certainly brought back happy memories and confidence for the patients to talk to each other on the ward.

AFTER A FEW WEEKS, Gloria's mood started to lift, and her anxiety seemed to subside, through good diet, different therapies, medication, and good old-fashioned company. So, I discussed her discharge plans. Gloria and her son had decided that moving to a residential home or independent warden controlled flat might be the best thing to do, so she wasn't as lonely, and be able to keep their eye on her diet.

The following Saturday, her son arrived on the ward to take Gloria to look at a few private residential homes. He set all the nurses' temperatures, pulses, and blood pressure off the scale. He was tall, dark, and handsome. A bit like George Clooney, but with George Michael hair. Luckily, I could pull rank and be the one that chatted to him about his mum's care. I had to have some perks to my job. When they returned to the ward, Gloria was excited as they had found a beautiful small twenty-bedded residential home only a few miles from Gloria's house. They decided that her son and family's best option was to move into Gloria's home, give up their rented house, and then pay towards the residential home for Gloria's care. It seemed a win-win situation with which they were all happy.

Gloria was discharged a week later with her supply of anti-depressants to hopefully settle well into her new environment, never to return to the ward again. That week I also got my results back from my needle injury. Thank God, it was negative.

MY RESEARCH on discharge and continuing care at home identified the failings that the care staff in the community were not trained sufficiently and didn't follow the ward's care plan. No wonder some patients were re-admitted a few weeks later when care failed at home. As a unit, we decided to involve the care companies with discharge planning and gave relevant training for personal care and psychiatric illnesses. Unfortunately, it wasn't sustainable because of the staff's high turnover in the community and the number of staff visiting the patient during the week. I arranged with a care company to shadow a carer in the community for a day and was shocked at the lack of support and training and the care companies' inadequate assessments. It wasn't the carers fault; they were trying their best. I was even more shocked that there wasn't a care company that specialised in psychiatric clients. I began to give it a great deal of thought into how to resolve this situation.

Derek was admitted one afternoon after being talked down by a police officer from a bridge over a dual carriageway. It caused havoc with traffic in Oxford as the dual carriageway had to be closed until they resolved the situation. Derek was suffering from severe depression and suicidal thoughts. He looked young for his age of sixty but looked dishevelled and expressionless. On admission, Derek stated that he just wanted to end it all because he had nothing to live for, as his girlfriend of thirty years had left him for a younger man. He had lost his job at the Mini car manufacturer in Cowley after BMW took it over, and was in lots of debt due to an inadequate redundancy package. Because of his suicidal thoughts, we nursed Derek one-to-one to ensure his safety. He also received a prescription for antidepressants and ECT.

The first week, he kept himself aloof, only talking when spoken to, but minimal conversation. He sat most of the day nursing his head in his hands or watching a little television. He ate extraordinarily little, not even enough for a child. We were genuinely concerned about him and tried to give one-to-one counselling, but he didn't cooperate and just sat silent. His one-to-one observation continued for a few weeks, and we could see some improvement in his mood very slowly. He became a little more talkative and interacted with staff and other patients. He told the ward doctor that he felt ashamed that he had tried to kill himself and didn't feel suicidal anymore.

We decided to ease off the one-to-one and just put him on general observation. Derek was quite a kind man, helping get elderly patients cups of tea, and chatting to them about their lives. For six weeks, he continued to improve and even went to the local shop for cigarettes and papers. We helped him look for local jobs that might suit his skills and arranged interviews for the following week. The medical team discussed the possibility of discharging him home with a CPN community psychiatric nurse to support him. He was ecstatic at the thought of going home and couldn't wait until Monday morning. Derek hugged and said, "Thank you," to every nurse on duty, he made us quite emotional with all his kind words. His taxi arrived, and he certainly looked so happy and couldn't wait to get out the door into his taxi home. He waved to us as he left.

One hour later, the ward manager received a phone call

from the police to say that Derek had taken his own life by hanging himself. They found his discharge letter from the hospital in his pocket and knew he was a patient of ours. The ward manager got the staff together on duty that day to inform us of this tragic ending for Derek. We were all in total disbelief and utter shock. We could have never imagined he was still so suicidal; he had hidden it from all of us. He left a suicide note stating that even though people had been kind to him, he still didn't want to live anymore. It knocked all of us for six. We repeatedly tried to think if we saw any signs of his suicidal thoughts, but all doctors and nurses drew a blank. We all felt we had failed him. The consultant said, "In some cases, patients who are determined to kill themselves give a false sense of security and happiness to others so they can eventually end their lives," and this exactly is what Derek had done. We all felt incredibly guilty for not seeing the signs—a lovely guy, whose life ended too soon.

I BECAME good friends with Janet, one of the nursing staff. She was like-minded about how she nursed the patients, giving her all; she also had a great sense of humour, which the patients loved. Over a coffee, we chatted about the situation of failing home care. She said, "Mel, you could start your own care company. You're confident, organised and a good teacher. Why don't you talk to my friend, who has her own care company, and find out more about it?"

I was intrigued by her comment and thought about it throughout the shift. I told her, "I'll think about it and talk it over with Steve."

Steve and I discussed it at length. At first, he thought it a bad idea, because of the cost, and amount of hard work that I would have to do setting the care company up. I already had a fantastic job that paid enough for us to have a good life. I understood his way of thinking, but it intrigued me. Could I set it up? Could I write all the policies and procedures? Could I interview and train staff? Could I design all the assessments and delivery of care plans? Could I do the accounts and invoicing? What did I know about the legalities and legislation? The list went on. It seemed an impossibility for me to do, but an inner thought fancied a chat with a care company to find out more. Janet arranged for me to talk to the director of another care company the following week. I couldn't wait. After all, I had nothing to lose except curiosity. The seed now sewn; I could think of nothing else.

A REQUEST TO assess a gentleman called James at his home came through. James was due to be admitted on the ward but was refusing to come into hospital. I looked up his address on a local map and drove my way into the countryside, just outside the city centre where he lived. It was an old farm up a long track hidden from the main road; I had passed it several times before while looking for his farm and eventually decided to look up the track. An ambulance was already waiting outside the farm, as they were supposed to be taking him into the hospital. The crew told me that James was adamant he wasn't coming into the hospital and hoped I had brought my magic wand to persuade him. The farm wasn't a working one anymore, and looked very run down, with broken windows and broken barn doors. I knocked on the door several times and shouted, "Hello, I'm Mel. I'm the nurse from the ward at the hospital."

A very tall, long-bearded man, with dishevelled hair and appearance, opened the door to me. He stood and smiled at me for a moment and said with a twinkle in his eyes, "I suppose you want to come inside, young lady."

I said, "That's kind of you. I can't remember the last time anyone called me a young lady," as I entered.

The farmhouse was like stepping back into the 1940s, with cobwebs and dust to match. James gestured with his hand to a chair and said, "You can sit there."

I introduced myself again and said, "The hospital has asked me to find out why you didn't want to come into the hospital for your assessment."

He sat, rocking in his rocking chair, and said, "I have my reasons; you wouldn't understand."

"You can trust me and tell me anything, and I will try to understand the problem, and even help you in any way possible to solve the problem together," I said earnestly.

He rocked some more in his chair, lit his pipe and puffed and sucked until it lit.

"I love the smell of pipe tobacco," I said, "as it reminds me of when I was a child, as my dad alternated between hand-rolled cigarettes and a pipe, and I loved to watch him light his pipe and inhale the smell of his Old Holborn tobacco."

James smiled and passed me his pipe and said, "You can have a puff if you want."

I declined politely stating I didn't smoke myself. "So," I asked again, "can you tell me why you don't want to come into the hospital today?"

He said, "It's not that I don't want to come into the hospital; it's because I can't."

"What's stopping you?"

He stopped rocking and said, "Can I trust you?"

Immediately I said, "Yes, of course, you can, James; tell me your problem."

He waited a few moments, then said, "It's because of my brown bear. I can't leave the house without my brown bear."

Confused, I said, "Okay, well, why don't we take the brown

bear with us in the ambulance to the hospital, because I'm sure that won't be a problem."

James seemed surprised but happy with my answer. "He's called Oscar. He's in the other room. Would you like to meet him?"

"Of course, I would love to meet Oscar," I replied, thinking I had solved the problem of the teddy bear. I entered the next room, which looked between an antique shop and Steptoe and son's backyard, it had everything and anything you could ever think of having.

Then my eyes met Oscar, the beautiful brown bear. He wasn't a teddy bear at all, but a life-sized stuffed real brown bear. James put his arms around Oscar and lovingly cuddled him. James stated, "We've been together for over fifty years." James was at least six-foot-tall, and the bear was much taller. I just stood open-mouthed and thought, *What the hell do I say or do now?* No amount of twenty-odd years of psychiatric nursing had prepared me for this moment. James then said, "I know I have been depressed and a bit forgetful, that's why the doc wants me assessed, but I can't leave Oscar. He has always been by my side."

My mind raced to find an answer to what to do. Do I retract from my solution and say, I'm sorry, I don't think we can get Oscar to the hospital? Or do I say, Okay, I will talk to the ambulance men and see if we can bring him with you to the hospital?

I walked outside to speak to the ambulance crew and gave them the scenario we were facing. The paramedics looked at me as if I had gone insane. At first, they laughed, but then realised that I was serious. I explained, "If it's the only way we can get James admitted then so be it, the bear must come too." I just hoped Oscar could fit inside the ambulance.

The paramedics came and looked at Oscar and tried to lift him. He was heavy but movable, so they brought the ambulance trolley stretcher into the house and laid Oscar the brown bear, onto the trolley, with his feet slightly hanging off the end of the stretcher.

James never left the bear's side and calmly collected his hospital bag and house keys to walk with Oscar to the ambulance. Surprisingly, the stretcher and bear fit inside the ambulance.

I helped James lock up and get into the seat of the ambulance.

I got in my car and followed on behind. While driving behind the ambulance, I started to laugh to myself. It was like an episode from *Beagles About* or *Carry-on Nursing*. I asked myself: was I honestly following an ambulance with a big brown bear on the stretcher? The more I thought about it, the more I laughed, but reality soon hit me when I thought, *What the hell had I done?* How the hell would I explain it to the ward manager and other staff? They were going to crucify and probably ridicule me for the rest of my life. But at least James could now get assessed. I was apprehensive but reasonably happy with my decision.

I walked onto the ward with a big stupid grin on my face. After all, what else could I do as James and I arrived on the ward? The staff on duty greeted him with a "Good afternoon, James, glad you decided to come and see us." Their smiles turned to puzzled expressions at the sight of a big brown bear being wheeled behind us.

The ambulance crew asked, "Where do you want Brown bear to go, Mel?"

I pointed to a single room where James would be sleeping. The staff just stood open-mouthed, until one of the nurses said, "What the hell's going on, Mel? What's with the bear?"

I whispered, "That's the only way James would agree to come in for an assessment." The nurses just looked surprised as they couldn't find an answer. "James," I said, "you can unpack your case in your room and take ten minutes to have a cuppa, then I will assess you, and devise your care plan."

"Okay, my lovely," he said and walked into his room to unpack. I sat with my coffee and didn't know whether to laugh or cry. Either way, I knew I was probably in for some stick from the powers up above, as I'm sure never had anyone before admitted a man and his bear. I didn't even know if it would cause a problem for health and safety.

I admitted James and devised his care plan for the present time for just general observation and arranged for the ward doctor, Tom, to medically assess him in the morning. I was exhausted and looked forward to going home, have a shower and put my mind in order, to explain the bear thing tomorrow.

The next morning, all the staff took the piss out of me, "Here comes the grizzly bear catcher." The powers up above and medical staff didn't seem to mind our new visitor. It wasn't causing a problem except curiosity, and it certainly created a talking point. James liked to sit in a chair in the lounge area, directly opposite his room, so he could see Oscar as he didn't want to let him out of his sight. We thought this might be delusional behaviour and continued to observe James' mental state and behaviour. After a few weeks, James was diagnosed with early stages of dementia. One morning after breakfast, I asked James to join me in the office. "How are you feeling? How do you think we could help you with your memory and dementia for the future?" We discussed different options of assistance at home, day-care or even nursing home.

He was very anxious and agitated, and didn't seem to want to engage in conversation. James asked, "Could we either go to my room so I could be with Brown Bear or in the lounge so I could have him in view?"

I agreed we could sit in his room to discuss his care package for the future with the brown bear at his side. He seemed relieved and quickly made his way back to his room. "James," I asked curiously, "can you tell me why Oscar is so important to you? Because I can see you want to see, or be with him at all times and when you can't, you become very anxious." He sat for a few minutes and looked at the floor, hesitant how to answer. I asked, "Is it a special reason, or is it just companionship? Or something else?"

Eventually, he said, "I know I can trust you, but you might think I'm crazy or foolish if I tell you."

"I have heard many things from patients over the years, and I promise I wouldn't think you crazy or foolish."

He blurted out, "I don't trust banks; my father before me didn't trust banks, so that's why I have Oscar." I didn't understand why he said this and probed into why Oscar was so important to him. He then said, "Oscar has all my money, keeping it safe." James could tell I was still puzzled and said, "Look nurse," and showed me a small cut out panel in the bear's back that fit in and out of the bear. James then asked me to shut his bedroom door, and he would show me. I closed the door, but left it just ajar, as I had learned in the past to have an escape route in case of emergencies. He pulled the panel out, and two twenty-pound notes fell out the hole. I looked closer and could see paper money crammed into the hole, tens, twenties, and fifty-pound notes.

The penny dropped. He kept all his money in Oscar and not a bank, no wonder he didn't want the bear out of his sight. "James, my love, we can't keep all this money on the ward, it's ward policy to put it into a safe in the finance office, where it can be collected when you leave." He became anxious and paced the few steps up and down his room and plopped himself onto his bed. I continued, "I'm afraid I will need to count it but, of course, with you and another witness to record the money before we put it into hospital finance." James stood up and looked even more anxious. I took his hand and said, "James, you said you trusted me, and I can assure you that you can, but

I have to do my job correctly, or I might get into trouble, okay?"

Eventually, James agreed. I called another nurse to help, and we started to take the money out the back of the bear and placed it on his bed. OMG, it was unbelievable—big wads of notes with elastic bands around them. The more I took out of the bear, the more they just kept coming. After a few hours of disembowelling the bear, James' single bed was full of wads of notes. The counting and recording task came next, which wasn't easy because each wad wasn't of the same value but a mixture, so every note was put into piles of fifty-, twenty- and ten-Pound notes.

We counted each pile several times, checking with all three of us the total value. The total value was over £25,000.00. I contacted finance, and two personnel came to collect the money. Before they accepted it and gave the receipt, they had to recount it. Never had they ever received such a high amount of money, and hoped that the large safe would be big enough to house it. James was genuinely concerned. However, I assured him it was safe, and he seemed to take my word for it, after I reassured him that he could go to the finance office with the staff to witness them putting it into the safe.

The next day, I drove to the care company that Janet had arranged for me to visit. The company director, a middle-aged lady, called Jenny, met me. She was very friendly and incredibly open about the care they provided and how she had set up her company five years before; after being a nurse herself and being frustrated at the community's lack of reasonable care. She agreed that there was a lack of psychiatric training for staff and wasn't aware of any other company specialising in that type of patient. She let me look at the legislation, assessments, and care plans. She also gave me contact numbers for social services and NHS personnel that organised contracts with care companies. She was very encouraging and told me to contact her at any time if I had any more questions. I thanked her very much for her time and left, absolutely buzzing at the thought that it could be possible. She had done it so why couldn't I? But I was aware that it would take months of organising and preparation, and I needed Steve on my side to support me. Personally, it would mean a lot of sacrifice of my time and finances if I did start my own company. There was so much to think about, and so much to discuss. Deep down, surprisingly, I wasn't fazed at the idea of starting my own company.

LOST VOICE FOUND THROUGH COUNSELLING

*E*very Wednesday evening, I attended Brooks University for my counselling course. I was coming to the end of it. I had to choose a patient I was working with and give a written account of my counselling sessions, assessed by the university. I had chosen an eighty-nine-year-old gentleman called Archie, who was on the unit suffering from depression. He was a very tall, willowy man who looked awkward at being tall and hunched himself forward when walking to appear smaller. He lacked personal confidence and didn't give eye contact. He was undoubtedly a gentleman, genuinely kind, humble and had impeccable manners. Before he retired, he had been a professional tennis coach and lived in a house with his sister and brother-in-law. He had been admitted to the unit because he was isolating himself in his bedroom and not eating properly, which caused anaemia and confusion.

I asked the consultant's and Archie's permission to be my candidate for assessment for my course. They both agreed. My first session with Archie was mainly explaining what coun-selling was. He thought a counsellor worked at the town hall, helping make decisions for the community (I quite fancied myself becoming lady mayoress of the county, wearing the chains of office). He didn't seem all that impressed by my type of counselling but said, "I will give it a go. I've got nothing to lose."

The next session, I found out as much about Archie and his life as I could. He said, "I never married because I was too shy to have an intimate relationship with a woman. I enjoyed female company in the past, but not now." During the war, he had been in the Navy and worked on a submarine but said, "I don't want to talk about that time in my life because it was horrific, I buried those times when the war was over. After the war, I agreed to move on where I worked in a big department store in Oxford as the floor manager in the Men's department." He decided to change his career to become a professional coach of tennis. He had always loved tennis and had won a few competitions in his youth, and people used to ask him for coaching because he was so good. He liked sketching and painting and visited the Chiltern hills, sketching until he was in his seventies when it became too much of a chore. His eyesight had deteriorated too much to enable him to catch detail in his drawings. He said, "I'm a bit of a loner, but enjoy some company. However, I prefer to sit and read, getting lost into a fictional story, but recently I couldn't concentrate on reading either."

I asked, "When did you first notice feeling depressed?"

"I was ill with the flu six months ago. I felt like the bedroom was closing around me, and had thoughts of killing myself, because now, as an old man, I have nothing to look forward to as everything is failing me. I wake every morning feeling sad that God hadn't taken me in my sleep."

"Was there something you had wished you had done in the past?"

He replied, "Finding a wife and having children, but I was too shy to go courting, so stayed alone by choice."

I asked Archie about his daily routine at home.

He woke at 7 am and waited in bed until his sister called him downstairs for breakfast, as she didn't like him coming down-stairs before. He had a cup of tea, and usually cornflakes, but sometimes toast. Then he would go back upstairs to get washed, shaved, and changed into his clothes. He listened to the radio for a while in his bedroom. At 1 pm his sister called him for his lunch to have a ham or cheese sandwich and a cup of tea, then he would retire back to his bedroom and have a nap. At 6 pm, he would have dinner in the kitchen, and retire back to his bedroom, to change into his pyjamas to go to bed.

My God, this poor man only left his bedroom to eat and drink and had no other activities or communication with anyone except his sister. No wonder depression had crept upon him.

Archie went on to explain, "My brother-in-law doesn't like me. Nor wants me in the rest of the house."

"Was the house rented or does your sister own the house?" I asked.

He replied, "It's my house, and my sister and brother-in-law moved in with me a few years ago because I was getting too old to run the house alone."

I was shocked. "Why didn't you go downstairs into the lounge or garden if it was your own house?"

He shrugged. "They didn't like me to listen to their conver-sations."

Counselling started with what he thought everyday life would be and how he may want to move forward to be more involved in ordinary life. We then moved on to when he stopped making decisions for himself and what he wanted to do in the future? Whether choosing when he got up in the morn-ing, or what he had for breakfast, or sitting in the garden.

As Archie had more sessions, he became more confident and wanted to change his life for the better. He felt that moving to a residential home might be the answer because he would have company or privacy when and how much he wanted. Archie felt having a much better diet and not burdening anyone was best. As that's how he felt his sister and brother-in-law saw him. "Have you ever voiced your feelings to your sister before about what you wanted out of life?" I asked.

"No," he said. "I didn't want to upset her."

I probed further, "So, do you think that by not choosing the life you wanted, it's affected your mood?"

"It probably did," he said, but he didn't like confrontation or arguments, so it was easier for him to stay silent and not to make a fuss.

His sister was on holiday for a week. Archie asked if I could take him home to collect some warmer clothing as it had now turned a bit chilly. "I'm sorry," I apologised, "I'm busy while working on the ward, but I will happily take you after my shift has finished." He only lived fifteen minutes away from the hospital, which meant the visit wouldn't take long.

After I finished my shift, we collected his small suitcase and drove to his house. It was a beautiful 1930s style semi-detached house, with a big bay window at the front. It had a very over-grown garden at the back of the house, but you could tell it could be beautiful with some care with many flowers and a couple of apple trees. Tastefully decorated inside, it was conservative but old fashioned.

We walked upstairs to his bedroom. My God, I was so shocked. It was a tiny box room probably eight-foot-long and six-foot-wide with a single bed that just fitted to the window wall and the opposite wall with no inches to spare. The curtains unevenly hung because they didn't have enough hooks to hold them on the rail. The light from the ceiling was a wire with a light bulb. He had a small three-drawer chest of draws with a radio sat on top, and that was it: no photos, no ornaments or mirror, none of his sketches and no personal belongings. I think a prison cell would be larger and have better light and comfort.

I asked Archie, "Why is your bedroom like this? The rest of the house is nicely decorated."

He shrugged, "I don't know; it's been the same for years as it was the junk room."

"How many bedrooms are there?"

"Three," he said. "One for my sister and husband and the other used as a study and sewing room for my sister.

"Could I see them?" I asked, and he obligingly showed me.

The master bedroom was at least three times bigger than his bedroom and nicely decorated with matching bedding and pale blue curtains. The study was at least twice as big as his bedroom, with a wardrobe and a desk for a sewing machine and mannikin doll and pink blinds. I couldn't believe that though he owned the house, his room was the worst. No wonder he felt depressed. The few minutes I was in there was enough for me. It was true the walls felt like they came in on you, and it was so dark, dingy, and impersonalised. Archie collected his jumpers, and I took him back to the ward.

My next session with Archie, I asked him how he felt about going back to his house yesterday. "I felt nothing really," he said, shaking his head in disbelief, "but realised how small my bedroom was since I had been away from it for a few weeks."

I nodded in understanding, then asked, "Would you prefer to be in one of the more oversized bedrooms?"

"I would. I used to sleep in the middle room, which is the sewing room. My sister said the box room was too small for the sewing room, so I moved out to keep the peace and please her." He shrugged then said, "I like to keep a quiet life and doubt that I could do anything about it now."

"As part of your therapy," I suggested. "I would like you to make notes for me of the things you would like to change in your life so that you can achieve a better quality of life. Also, by changing them, how you think it would make you feel."

Archie realised that by staying in the box room all day and

night, it was probably contributing towards his depression. "I would give it some thought," he said, "of the changes I want to make. I'll have it ready for our next session." When Archie arrived for the next counselling session, I was surprised to find Archie waving his list in the air. He proudly said, "I've made my list, and I'm eager to show you."

I felt I was beginning to see the old Archie emerging as it certainly wasn't the man, I knew a few weeks ago. He was more talkative and confident but still humble and shy. I opened the list and was amazed at how much he had written. Slowly I read the comprehensive list.

He wanted to move back into the middle bedroom when discharged home because he felt it would be airier and lighter. He intended to put the house on the market to sell because he wanted to live in a residential home where he could be cared for until the end of his days. He desired to write a will, and he wanted to hire a gardener to tackle the garden and look at it from the dining room window. It would also help with the sale of the house. He wanted his pension book as his sister sorted all the bills and food. He intended to sell his car. He no longer used it as traffic was too scary for him to drive.

"Wow," I said to Archie, "that was a hell of a list. How did it make you feel when writing it?"

"It felt like I was finding myself again as I had forgotten how it made me feel—empowered to make decisions. It was like lighting the litmus paper to my new life and destiny."

Impressed, I asked my next questions, "How are you going to achieve these goals? Which ones would you deal with first? To deal with them all at once could be quite daunting."

"I want move into the middle bedroom once discharged home. I want to talk to my sister and husband to help me spruce the house up a bit, get a gardener, and then put the house on the market." He wanted to find a residential home nearby as he liked the area and move in once he had sold the house.

"Wow, Archie," I exclaimed, "you have put a lot of thought to it. But maybe you need to talk it over first with your sister and not deal with this like a bull in a china shop."

He agreed and couldn't wait for them to visit that afternoon after being away on holiday to Cornwall.

I sat, writing my reflection of Archie's counselling session, and stated that he had now found his voice and how it had given him empowerment and purpose in life in just six weeks of counselling.

At 2 pm, Archie's sister and brother-in-law arrived on the ward. Archie was pleased to see them. For the first time, I saw him smiling at them as they entered the ward. I made them a pot of tea and took them to a quiet area of the ward to chat. "Archie's counselling sessions have gone well," I said, "and he now feels empowered to make more decisions regarding his future."

His sister smiled and seemed pleased he was improving, but the brother-in-law didn't look so happy and said, "I hope you've not been filling his head with nonsense because it will be us to get it in the neck."

Surprised, I assured him that all these thoughts were all Archie's, I just facilitated and encouraged his decision making. "Is it okay to record the conversation for my counselling course?"

They agreed.

Archie's whole-body language changed, he didn't give eye contact and hunched over, his body rocking a little because he was nervous, and I detected he seemed scared of the brother-in-law. Archie decided not to speak, and handed them the notes of changes he wanted for his future. His sister put her reading glasses on and read the note. She inhaled deeply and passed the note to her husband. Well, the next second all hell broke loose. The brother-in-law stood up and shouted at me. He said, "This is all your fault, meddling with your talking counselling rubbish. He's fine where he is, and you shouldn't have encouraged him. Keep your nose out of our business, you nosy bitch!"

Archie reverted to his previous demeanour. He rubbed his hands together, rocked to and fro, with his head down and his eyes shut.

"I'm sorry you feel like this," I said, "but it's my job to enable Archie to make plans for his future, which he had bottled up inside while depressed. However, now he is improving and wants to make some changes."

The brother-in-law stood over me, wagged his finger and shouted at me, "You're an interfering old bag and a disgrace to your nursing profession."

Archie suddenly found his voice and stood up tall, over the brother-in-law. He said in a booming voice, "Leave her alone. It has nothing to do with her. She has helped me find me and my voice, which you and my sister have suppressed for years." They were both as shocked as I was at Archie's outburst as it was so out of character. He continued, "I will make these changes, you two have ripped me off for years. I know you want my money, car and house but you can't, I earned it, and I will decide how to spend the rest of my short life. So, you had better start looking for somewhere to live in the future, because I don't need you." His sister and husband just looked at Archie in disbelief. "In the meantime, I will be looking for a residential home where I could live in comfort because the box room was like sleeping in a dog kennel." Poor Archie was physically shaking by now and white as a ghost; years of pent-up frustrations had all surfaced and come out at once. I had helped open the lid of fireworks, and he'd exploded. I guided him to a chair and held his hand to comfort him.

"I think you all need to calm down and have a cup of tea so we can talk about this situation without frustrations and tempers flying," I said.

The brother-in-law grabbed his wife's arm and announced

they were leaving, "We are holding you responsible for this impossible situation. We intend to make a complaint about you to your senior officer. It's obvious to us. You are after his money."

I was so taken aback at their allegation but chose not to answer.

Archie just sat with his head in his hands and said quite calmly, "Don't punish the ward sister for me making my mind up on what I want in life, because it shows I was right about you both manipulating me all along." He looked at his sister and shook his head in dismay. They stormed off the ward, and Archie and I sat in silence for a few minutes.

Where was the brandy bottle when you needed it? I certainly needed a bottle, preferably with a drinking straw. I was in total shock as to what had just happened. Archie looked at me and said, "Don't worry, it's not your fault, it's mine for keeping quiet all these years. I should have confronted them well before now."

"So, what do you want to do now?" I asked Archie.

"I think tomorrow I will need to speak to a solicitor or someone about my rights."

"I could contact citizens' advice to sort out an advocate to help you tomorrow."

Archie agreed and said, "Do you mind if I go and lay down on my bed because I'm exhausted; it's been a bit of a traumatic day."

I helped Archie to his bed. He looked entirely wiped out. I reported the incident to the staff at hand over, so they were aware of the situation. I expected repercussions in the days ahead from the family. I would have to deal with it, whatever they accused me of doing. But indeed, I wouldn't be held responsible for helping an elderly man find his voice.

I drove home and bought a Chinese takeaway because of the day I had just had, and I certainly didn't want to cook. We ate our meal, and I encouraged Adrian to have a bath and checked he had washed his hair and cleaned his teeth, because he was of an age where all kids pretended, they adequately washed, it's like they were allergic to soap, and masters at lying. It had been a long, eventful day, and I was exhausted. I wasn't going to put up with his nonsense.

After dinner, I asked Steve if we could have a chat about my idea of starting my own home care company. We waited until Adrian had gone to bed so we could give it our full attention. We sat at our dining room table, and I began to tell him about my visit to the care company. He listened to my excitable presentation and said, "Why don't you do some more research, speak to social services and the NHS contacts. Look at what will be required to set up a home care company. Then we will discuss it again once you have all the facts." I was quite surprised that he took me seriously because I didn't even know how serious I was to take on this challenge. I just knew it felt exciting, and I was enthusiastic. I got into bed, and my brain went into overdrive, thinking of what I needed to find out tomorrow.

THE BEGINNING OF THE END

*T*he next day, I was on an afternoon shift, so I had the morning to make a few phone calls to the care manager's department. Unfortunately, there was a team meeting, and they wouldn't be available until after lunch. I would be at work myself by then. So, I asked if a care manager could ring me the following day on my day off after 9.30 am. The receptionist told me she would pass the message on for me. I was disappointed because I was eager to get more information and get the ball rolling. I had bought a blue file and put headings on a front sheet with all the questions I wanted answering. But tomorrow would have to do, and I would probably think of other things to ask during the day and add to my list. I changed into my uniform with an extra spring in my step and set off on my journey to work.

It had become a lovely sunny day after morning rain. I thought, *Thank God, some sun is on its way after a very wet and rainy few days.* I hated driving in the rain. As I passed the golf course on my left-hand side, I felt the back end of my old 3-series BMW swerve to the other side of the road, to witness a big lorry coming straight for me. I panicked; I swear I was so close I could see the whites of his eyes in shock. I over-corrected my steering wheel. I managed to miss a head-on colli-sion with the lorry. Unfortunately, ended up on the opposite side of the road, travelling through a thick roadside bush and into the field behind. It all seemed to happen in slow motion, but I guess it was within seconds.

I jolted as I hit the bush and the car leapt into the field and stopped. It was silent for a moment as I tried to orientate myself to what had just happened. I managed to turn off the engine just as the lorry driver came running towards me to help. The pain in my neck and mid-back area was instant. I held onto the steering wheel to support myself, as I was aware of my first aid training not to move in case, I had broken my back.

The lorry driver tried to open my door, but couldn't keep it open as it was too heavy due to the door's damage and a bush being in the way. "I've phoned for an ambulance," he said. "Keep as still as possible."

I heard the ambulance sirens in the distance, getting closer and closer. I began to shake uncontrollably, which aggravated my back and neck pain. I was in agony. I closed my eyes and silently cried. I then heard a familiar voice; it said, "Don't worry, Mel. We will get you out of the car, tell me where you hurt." I opened my eyes and saw Brian, one of the ambulance men I knew from the ward. That was a relief; to have someone I knew by my side because I was terrified.

With assistance from the lorry driver and a police officer who was now on the scene, they managed to pull the door open. Brian gave me a full medical assessment, especially my vertebra, before he attempted to move me. They placed a surgical collar on my neck and laid the seat back to lift me onto the stretcher, where they strapped me in and placed a strap around my head. I was in absolute agony, but they couldn't give me any long-term pain relief, as it might mask the pain when examined at the hospital. Thankfully, they gave me gas and air, which made me high as a kite and giggly and made me feel incredibly sick.

Brian's partner drove quite slowly to the John Radcliffe hospital because of my neck and back injury. Brian tried to keep my spirits up and even took a photo of me on the stretcher, then stated that it was blackmail material for later. I laughed and said, "You will be lucky to get any money from me because I'm skint." As we pulled into the hospital ground, I shouted to Brian, "I'm going to be sick. I'm going to choke due to being strapped in." I started to panic as the vomit came up from my stomach into my mouth.

Before I knew it, Brian had turned the whole trolly onto its side, and I vomited milk all over the ambulance floor, it smelt and looked disgusting. I was so embarrassed and ashamed because Brian would have to clean it up later. I felt ill and out of control. As it's a real phobia of mine, I hated being strapped down. They took me through into A&E and transferred me onto another trolly. The medical team were all over me like a rash, trying to evaluate my injuries. Fortunately, it was only my back and neck where I had pain. So, the doctor arranged for me to have an X-ray and a scan.

As I waited for my results, Steve arrived at A&E, a little pale and shocked as a police colleague who attended my accident contacted him to tell him I had been involved in a car accident and taken to the hospital. Steve said, "What the hell did you do? You must have been going far too fast to end up in a field."

"The back end of the car just went out of control. However, it was my fault, as I over-corrected the steering wheel to avoid hitting the lorry and ended up through the bush and into the field on the sharp bend," I said.

He didn't look as if he believed me, but I wasn't going to get into an argument. I had more things to worry about.

The A&E doctor arrived with my results. I had a whiplash neck injury that would probably take six weeks to heal, but more seriously, I had injured my L4 and L5 at the lumbar region. He explained, to my surprise, that I had two prolapsed discs. He thought the accident had exacerbated the injury, but the discs were from an older condition, probably from nursing for years. It was continuous wear-and-tear from moving and lifting people in the past.

I asked, "How did you know I was a nurse?"

He looked at me and laughed, then said, "Your uniform and badge saying ward sister gives it away." I had completely forgotten I was in uniform and been on my way to work; it must have been the drugs they had given me. I felt a proper fool.

They discharged me from A&E with a bag full of potent analgesia and told me to visit the GP in two weeks to discuss my long-term back problem further.

By the time I got home, my muscles had started to go into spasm. I didn't know if I wanted to stand, sit, or lay down because the pain was relentless in whatever position I was in.

For a full week, I couldn't do anything for myself because the pain was so bad. Every time I moved, I groaned in pain. Steve had to shower me, dry me, and dress me into nightdresses so that it was easier to take on and off. He had to help me on and off the toilet and make all my meals and drinks. I found it more comfortable with my back against the sofa back than a bed or a chair. A pillow between my knees eased the strain on my back. I drifted in and out of analgesia sleepiness and tried to watch a little TV, but it was impossible. I was so irritable and uncomfortable when awake. I thought I might have been able to sit and write questions for home care, but I couldn't sit in a chair and couldn't lift my arms to hold a pen without pain sweeping over my body. I never knew genuine whiplash was so painful until now, my neck and shoulder muscles seized up.

The second week was a little better, and I could walk around the house slowly and carefully, but still couldn't sit to write; this upset me because I had things in my head, I needed to record so that I didn't forget it. One night, I cried to Steve how frustrated I was, as this time off work could have allowed me to do my research. I knew he couldn't help as he worked and cared for Adrian and did all the household chores. The next day, Steve came home from shopping and said, "I have a little present for you, now close your eyes and put your hands out." He placed a small box into my hand. I opened my eyes and found he had bought me a Dictaphone. I had never used one before. It was battery-operated, but he had forgotten to buy any batteries for it to work. So, we had to search the house for AA batteries. Thank goodness I found some in an old toy dog of Adrian's. Steve showed me how to use it. I couldn't believe how easy it was, but hated the sound of my voice. You never really hear your own voice. I got cracking. I recorded everything I needed to ask about home care. I could write up my recordings later.

In week three, I continued to improve and was able for short periods to write notes from my Dictaphone. I was ready to make some phone calls, which was exciting yet daunting at the same time. My first phone call was to the local care managers office in the town where I lived. I had butterflies in my stomach as I dialled the number. "Hello, Social Services care manager's department, Joyce speaking, how can I help you?" the receptionist said. I introduced myself and asked if it was possible to speak to the senior care manager on duty. She didn't ask what it concerned and just said, "Okay, I will put you through."

A lady called Mary answered. As we had met on the ward, I knew her from discussing patients we discharged into the community needing their home care services, so I didn't feel as tongue-tied as I thought I would. I said, "Hi, Mary, its Melanie, the wards sister from the unit."

She remembered me immediately and said, "I heard you've had a car accident. How are you feeling? Are you okay now?" How she knew that I don't know, how gossip spreads like a horrid disease.

"I'm improving," I said, "but still have a way to go because I'm still in a bit of discomfort." Eventually, after all the chit chat, I got down to business. "I'm researching home care as I'm thinking of starting my own home care company in the future, specialising in care for psychiatric patients as well as all other types of patients."

She was thrilled and said, "It's a much-needed service. If I can help in any way, I will."

Wow, I was amazed at her response. I asked, "Do you have time now to answer my questions?"

"Yes," she said. "Fire away. I'm all yours because they cancelled my meeting, so I'm free for thirty minutes." I asked everything I had on my list. She replied by giving me names and contact numbers, advice on setting up systems, contracts, and what she thought I would need to do to start a credible care company. I couldn't thank her enough, because it was my starting point of working my way through what was required.

I needed to devise my care company's presentation to present to the NHS and social services care managers and contract teams; this included: Policies and procedures, Assessment plan for clients, Care plans and review plans, Training and rostering of staff working hours, Brochure about the care company, Provided care and for which categories of clients.

Well, that was enough to start with; I might as well take this opportunity while off sick to research and devise everything. I decided to write the assessment plans first as I was used to assessing patients for nursing care. But what I wasn't used to was assessing a house situation where they lived for access or dangers in the home. I decided to pretend I was the patient being sent home with specific needs. I walked around my house and wrote all the needs I thought I might require. First, my name, address, age, contact numbers of next of kin, GP, other family members. What problems did I have, both physically and mentally? Did I require any moving and handling equipment?

Who did I live with? How did I get into and out of the house? What dangers were there in the house like stairs, an open fire, pets, narrow doors for a wheelchair? What care did I require?

I started a file for all the documents on my computer. This client assessment took me four days to complete and type into a document. Then printed a paper copy folder.

I did the same for each part of my presentation and filed them together in a bundle for social services. There was only one thing I had forgotten to do; it had been in and out of my mind for weeks. It seemed today was the day to name my company. I stayed up until 3 am writing lists of company names. I had over twenty in total at one point, but eventually, I got it down to the last three. They were Oxfordshire Psychiatric home care, Oxfordshire Private home care, and Empathy private home care. I knew as soon as I looked at the three names, the one that slapped me in the face, the one that had been special to me all my nursing career, the one that resonated the type of care I wanted to provide. It was as if it was destiny. EMPATHY PRIVATE HOME CARE was named.

I WAS NOW ONLY a week off returning to work. Occupational health requested a visit to ensure I was fit for duty and return to the ward. It was my first long journey since my accident. It was only a twenty-minute drive, but I was very anxious at the thought of getting behind a wheel again. The insurance company had written off the BMW, so I was now driving a two-year-old Ford cabriolet in powder blue. I loved it aesthetically, but mainly because it had power steering. My BMW had been like driving a tank as it was old and didn't have power steering. But this new car was as light as a feather. I drove to the occupational health department with ease.

The doctor introduced himself and looked at my X-rays,

scans and reports and gave me a full examination. I was still a little stiff in the neck area, and my back pain was still niggling, but apart from that, I felt well enough to return to work. He sat in his chair, chewing on the end of his pen, re-reading my reports and pulling faces as if struggling to think. So, I asked, "Is everything okay?"

He said, "Mmmm. I don't think you will be able to go back to active duties that include any form of moving and handling, as your back has two prolapsed discs which will continue to deteriorate; severe damage from one false move could be for life."

"So, what does this mean?" I asked.

"It means we shall have to find you lighter duties that don't involve any movement of your back, mainly office-based, or we might have to retire you on medical grounds."

I was thirty-seven years of age, far too young to retire. I loved nursing and felt gutted by this announcement. I panicked as to whether this injury could affect me finding another suitable job, or even prevent me from starting my own care company in the future.

The doctor then said, "I will need you to have an assessment by another doctor for a second opinion." He arranged for me to see the second doctor for the following week.

I left the department. I felt like a bus had hit me. I couldn't take it in. I was completely and utterly shocked, as I didn't realise how serious my back problem was. I had suffered on and off for at least ten years with severe or niggling back pain. Always after rest, I improved. I suppose I should have been thankful for my car accident, who knows what further irreparable damage I might have done in the future.

I drove home deep in thought, and to be honest, I don't remember driving home because my brain was working overtime.

I told Steve my devastating news. He couldn't believe that other doctors hadn't picked up the prolapsed discs before. I told him I would have to put the presentations on hold regarding the care company saga, until I knew if I was returning to work or not. I would continue to make enquiries about home care contracts and what I needed to do if I decided to start my company. I decided to continue the paper exercise, as that didn't cost anything except my time, ink, and paper.

The following Friday, the new doctor stated that I should try and get back to work but on lighter duties, and if this failed, they would advise me to retire on medical grounds. He signed me off sick for another week as my back was still tender when touched.

I visited the ward manager and told her of my predicament. However, the doctor had already forewarned her. "The only position available," she said, "would be as the night sister covering several hospitals and wards during the night; mainly a managerial role." My job would be to organise staff rosters, staff training, travel to each area nightly, give controlled drugs, and sort any problems out on the different wards. I would not do any heavy duties using my back, like hands-on physical nursing care. I didn't want to work nights again, but it seemed I didn't have any other choice and I wasn't quite ready to retire just yet.

I did have another idea for the future. I had passed my diploma in counselling, which meant I had another option. I could leave nursing and become a professional counsellor. Maybe I could work for victim support, as they had helped me in the past.

A TRAGIC LOSS

$\mathcal{I}$ began my first nightshift the following Monday. I walked to my unit, where I had worked before my accident and the day staff greeted me. They missed me and were sad that I wouldn't be working with them again. The night staff were a little wary of me because quite often on handover to them I had asked for changes in how they worked. I was determined to make a go of it. Another night sister called Claire arrived on the ward to introduce herself to me. I have heard people say that you know when you're getting old when a police officer looks like a boy aged twelve, well this was the case with Claire, she was only twenty-two years of age but looked about twelve. We would work together and cover for each other's days off, so the hospitals had night sisters seven days a week. She said, "Right, Mel, are you ready for an adventure?"

She took me to the central building's large main office; this also was an old Victorian building. At night, it was bloody scary. There were lots of nooks and crannies, with shadows and creaks and probably ghosts to fill them too. My first job was to ring round the other wards and hospitals to see if everything was okay and see if they needed our assistance; this took about a half-hour to complete. In turn, we then prioritised what we had to do first. We split up at 10.30 pm to attend to the giving of controlled drugs, like Morphine, on two different wards, then met up in the foyer to drive to the Radcliffe Infirmary to deal with a problem on a ward, as a patient had deteriorated. By the time we had dealt with the medical problem and drove back, it was already 2 am.

I was starving. So, I ate my sandwich and crisps with a strong coffee to keep me awake and chatted to Claire to find out more about her. She was married and was trying for a baby. Her husband worked nights too as a staff nurse on one of the wards. They were keen motorcyclists and had a Harley Davidson, she was tiny in build, and I couldn't see her being able to climb on to it, never mind ride it. She was so mature for her young age. I could understand why they promoted her to a ward sister; she was an astute lady. Between 2.30 am and 5 am we visited the rest of the wards to discuss rosters and any problems and visited the porters' lodge to introduce myself.

The night porter was to become my saviour and partner in crime. If there were reports of a missing patient or an intruder, me, and the porter would take a torch and enter into the darkness. We would look around the grounds and all the hospital outer buildings before I contacted the police if suspicious. I disliked the thought of this scenario. I knew I would scare myself to death, or as, knowing what porters were like and their sick sense of humour, they would probably try to scare me on purpose. I'm not sure what I would do if ever I found a burglar or intruder, as I'm sure they wouldn't put their hands in the air and give themselves up, and apologise for being naughty. A nurse and a torch would be no match. So, I planned to observe from a distance, shit myself, and run like the wind back to the safety of the office, locking the outer and inner doors and ringing for the police.

A few weeks later, I received a bleep during the nightshift to ring the night porter, Ken. I rang, and he told me that one of the wards had said they thought they had seen an intruder in the garden and he was asking me to meet him in the reception with the emergency torches. I hated this part of my job, and to be honest, I didn't think it was in my job description, but I did it anyway. I met Ken at reception. "It's one of the wards away from the main building," he said.

Great, I thought to myself, *what the hell am I doing, trundling, and stumbling around in the grounds of a scary hospital, shining a torch at anything that moves, and scaring myself witless?*

I didn't understand why it was a trained nurse's job to play cops and robbers — as if we would make any difference to scaring the intruder. Ken said, "Come on, Mel, I thought you were a big strong Yorkshire lass," as he put his arm through mine and we walked into the darkness.

I had wanted it to be a quiet night because tomorrow was mine and Adrian's birthday. I needed to stay awake when I got home to watch Adrian open his birthday presents before going to school instead of just opening my door and falling into bed.

It seemed so dark despite having torches, as there was no moon to give extra light. I heard foxes squealing in the distance and owls hooting in the trees, but no sign of an intruder. Then Ken's torch went out. "The battery died," he said.

It was now even darker, and I was even more terrified. I clung on to Ken's arm so tightly that I practically stopped his blood supply to his arm. At last, we arrived at the last outbuilding. We approached slowly and listened; it was all quiet. Thank goodness. I could now get to the office's warmth and safety to write another report of the non-existent intruder. "Come on, Ken, my coffee is calling me." I turned on my toes and started to walk back.

Ken shouted, "Wait, Mel, there's someone inside. I can hear something."

I must admit I stifled a scream. I put my hand over my

mouth. I whispered to Ken, "Come on, let's just go back, and I will ring the police to come and check."

"Mel, calm down, we're here now, so let's just look inside, it's probably a fox or a rat, then we can go and have that coffee and a well-deserved biscuit. I promise."

Foolishly, I agreed. I was trying to keep my reputation as a tuff old northern bird. I held the torchlight over the handle area so Ken could open the door. Before Ken could open it, we heard another noise, like whatever was inside had knocked over something. I nearly shit myself and could hardly keep the torch still. I was shaking too much.

The door handle pushed downwards as if an intruder intended to come out. I screamed so loud and began to run away. I shouted, "Come on, Ken, run!"

Then I heard voices burst into song, "Happy birthday to you, happy birthday to you; happy birth-day dear Mel-anie, happy birthday to you!"

I turned round to see two of the nurses, and another porter stood with Ken. They had pranked me for my birthday. "You bastards!" I shouted. "You've scared me half to death. Surely you could have just sung *Happy Birthday* down the phone to me." I laughed with pure relief and punched Ken on the arm, calling him a bastard yet again. What was it with hospital staff who surprised me with birthday surprises? Last time was scary but thrilling with the firemen a few years ago, but this time was utter fright.

Ken said, "Follow me, young lady," and linked my arm again and took me on to one of the wards. In the staff room, they had made a little birthday buffet.

"Ahhhhhh, how lovely of you all," I said and hugged them. The staff handed me a big card. I opened it to find all the night staff had signed it with lovely birthday messages. They also handed me a present wrapped beautifully with a big red bow. I opened it and burst out laughing. It was a pair of big bloomer pants with a note pinned to the big gusset that said, *A spare pair just in case you shit yourself from our scary birthday surprise.*

The buggers had planned all this, knowing I hated looking for intruders at night. I suppose I deserved it as I was always a prankster to other staff too. I guess it was payback.

Clare joined me, and other staff took turns in coming for their break and a sandwich and a natter. They also handed me a lovely bunch of flowers. I was well and truly spoilt. After an hour, it was back to reality, and back to filling in the rostering, visiting wards and answering my bleep.

Working nights did indeed fit in well with my family. I worked four nights per week with three days off. Plus, I got a financial night enhancement, which paid me an extra few hundred pounds per month. It meant I could save for a holiday the following year; Adrian had set his heart on Disneyland in Florida.

A few weeks later, I was working with Claire again. We arranged to split the duties. I would travel to the other hospitals, and she would cover the wards in the main hospital and meet at 2.30 am for our break together. I travelled to the Radcliffe Infirmary to check and administer controlled drugs to two patients and chatted with the staff about any problems and gossip, of course. Claire told me of a quicker way back to the hospital, cutting through a housing estate, so I thought I would give it a try. She had written directions on a piece of paper: turn left on to the estate, take the second right, go over two road humps and turn down the third exit on the right, travel to a T junction which joins onto the dual carriageway to the roundabout and then turn left to the hospital. I had heard that this estate had a bit of a reputation for being a bit rough, so I ensured I locked my doors and had the windows up. I turned left onto the estate then second right and could see a large group of young men, probably about fifteen of them, all dressed in tracksuits and hoodies. I carried on towards the first hump in the road.

Meanwhile, the lads decided to block me by standing in the middle of the road. I panicked. Immediately I went straight back to my sexual assault in my mind. So, the Evil Knievel in me put my foot on the accelerator and floored it. It was a case of survival — them or me. They jumped out of the way as I drove at speed towards them and the first hump, it was as if I had driving lessons from Starsky and Hutch. I hit the hump and flew into the air and landed with a loud thump. I looked in my rear-view mirror. I could see they were still behind me running towards the car, so I kept up the speed and hit the second hump, flew through the air, and landed with a thump again.

I sped away from the lads. I then began to panic even more as I couldn't remember if it were the second or third right to meet the dual carriageway. If I took the wrong one, I might be in trouble as I didn't know how to get off the estate. I took the second right and realised it didn't look like the right one and drove through the estate, hoping I had lost the lads. Eventually, after a few minutes, I found the dual carriageway, but not the exit I should have arrived, and slowed down to the correct speed.

My heart was beating so fast I could hardly get my breath as I drove the next few miles to the hospital. I got out of the car and flew into the main hospital area to the nurse's admin office, where Claire was waiting. She could see I was out of breath and a bit traumatised. "Christ, Mel, what's happened to you?" she said as she bit into her sandwich.

I began to laugh inappropriately and told her of my ordeal. It was exhilarating, but very scary too. Claire couldn't stop laughing as I told her how I drove to escape the lads. I decided to phone the police to tell them that several young men were walking around the estate. However, I didn't say they tried to intimidate me into stopping, because they had seen me and my distinctive car, and I didn't want any repercussions. Honestly, I could have done with a large brandy at this point, but a large mug of coffee and chocolate had to do.

Claire hugged me as she left the office and parted with the sarcastic words, "See you tonight, Mrs crime buster." On my way home from work, I heard on the news that there had been trouble on the estate. Cars were being stopped by a group of youths, and the occupants threatened until they gave their belongings, like bags and jewellery. I realised I had been so lucky. I didn't take the shortcut through the estate ever again.

THE NEXT NIGHT SHIFT, I expected to meet up with Claire but was greeted by the nursing officer in the main office. I thought he might have come to talk about the incident last night while driving through the estate as I had left him a message, which said: *in future, perhaps it would be safer for the night nurses to keep to the main roads,* as I didn't want any other member of staff to go through what I had. He asked me to take a seat, "I have some tragic news for you, Mel." He took a deep breath, "Claire and her husband had a fatal motorbike accident earlier this morning on their way home from work. They had skidded on an oil patch, hit a fence in the countryside and been hurled about twenty feet into the air. Both had broken their necks on landing and instantly died at the scene."

I was in utter shock; it was like a bolt of lightning struck me. I couldn't believe that less than thirteen hours before I had been sat with Claire, laughing at my ordeal on the estate in this very office.

The nursing officer was very teary-eyed, so I made us both a mug of sweet tea. He told me he was in bed at home when he got the phone call from the police. They had rung him because Claire and her husband were still in uniform and they didn't know if they were on their way to work. "They also asked if I would mind going to identify their bodies at the scene. They were side by side, facing each other in the field." He explained how traumatic it was for him.

I was so sad. Uncontrollable tears ran down my cheeks. What a beautiful, intelligent, woman Claire was, she had her remarkable career and life planned out before her, but now had it tragically taken away. We just sat drinking our tea in silence, deep in thought and mourning our loss of our friend and colleague.

I received a request to work extra shifts until they could find someone to take Claire's post temporarily until they advertised the following week. Of course, I didn't mind. It was the least I could do in the circumstances. My shift started with a phone call from a ward asking for my help as an elderly confused lady had trapped her leg in a cot side, and they couldn't free her leg. I walked onto the ward and heard screaming and voices trying to calm the patient down.

Mary was a ninety-year-old lady who had severe dementia. She was very restless at night and had to sleep in a bed with a cot side to stop her from falling off the bed. Unfortunately, tonight, she had managed to find the button to release the cot side while her leg draped through it. The catch released and the cot side enclosed around her tiny leg and nipped into her skin; this small cut made it look like there was a massacre, blood was all over her and the white sheets.

We had to try between us to plan how we could get the leg out, as it seemed to wrap itself around the cot side and she was still screaming and trying to get her leg free but didn't understand what was happening to her, due to her confusion. I decided to try to calm Mary first of all, so I put some lavender oil on my hands. I took her hand off the cot side and started to massage it. I said in a calm and lilting voice, "You're going to be okay," and hummed a little tune. It took a few minutes to calm her down enough for me to instruct the staff to move her leg quickly and free her from the cot. We had to be as swift as possible to cause as little distress or further injury. Within a few seconds, and a piercing scream from Mary, she was free. The nurses lifted her onto a commode. Then took her to the bathroom to wash off the blood and change her into a clean nightdress. She had a small skin flap behind her knee where the cot side's mechanism had nipped her leg. It had bled a lot because she was on Warfarin, a drug that thins the blood, and caused her to bleed much more than usual. I placed a dressing on the injury, and she was put back into a blood-free, nice clean bed. Her ordeal must have worn her out as she instantly fell asleep.

Every ward I visited that night, the discussion of poor Claire and her husband's accident was on everyone's lips. It was mentally exhausting for me, listening and comforting her friends and colleagues, it was devastating to all.

Halfway through the night, I realised I was in quite a bit of discomfort with my back. I now had a numb patch on my outer left thigh, which was a new symptom. I think the flying over the ramps and landing heavy a few nights before might have irritated the discs, which caused compression on a nerve. I just wanted to go home, take some pain relief and lay on our sofa, supporting my back again. But I had to finish off staff rostering, filing, and some controlled drugs to give on two of the wards at 6 am.

At 7 am I was so pleased it was home time. I had to drive a lot slower than usual due to the discomfort. When I walked into the house, I was so relieved that I could now rest my back and take some pain relief. I laid on the sofa and burst into tears, thinking about the loss of my friend, Claire. The more I cried, the more I became angry and guilty with myself that here I was, complaining about my back pain when my beautiful friend was tragically dead.

∾

I WAS RELIEVED that I had two days off as my pain was relentless. Most of that first day, I lay on my side with the cushion between my legs, taking strong pain relief. My back over the past few months seemed to be getting worse, not better. Probably because of the car accident and now flying over the ramps at speed had caused even more damage. I made an appointment with the GP for a referral to a specialist to find out exactly what the diagnosis and prognosis were. Fortunately for me, Steve had private health insurance for both of us, so I could make an appointment with a private specialist and not wait weeks for an NHS appointment. I rang to see when the next appointment was available at the private hospital. To my surprise, they had a cancellation that day at 6 pm, so of course, I snapped it up.

I walked into this beautiful old grand house converted into a private hospital with only twenty inpatient beds. Outside had beautiful grounds, mature trees and colourful bushes and flowers with an aviary full of budgies and parrots. I thought to myself, *What a wonderful place to sit while recovering from an operation.* The consultant's assistant called me to meet with him in his office. I was surprised to find he was a young consultant, maybe in his early forties. I always associate private consultants as retired. He shook my hand and asked me to take a seat. He had read through my referral letter and said, "The best way forward is to have an MRI scan on your back, so I can exactly see what the problem is." I couldn't believe it. The consultant immediately made a phone call and arranged for the following day for my scan at 2 pm and asked me, "Make an appointment to see me the following day, please?" He didn't even examine me, just shook my hand again and said, "See you on Friday." If I had paid for him privately, it would have cost me £150 for the five minutes I had been with him.

The following Friday at 6 pm, I was back, waiting in Mr Brown's office. He burst through his office door and said, "Sorry, I'm late. I was just finding your MRI results, which had gone walkabouts. I have bad news; you have two crumbling vertebrae and two prolapsed discs of L4 and L5. We can operate on them, but I could not guarantee the operation would be successful and might cause further discomfort in the future."

Once again, even though it was a private hospital, you would think they would deliver medical news a bit more empathetically. But no, it was delivered with the softness of a sledgehammer. I wondered if all consultants had a lecture while training to deliver bad news to a patient with zero sensitivity. I was not too fond of the thought of a spinal operation, so I asked, "What other options are there?"

He replied in his appallingly blunt manner, "Firstly, you need to lose weight. Secondly, you need to retire from your nursing career. Thirdly, take care of everything you do when using your back, and finally, take pain relief as required for the rest of your life." The worst part of that sentence was 'finishing your nursing career'.

Inside I was undoubtedly crushed. I loved working with patients. I asked him, "Could I do a managerial post in nursing with no physical handling of patients?"

He answered, "I don't think you should because of the type of patients you look after; they could be unpredictable and aggressive. The next sudden movement could cause even more severe injury." He shook my hand again and wished me good luck for my future.

I left the consulting room, numb and heavy-hearted, but excited that it may be the sign I had been waiting for, enabling me to start my own home care company. The following Monday morning, I took my letter and results into the occupational health department, and asked about retiring from nursing on medical grounds; they told me that my application would be processed and potentially take up to six weeks to go through. However, they were sure that I would be a medical retirement candidate due to my back injury. They instructed me not to return to work until an assessment of my case.

I took regular pain relief and rested for the first week. I did nothing, no washing, ironing, shopping, cleaning, or driving, just complete rest. My back did improve a little, but it was still apparent that my back was vulnerable, the deterioration had happened so quickly that I found it hard to keep up.

A NEW CAREER IN SIGHT

The second week, I decided to look through all my home care paperwork and tweaked it, until no more tweaks were possible. The only thing I needed to do now was to give presentations to social services and care managers in the hospital. I rang Mary at my local social service office and asked, "Could I give a presentation about what my care company could offer?" Mary was thrilled I was still going ahead with starting the care company. She arranged a meeting with the local care managers for the following week; this would allow me to print off the information and practice my presentation.

I stood in front of my bedroom long-mirror and practised my presentation. I completely fluffed my first try. I stuttered, made up words, and lost my train of thought several times. So, I started again; this time talking to my teddy bear sitting on the bed because talking to my reflection was very off-putting. I hadn't realised how many facial expressions I used when talking and how much weight I was putting on due to low mobility. How could I get some weight off when I was sitting around the house all day? I cast my mind back to when I worked one-to-one with a young girl called Abby, who suffered from Anorexia.

My shift with her was exhausting. she would continuously walk around the ward, trying to keep moving at all times. Even if I managed to get her to sit and rest, she would wriggle her body in the chair and swing her upper crossed leg backwards and forwards, all in the aid to burn calories. Mealtimes with her were personally a nightmare for me. I'm a northern girl brought up to love her grub and eat it with gusto, never leaving a morsel of food on my plate.

At mealtimes, I would sit with Abby for an hour or more with her tiny portion of food. She just moved it around her plate, making every excuse why she wasn't hungry or couldn't eat her food. My job was to encourage her to eat, even if it were a little; when she did eat a few mouthfuls, she physically retched and would run to the loo to make herself sick.

Anorexia is a terrible Psychiatric illness. Those afflicted suffer from delusional thoughts that they see themselves as fat. Even when they look in the mirror weighing five stone and bones protruding, they still visually see themselves as fat. These thoughts can tragically take the patient's life within months, due to lack of nutrition and organ failure. If only I could transfer some of Abby's willpower and exercise more to lose a bit of weight, but that wasn't healthy and a bit overly dramatic.

I realised that I needed to print off more assessment sheets and care plans so each care manager could follow with a copy of their own, because just standing in front of them showing the paperwork at a distance just wouldn't work. I practised my presentation every day and began to feel more confident. I only hoped that on the day I would feel the same.

The day of the presentation arrived far too quickly for my liking. I dressed in my new navy trouser suit with a white blouse, navy handbag and shoes to match. I put my hair up in a small clip and wore my new best pink lipstick. I looked in the mirror and felt like the Director of Care, as only an hour before I realised that I needed a title for myself.

I arrived at Social Services with my legs wobbling like jelly. Mary met me with a shake of the hand and took me through to the meeting room to meet ten care managers. I wasn't expecting so many. I thought to myself, *Well, you've practised at home in the mirror and to your teddy, now's the real thing. Keep calm, look confident and don't balls this up, Mel.*

"Good morning everyone, my name is Melanie, and I'm here today to tell you about my care company, Empathy Private Home Care. I have been a registered psychiatric nurse for over twenty years, and I'm a trainer for degree students, a counsellor, and a cognitive behaviour therapist." I took a deep breath and continued, "I started the company because when I was a ward sister on a rehabilitation assessment ward in Oxford, I found that it would often fail when we sent patients home with a care package into the community. The patient would be back on the ward after a few weeks. I decided to do some research into the reasons care was failing. I worked with a carer in the community. I found that patients were not being assessed correctly by the care company. The care plan devised by the care company for carers to follow was flawed and not informative to the patients' specific needs. The carers had little training or support, and there wasn't any reassessment after a week of the patient arriving home to tailor the care to the patient any further. The turnover of staff was huge so the patient couldn't get continuity or to know the carers." Getting more comfortable as I talked, I relaxed. "At first, I tried to train care staff before the discharge of the patient from the ward, but due to the high turnover, it was impossible. A friend of mine, Janet, a nurse on the unit said, 'why don't you start your own care company, especially for psychiatric patients?' So, it's all her fault I'm here today." The care managers laughed, which made me feel a little less anxious. I asked them to look at the assessment document first, go through it a page at a time, and asked if there was anything else as care managers, they thought I could add.

They were silent, then a care manager called Brenda said, "I think it's a fantastic, thorough assessment."

I then talked about the care plan, and how it would be split into visits and made specific to everything a carer would do on each visit, and gave them an example of care for a morning visit and the record of the morning visit a carer would complete and sign. I then got them to look at the training program I had put together for every carer. They would have a week's training in-house before they met clients and would work with an experienced carer or me the second week, and if the trainees were to my standard, they would work independently on a specific run of clients on the third week.

The training included: First and foremost, the meaning of Empathy and how I wanted them to provide empathetic care; Moving and handling, including use of equipment; Basic First aid; All personal care needs; Health and food hygiene; Medical and Psychiatric conditions; Assessments and Following care plans, and Policies and procedures.

The care managers were still and silent after my presentation, you could have heard a pin drop. I felt extremely uncomfortable. Then Mary stood up and said, "I think I can speak for everyone in this room when I say that was a fantastic presentation, well done. We have been waiting for years for someone like you."

I breathed a sigh of relief. I asked, "Does anyone have any questions?"

Brenda piped up from the back of the room, "When can you start? Because I have patients, I want to refer to you right now?" the room exploded into laughter.

"You are the first to receive my presentation, and I have a meeting with the contracts team in two days, then other care managers over Oxfordshire county. If successful and offered a contract with Social Services, then that would be the start of Empathy. I need to advertise for staff, interview and train them, so I was probably looking at three months, which made it January 1996."

I joined them for coffee, and they bombarded me with millions of questions and gave me their contact cards. My throat was sore from talking so much, but I bloody loved the experience. I was euphoric. They thanked me for my presentation and stated they were confident I would get a contract, and couldn't wait to work with my company soon. All I had to do next was convince the contracts team, and achieve a contract to provide care in the community.

When I arrived home, I found my letter from the hospital had arrived. Due to my medical condition, it said, I would be medically retired from the NHS from this date. I was required to return any property belonging to the NHS within the next seven days. But the one thing that upset me most was that despite me working hard and giving over twenty years of my life's work for the NHS, I didn't even get an acknowledgement, or a thank you. I guess I should be grateful and thank the NHS for training me and giving me endless experiences. I must admit I burst into tears with sadness and joy; hurt by the fact that this was the end of a nursing career that I had loved so much, but the start of something new.

I had met some lovely patients, some horrid ones too. All of which were a pleasure to have nursed, and they had helped me obtain skills that saved my life and aided my future plans. I had met wonderful nurses and doctors who had taught me so much about life and care. I was so proud to say I was a nurse for the NHS, even though underpaid for the amount of responsibility, and personal dedication involved. I was sad to leave it behind. I was also excited at my new beginning, my new adventure, where I could use my knowledge and skills learned working for the NHS to provide better care in the community.

. . .

THE FOLLOWING DAY, I arrived at the contracts department early at 1.45 pm, my appointment being at 2 pm. I decided to go to the loo to look at my notes. I needed to go through my presentation and recall the questions asked previously by the care managers. I looked in my case for the umpteenth time to ensure I hadn't forgotten the bundles of paperwork to give to the panellists. Phew, they were still there. Unfortunately, the nerves were getting the better of me. I told myself, *You can do this, it's just a presentation. Go in and sell you and your company. After all, you have done all the hard work to get to this very day.* I looked in the mirror and smiled and nodded at myself and walked to wait in the foyer.

I had no sooner sat my backside on the chair when a tall, smiling blonde lady came to greet me and took me through to the meeting room. It had a big half-moon shaped table with six people sitting behind it. The blonde lady introduced herself as Claire, the Director of contracts, and continued introducing her team. Claire said, "It's a pleasure for me to put a face to a name now, as I had heard all sorts of wonderful things about you from care managers."

I blushed and smiled, and said, "Thank you," but that statement gave me the boost of confidence I needed to get on with my presentation.

I gave out six bundles of paperwork and asked them to follow with their copies. Once again, I gave the same presentation as before to the care managers, they followed me with their paperwork and seemed to be nodding in the right places and looking at me encouragingly. I finished by asking if they had any questions for me.

Claire asked, "What is your goal for the future with your care company?"

I replied, "I want to be known as the best care company because I strive to have the best reputation of delivery of care by introducing standards and training for all my staff. I want the company to achieve a contract with the NHS and Social Services of guaranteed hours to have the staff ready and trained, and I want my company to be at the forefront of care in the community."

They all nodded simultaneously.

The next question Claire asked was the one I was dreading, "How many staff do you have working for you presently?"

I took a big gulp and grinned and said, "I have one member of staff; she is a real asset to my company, and you're looking at her." They looked at me and smiled, not wanting to be unkind. "I'm in the process of recruiting and interviewing staff and would have them trained and ready in six weeks as I intend to start slowly and build up the business as required." But then told them a little white lie, "I do have many private clients who want care from January."

Once again, they smiled and nodded as they digested my answer.

Claire then asked, "Do you have any questions for my team and me?"

"Yes," I said. "Do you think my company and the fact it would specialise in mental health be a welcomed addition to Social Services?"

Claire replied, "It certainly would be a welcome addition as we have no specialist care company providing home care for this category of client, and as you rightly pointed out in your presentation, that the care tended to fail. However, at this present time, we couldn't take on a new care company for a guaranteed contract."

I swear my world fell out of my body as I heard these words. I was devastated, and my face must have shown it too. I just said, "Oh, I see."

Then Claire continued, "We could offer you a temporary contract for a few months until April, as this was the end of the old contract year. But in April the new contracts would be awarded to care companies for guaranteed hours. We have witnessed your quality of care and assessments, and we would invite you to apply for a permanent contract then."

I smiled and said, "I would be honoured to take a temporary contract and look forward to working with you permanently in the future."

"I've been extremely impressed with your presentation," Claire went on, "and love your enthusiasm and professionalism, and hope we have a professional future together."

We shook hands and said goodbye.

I drove home with a silly smile on my face, and I swear the car drove itself in a wave of euphoria. I called in at the supermarket and bought ingredients for beef stroganoff, strawberries and cream and a bottle of champagne, our family's favourite celebratory meal. I had two things to celebrate, my retirement and my bright and shiny new future as Director of Care for Empathy Private Home Care. My dreams were now a reality, all thanks to the beautiful meaning of the word EMPATHY.

I will share with you my continuing journey of EMPATHY, the fun, laughter and heart break of the day to day running of the care company in my next book.

ACKNOWLEDGMENTS

My first attempt at writing a book was cathartic, totally out of my comfort zone; it made me anxious and brought out many personal feelings and emotions. Some good, and some not so good. But without the support of my family and friends around me, I wouldn't have had the courage to complete and finally publish this book.

Special thanks to my loyal friends.

Debbie Begley, my best friend, gave me encouragement, advice, and strength to keep on writing daily, even when my confidence in my ability to continue was at a low, she kept me focused with her love and support.

Sharon Dickens, my unofficial PA. My thanks for explaining time and time again how to use my new laptop, wiping my tears of frustration, taking notes, and pouring me endless glasses of wine.

Deborah Kinloch. Thanks for taking the time to read my book in the early stages, and giving me such excellent feedback.

Sue Bedford for being there for me from day one, encouraging me to keep going, and taking the fantastic portrait photo of me for my book, I hardly recognise myself. You're an incredibly talented photographer.

Richie Cumberlidge, the book cover designer from More Visual. Who embraced my childlike drawing and transformed it into my perfect book cover.

Lynn Worton, my editor; my thanks for her patience wading through all grammar and punctuation errors.

Helen Bright; a fantastic author in her own right. Writing a book created anxiety within me, but publishing a book, I found overwhelming. There were so many things to do and understand. Helen gave me advice and information at a pace I could understand when I fell apart and was at the end of the phone when I needed her. You have become a true friend.

Unconditional love and thanks to my wonderful family.

My mum, Madeline Auld, whom at the tender age of ninety-eight, learned how to use a tablet just for me, so that I could read her each chapter when we were both shielding due to COVID-19. As always, her love and support in anything I do in life.

My sister Sondra Lilley, for her love, and encouragement to continue writing.

My handsome son, Adrian Baker, for listening and encouraging me to be more confident in writing my book and designing my social media platforms. Without your love and guidance, I would have floundered at the first hurdle.

My loving husband, Steven Baker, who reminded me of so many memories in my life and career; for his patience with me, when shouting in a panicked voice, 'STEVEN, HELP!', whenever I lost or deleted a file by accident on my laptop. Your love and protection kept me grounded. You deserve a medal for putting up with me.

Finally, to my ten-year-old grandson, Jacob Baker Staples. Because of COVID-19, sadly, it's been over a year since we were together. My last visit we laid in bed cuddling as you listened to nanny's nursing stories. You sat up from your pillow and said the magic words that inspired me, 'You should write a book, Nanny.' So, I did just that. I wrote a book just for you, my darling boy.

ABOUT THE AUTHOR

Melanie Baker was born and raised in Darfield, a small village in South Yorkshire, U.K. Melanie is married and has a son who also decided on a career in nursing, and now specialises in aesthetics.

Her first book *Discovering my Empathetic Heart* is based on her memoirs of life experiences from childhood to adulthood, guiding her to a career in psychiatric nursing. Her book is filled with love, laughter and heartbreak.

After twenty years of nursing experiences, and achieving additional skills as a degree student mentor, counsellor and CBT therapist, she recognised as a ward sister a major problem in psychiatric care in the community. Melanie left the NHS and started her own company, specialising in care for clients with mental health issues.

The company, Empathy Private Home Care, developed into an award-winning organisation, serving clients across Oxford-shire and Buckinghamshire.

Though her first book is about her early nursing career, her second book will cover care in the community, sharing stories of carers going beyond the call of duty; the challenges of social services and the NHS, and many heart-warming characters.

Lightning Source UK Ltd.
Milton Keynes UK
UKHW041250100321
380104UK00002B/555